The University Libraries at Penn State
and the Penn State University Press, through the
Office of Digital Scholarly Publishing, produced
this volume to preserve the informational content
of the original. This reprint edition was created
by means of digital technology and is printed on
paper that complies with the permanent Paper
Standard issued by the National Information
Standards Organization (z39.48-1984).

2008

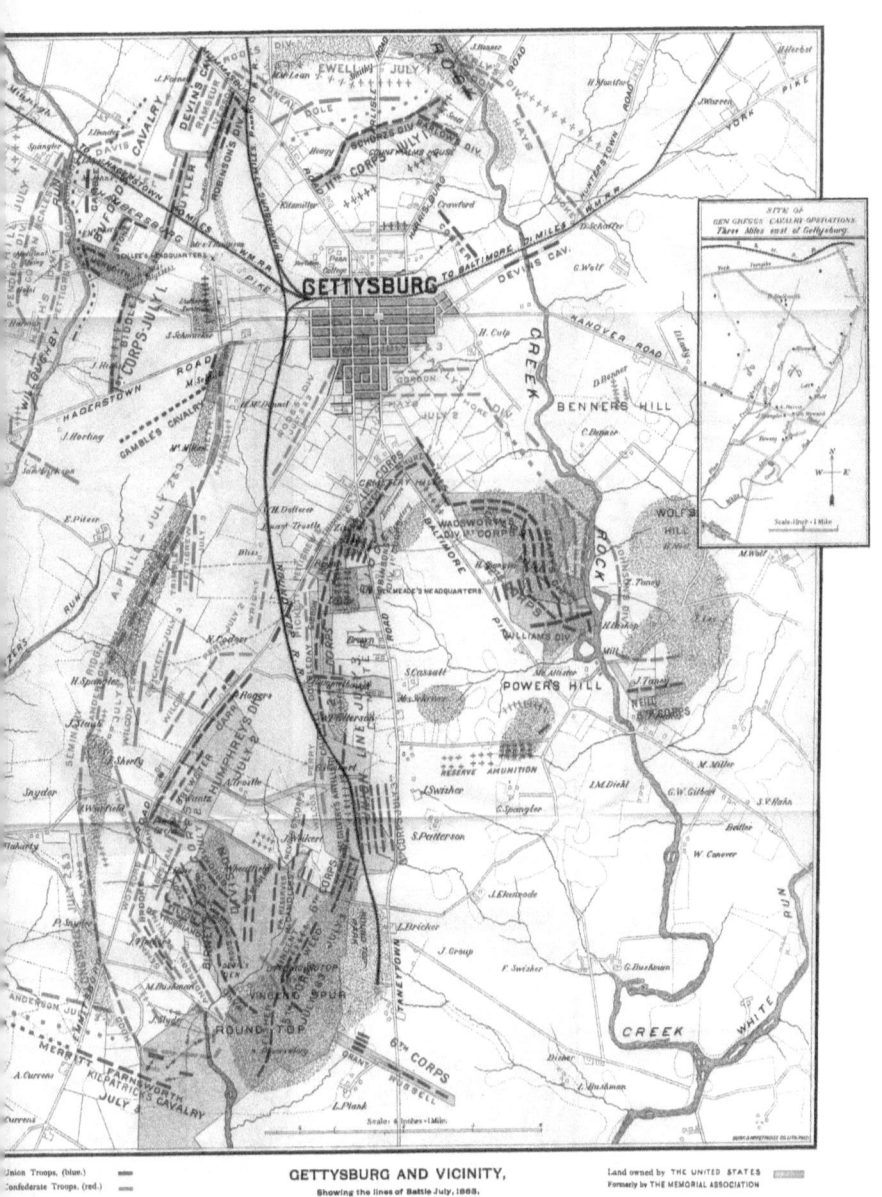

GETTYSBURG AND VICINITY,
Showing the lines of Battle July, 1863.

GETTYSBURG

A HISTORY

OF THE

Gettysburg Battle-field Memorial Association

WITH AN ACCOUNT OF THE BATTLE

GIVING

MOVEMENTS, POSITIONS, AND LOSSES OF THE COMMANDS ENGAGED

BY

JOHN M. VANDERSLICE

PUBLISHED BY THE MEMORIAL ASSOCIATION

PHILADELPHIA
1897

3 973.7349
V285g
1897

COPYRIGHT, 1896,
BY
JOHN M. VANDERSLICE,

PHILADELPHIA.

PREFACE.

At a stated meeting, held October 3, 1894, of the Directors of the Gettysburg Battle-field Memorial Association, a resolution was adopted authorizing the appointment of a committee to prepare and publish a history of the Association.

At the stated meeting, May 22, 1895, Hon. Edward McPherson, chairman of the committee appointed in accordance with the resolution, submitted a report upon the history and its cost of publication.

Major-General Daniel E. Sickles, U.S.A., offered a resolution, which was unanimously adopted, authorizing, under the supervision of Vice-President Colonel C. H. Buehler, the publication of two hundred and fifty copies of the history of the Memorial Association, and making an appropriation for the expense thereof.

Vice-President Buehler appointed Mr. McPherson to compile and publish the history.

Upon the deaths of Colonel Buehler and Mr. McPherson, the duty devolved upon the Executive Committee of the Association to select an historian.

PREFACE.

At a stated meeting of the committee, John M. Vanderslice, Esq., whose long and faithful service to the Association as a Director and as Secretary of the Committee on Tablets and Inscriptions made him especially qualified for the work, was unanimously selected to prepare the history, and a sub-committee was appointed to supervise the publication.

This book is the result of his labors, and it is believed that the important work of the Association in connection with the preservation of the historic battle-field of Gettysburg is fully and fairly set forth for future reference.

LOUIS WAGNER,
JOHN P. NICHOLSON,
Committee.

CONTENTS.

	PAGE
Map . . . . *Frontispiece.*	
Introduction	9
Gettysburg	15
Losses in the Twelve Greatest Battles of the War	17
The Town and Field	19
The Ten Roads leading into the Town	21
The Advance of the Army	22
The Cavalry Fight at Hanover	27
Forces Engaged and the States represented in the Battle	29

FIRST DAY'S BATTLE.

Approach of the Confederates	33
Encountered by Buford's Cavalry	34
The First Federal Corps arrives and opens Fire	36
Meredith's Federal Brigade charges Archer's	37
Death of General Reynolds	38
Davis's Confederate Brigade attacks Cutler's	39
General Heth reforms his Line	39
Doubleday's Federal Division goes into Position	41
Robinson's Division meets Rodes's upon Oak Ridge	41
The Federal Eleventh Corps arrives upon the Right	43
Attacked in Flank by Early's Confederate Division	45
Its Withdrawal to Cemetery Hill	45
Robinson's Division forced to abandon Oak Ridge	45
The Fight continued on the Left by the First Corps	47
The Corps retires to Cemetery Hill	49
Losses at Reynolds's Grove	56
Losses upon Oak Ridge	62
Losses upon Eleventh Corps Line	64
Number of Regiments of each State Engaged	67

SECOND DAY'S BATTLE.

Position of the Several Corps	68
Sickles moves Federal Third Corps forward to New Line	71

CONTENTS.

	PAGE
Opening of the Battle at Devil's Den	72
It extends into the Wheat-Field	73
Arrival of the Federal Fifth Corps upon the Field	75
Confederates attack Little Round Top	76
Battle in the Wheat-Field continued	78
First Division of the Federal Second Corps goes into Action	79
Ayres's Division of United States Regulars enters the Field	82
The Federal Troops forced to abandon the Field	82
The Fight at the Peach Orchard	83
Struggle of Humphreys's Federal Division along the Emmittsburg Road	85
Withdrawal of Federals to Cemetery Ridge	87
The Battle continued there	88
Confederates capture Works upon Culp's Hill	91
Confederate Assault upon East Cemetery Hill	93
Losses at Round Top	96
Losses in Wheat-Field	98
Losses in Peach Orchard	104
Losses upon Emmittsburg Road	107
Losses upon East Cemetery Hill	110

THIRD DAY'S BATTLE.

Battle opens upon Culp's Hill	115
Confederate Assault upon Cemetery Ridge	122
Charge of Pickett's, Pettigrew's, and Trimble's Divisions	124
They reach the Wall held by the Federal Second Corps	125
They are repulsed with Great Loss	129
Injustice done to Pettigrew's and Trimble's Divisions	130
The Troops engaged in the Assault and Repulse	132
Gregg's Cavalry Fight on the Right Flank	134
Final Charge and Repulse of Confederate Cavalry	137
Federal Cavalry Charge upon the Left Flank	140
McCandless's Pennsylvania Reserves capture a Battery	141
Losses at Culp's Hill	142
Losses in Assault upon Cemetery Ridge	146
Losses in Pickett's, Pettigrew's, and Trimble's Divisions compared	150
Regiments engaged and States represented	153
Cavalry Losses	154

CONTENTS.

	PAGE
Retreat of Confederate Army	156
Points where Principal Fighting was done according to Losses	161
Losses by Divisions	162
Losses by States	163

THE NATIONAL CEMETERY.

Location	171
Arrangement of Graves	179
Dedicatory Services	180
Speech of Secretary Seward	182
Prayer of Rev. Dr. Stockton	184
Oration of the Hon. Edward Everett	187
The Memorable Address of President Lincoln	193
Design of the Monument	195

THE BATTLE-FIELD MEMORIAL ASSOCIATION.

First Appropriation by Pennsylvania	202
First Appropriation by Minnesota	206
Reorganization of the Association	211
Encampment of the Grand Army of the Republic upon the Field	213
First Appropriation for Monuments by Massachusetts	216
Death of Vice-President McCreary	217
Inscriptions required upon Monuments	221
Death of Vice-President Buehler	228
No Memorials but those constructed of Granite or Bronze allowed upon the Field	229
Monuments to be located in Positions occupied by Commands in Line of Battle	232
Markers at Advanced Positions allowed	232
Monument of Pickett's Confederate Division directed to be placed on the Line occupied by it	233
Spot where Confederate General Armistead fell, July 3, marked by the Association	234
Avenues named	235
Rules and Regulations for Erection of Monuments	236
Death of Secretary Krauth	248
Deaths of Generals Barnum and Crawford	252
Death of General Slocum	256

CONTENTS.

	PAGE
Lands, Monuments, etc., transferred to the United States Government	257
Deaths of Colonel Bachelder and General Carr	257
Last Meeting of the Association	258
List of Directors of the Association during its Existence	259
Abstract of all Receipts and Expenditures	261
List of Federal Regiments, Batteries, and General Officers from each State	263
Appropriations to Association for Monuments and Description of Principal Monuments	263
List of Regiments and Batteries of the United States Regular Army	305
List of Confederate Commands	307
Act establishing National Military Park	316

INTRODUCTION.

CONGRESS having passed an act on February 11, 1895, "to establish a National Military Park at Gettysburg," the Board of Directors of the Gettysburg Battle-field Memorial Association, at a meeting held May 22, 1895, having been previously authorized to do so by a vote of the stockholders, decided to transfer to the United States government the six hundred acres of land which had been acquired by the Association, upon which seventeen miles of avenues had been constructed, giving access to the most interesting points of the battle-field, and to consign to the care and protection of the general government the three hundred and twenty monuments which had been erected upon the field by the several States and by regimental associations.

There were present at this meeting of the Board: Colonel C. H. Buehler, of Pennsylvania, vice-president; General Daniel E. Sickles and General Alex. S. Webb, of New York; General Lucius Fairchild, of Wisconsin; Colonel Frank D. Sloat, of Connecticut; Colonel Charles L.

Young, of Ohio; Colonel George E. Briggs, of Michigan; Colonel Wheelock G. Veazey, of Vermont; General D. McM. Gregg, General Louis Wagner, Hon. Edward McPherson, Hon. S. McSwope, Captain H. W. McKnight, D D., and Messrs. J. M. Vanderslice, J. L. Schick, J. A. Kitzmiller, Dr. C. E. Goldsborough, and Calvin Hamilton, the Secretary of Pennsylvania; General Joseph B. Carr, of New York, and Colonel John B. Bachelder, of Massachusetts, having died since the previous meeting in October. There were also present Colonel John P. Nicholson, of Pennsylvania, also a member of the Board; Major W. M. Robins, of North Carolina, and Major C. A. Richardson, of New York, composing the United States Board of Battle-field Commissioners.

After the transaction of the important business attending the formal transfer to the national government of the property of the Association, and the practical completion of the work for which it had been organized thirty-one years before, upon motion of General Sickles, it was decided to publish a brief history of "The Gettysburg Battle-field Memorial Association." It was considered of importance, historically, that there should be preserved a record of the great results accomplished by the Memorial Association, the first of like character ever organized. It was also deemed proper that there should be some recognition of the generous and patriotic support accorded the Association by the people of the several States, whose legislatures had made liberal appropriations in furtherance of its objects, and of the zealous and effective co-operation given it by the survivors of many of the commands which participated in the battle; for, by the aid thus rendered, the Association was enabled to acquire much of the most important part of the battle-field and to correctly mark the lines of battle, so that at the conclusion of its work the position of every volunteer command in the Union army except three had been appropriately marked by enduring, and many of them by artistic and costly, monuments or memorials, representing in the aggregate an expenditure of more than three-fourths of a million dollars, and Gettysburg was not only more visited but better marked and understood than any battle-field in the world.

It was suggested that in connection with the history of the Memorial Association there should be published a concise history of the battle, so that the work of the Association might be better understood and the difficulties attending its efforts to secure and accurately mark the battle-field be better appreciated, as well as to show how fitting was the work it attempted to accomplish, how richly the troops who fought upon the field deserved that it should be preserved as it was when hallowed by their services and sacrifices, how appropriate, too, that their States should erect thereon memorials to commemorate for all time their devotion and valor, and why the care and attention the field is now receiving from the national government in liberal appropriations and intelligent management by able and judicious commissioners meets the approbation of all patriotic people.

The writer was selected by the Board of Directors to write this history. As he had been actively identified with the work of the Association for sixteen years, for the most of that time being a member of the Executive Committee and Secretary of the Committee on the Location of and Inscriptions on Monuments, it was probably thought that his familiarity with the work and the information he had acquired might in a measure qualify him for the duty.

While highly appreciative of its confidence in him, as evinced by this action of the Board, he is equally appreciative of the responsibility he assumes and of probable disappointment with the results of his work.

It is proposed to briefly and accurately describe the position, movement, services, and losses of every regiment and battery engaged in the battle, as established by the information gathered and collated by the Association, by the official reports, and by statements of officers and men of both armies, who, by its invitation upon several occasions, met and conferred upon the field for the purpose of marking the lines of battle, which statements have been most carefully examined, compared, and verified.

There will be no criticisms upon strategical or tactical movements upon the field. In fact, there were few such. As has been well said, "Gettysburg was, in a measure, the American soldiers' battle," a battle of the ranks, a struggle of American prowess and courage, of discipline and tenacity, of unwavering fidelity and unselfish devotion, a contest of American manhood.

GETTYSBURG.

There are many reasons why Gettysburg was selected at such an early period for preservation, and why it has attracted more attention and been visited by more people than all the other battle-fields of the Rebellion.

In every epoch of history there will be found some battle which ever remains prominent above others of the same period, though they be of greater magnitude. As in Napoleon's campaigns, Lodi, Arcole, Rivoli, Jaffa, Aboukir, Marengo, Austerlitz, Jena, Eylau, Friedland, Burgos, Wagram, Lutzen, Dresden, and even Borodino, when Russia and the whole continent lay at the feet of the invincible conqueror, and Leipsic, his first serious and decisive defeat, are eclipsed by the memories of Waterloo, because of its effects upon the destinies of Europe and of civilization, so Gettysburg will ever be preeminently the most renowned of all the battles of the war for the Union, not only because of its magnitude and immediate results, but also by reason of the grave consequences dependent upon the issue.

But Gettysburg should not, as is so often erroneously done, be considered the Waterloo of the Rebellion. As one able writer well says, "It was more like Leipsic, decisive as to the field but not as to the struggle." For it must not be forgotten that while the Army of the Potomac and the other Federal troops operating in Virginia, up to and including Gettysburg, lost 89,175 killed and wounded and 48,638 missing, they after Gettysburg lost 110,820 killed and wounded and 35,586 missing before the final victory at Appomattox.

Gettysburg was, however, fought at the gloomiest period of the war, which had then been carried on for two years upon a tremendous scale, with the expenditure of so much blood and treasure, so many severe battles having been fought and so many lives sacrificed without decisive results. The campaign of 1862 had ended with defeats in the East and West, and that of 1863 had opened with one. The Rebellion had reached its very zenith of success and triumph. Foreign intervention in behalf of the Confederacy was imminent.

Gettysburg, too, was the only battle fought on Northern soil during those four years of terrible war, north of Mason and Dixon's line, the then line of demarcation between North and South.

It was also the bloodiest single battle of the war. The losses of the Union or Federal army in the twelve greatest battles of the war were as follows:

	Killed.	Wounded.	Missing.	Aggregate.
Gettysburg	3070	14,497	5434	23,001
Spottsylvania	2725	13,416	2258	18,399
Wilderness	2246	12,037	3383	17,666
Antietam	2108	9,549	753	12,410
Chancellorsville	1606	9,762	5919	17,287
Chickamauga	1656	9,749	4774	16,179
Cold Harbor	1844	9,077	1816	12,737
Fredericksburg	1284	9,600	1769	12,653
Manassas (1862)	1747	8,452	4263	14,462
Shiloh	1754	8,408	2885	13,047
Stone's River	1730	7,808	3717	13,255
Petersburg (first assault, 1864)	1688	8,513	1185	11,386

Many of the wounded died of their wounds, and should be added to the killed, while many accounted for as missing were either killed or wounded, and at Fredericksburg and Cold Harbor nearly all such were among the killed, as but few if any were captured in those assaults.

Then, too, Gettysburg, being located in a populous Northern State, and being comparatively easy of access, has ever since the battle been visited by great numbers of the people of our own and other lands. The smoke of battle had scarcely cleared away before thousands of patriotic people were thronging to the place, with supplies and comforts, to render what aid they could to the wounded and help bury the dead. And all through the months the immense hospitals were located there, multitudes came and went, many tenderly carrying with them a stricken dear one, that he might die at home, amid the scenes of his childhood, or a lifeless body, to inter it beside those of kindred and friends. From no other field were so many of the fallen taken to their homes as from Gettysburg. The interest thus early awakened in the place has never abated, and each year the number of visitors increases, and seldom does one leave Gettysburg without a strong desire to revisit it.

Aside from the historic association and interest, there is much that is attractive in the magnificent and beautiful surrounding scenery which enhances the pleasure of the visitor. In the woods and meadows, in the glens and vales of the battle-field, there is many a romantic and charming bit of landscape, while from the elevated portions of the field there are splendid and delightful views extending for miles in every direction. The prospect from the National Cemetery, as the sun is setting behind the South Mountain, is one that is unexcelled in beauty and impressiveness.

THE TOWN AND FIELD.

The old town of Gettysburg, founded in 1780, is the county-seat of Adams County, Pennsylvania, and is about seven miles from the southern border of the State. It has, as it had at the time of the battle, a population of a little more than three thousand. It was little known before those memorable July days that were to make it forever historic. Until then its chief distinction was that it had been for many years the home of Thaddeus Stevens, "the great Commoner," the brilliant leader of the House of Representatives during the war, and the lifelong and unyielding champion of human rights. It furnished its full quota of splendid soldiers, though none of its companies, except one in the 1st Pennsylvania Reserves, participated in the battle, the rest being on duty elsewhere,—by a strange occurrence several of them being in two of the regiments under French at Harper's Ferry, which were not permitted to join the Army of the Potomac until after the battle.

The town is in the centre of the battle-field, as the fighting on July 1 was north and west of it, while on the 2d and 3d it was on the south and east, it being peculiar that during the battle the Northern army should be in a position to the south of that of the Southern army, completely reversing the positions that the two armies would naturally be expected to occupy.

The town is situated in a beautiful valley between two ridges, which are now classic by reason of the importance attaching to them in the battle. The hill north and west of the town and about a mile from the centre thereof is Seminary Ridge, the Lutheran Theological Seminary located there giving it the name. The ridge runs for many miles northeast and southwest, a portion of it being the line held by the Federal troops during the first day's battle, and forming the principal line of defence of the Confederate army during the remainder of the battle. The ridge south and southwest of the town is Cemetery Hill, so named because Evergreen, the town cemetery, was located thereon, on the Baltimore Pike, a half-mile from the town, the National Cemetery being placed there also after the battle. This ridge begins a few hundred yards northeast of the cemetery entrance and extends in a line nearly parallel with Seminary Ridge. Big and Little Round Tops are spurs of this ridge, which formed the main line of the Federal army during the second and third days' battles. A short distance east of the cemetery this ridge bends sharply to the right, forming two rocky and wooded prominences, Culp's and

THE TOWN AND FIELD. 21

Spangler's Hills, terminating in Wolf's Hill, a steep knob beyond Rock Creek.

Ten roads concentrate in the town almost as regularly as the spokes of a wagon-wheel at the hub. That from Emmittsburg, upon which Buford's cavalry, the First, Third, and Eleventh Corps, marched, comes from the southwest; that from Taneytown, upon which the Second Corps marched, from the south; the Baltimore Pike, upon which the Sixth and Twelfth Corps marched, from the southeast; that from Hanover, upon which Gregg's and Kilpatrick's cavalry and the Fifth Corps marched, from the east; those from Mummasburg, Carlisle, Harrisburg, and York, upon which Ewell's corps marched, from the north and northeast; that from Chambersburg, upon which Hill's and Longstreet's corps marched, from the northwest; and that from Hagerstown from the west, or, rather, southwest.

[margin note: Avenues of Approach]

From these unusual facilities for the movement and concentration of large bodies of troops, together with the conformation of the surrounding hills and fields, it would seem as if Gettysburg had been designed by nature for a battle-field.

While the field is said to cover twenty-five square miles, the principal and important operations were confined to a much more limited space, and there are many points upon it from which can be had a good view of the whole battle-field, with the exception of that upon which Gregg's cavalry fought, three miles east of the town; and, except where a piece of woodland may intervene, the Federal lines of battle can be readily traced by the monuments which now mark the positions of the different regiments and batteries, even some of those of Gregg's cavalry being seen off in the distance.

THE ADVANCE OF THE ARMIES.

In the beginning of June, 1863, the Army of the Potomac under Hooker lay north of the Rappahannock River in Virginia. The campaign of 1862 had ended with Fredericksburg, where superb valor had been wasted in five successive reckless assaults which for desperate courage have never been excelled in the world's wars, and that of 1863 had opened with the brilliantly planned but miserably conducted struggle in the woods around Chancellorsville, whence the veteran army, after a loss of over 17,000 with less than half its number engaged, had been again withdrawn to the north side of the river. It retained its splendid discipline and incomparable, unfaltering devotion, and was, as ever, hopeful, ready, confident.

It was composed of the First, Second, Third, Fifth, Sixth, Eleventh, Twelfth, and the Cavalry Corps, the Ninth Corps having, after Fredericksburg, been sent west to reinforce Grant.

Upon the other hand, in the Confederate army, after the death of Jackson, his corps, with Anderson's division of Longstreet's, had been reorganized into the Second and Third Corps under Ewell and Hill, Longstreet still commanding the First Corps, and this army was never in better, more effective, and more promising condition. In its camps were reviews and inspections, and everything indicated important offensive movements.

It being reported that the enemy was moving towards the Blue Ridge, Hooker ordered Pleasonton to make a reconnoissance with the Cavalry Corps, and on June 8 Buford's division moved to Beverly Ford and Gregg's to Kelly's Ford, they together numbering about 9000. Before daylight on the 9th they crossed the river and found Stuart's cavalry, about 12,000 strong, which had been reviewed the day before by General Lee amid much enthusiasm. Buford attacked at once, and Gregg, moving rapidly to Brandy Station, attacked from that point. Regiment met regiment and brigade met brigade, and from sunrise until near sunset these 20,000 troopers fought upon the plains around

Brandy Station one of the most brilliant cavalry battles of history.

It was not only ascertained that Lee's infantry was already at Culpeper, but in one of the charges Stuart's head-quarters baggage and official papers were captured, and among them was the order for the march into Pennsylvania.

With this information the Federal cavalry withdrew across the river.

The great march northward now commenced, the Army of the Potomac moving to Fairfax and Manassas, while the Confederate army moved northwestwardly into the Shenandoah Valley, Ewell's corps, in the advance, falling upon and dispersing Milroy's command at Winchester on the 14th. Stuart's cavalry was assigned the duty of protecting the flank of Lee's army and concealing its movements, and at the same time of watching the movements of Hooker's army; but on June 17 it was encountered at Aldie by the Federal cavalry and driven beyond the Bull Run Mountains, and after three or four days of severe fighting it was driven through Middleburg and Upperville to the Blue Ridge. The Federal cavalry thus not only masked the movements of its own army, but a reconnoissance to the top of the mountain discovered Lee's whole army in the Shenandoah Valley, about to cross the Potomac.

THE ADVANCE OF THE ARMIES.

Ewell's corps crossed at Williamsport and Sheppardstown on June 22, and was followed shortly afterwards by Longstreet's and Hill's. Ewell, with Rodes's and Johnson's divisions, and Jenkins's cavalry, moved rapidly to Chambersburg, Pennsylvania, and up the Cumberland Valley to Carlisle, arriving there June 27, while Early's division moved to Cashtown, eight miles from Gettysburg, and on the 26th moved to York *via* Mummasburg, except Gordon's brigade, which, accompanied by Early in person, entered Gettysburg. This brigade was preceded by White's cavalry, which charged through the town, yelling and firing. On this day the 26th Emergency Regiment of Pennsylvania, in which there was a company of college boys from Gettysburg, arrived from Harrisburg and moved out some three miles towards Cashtown, where it encountered White's cavalry and after some skirmishing retreated towards Harrisburg. A home company of the 21st Pennsylvania Cavalry, under Captain, afterwards Major, Bell, for many years a member of the Memorial Association, rendered efficient service as scouts, and the first soldier killed at Gettysburg was of this company. The Confederates left on the 27th for York, before Early's requisition for money and supplies was complied with.

In the mean time the Federal army had moved

rapidly across the Potomac to Frederick, Maryland. Here, on June 27, General Hooker, having asked that the ten thousand troops at Harper's Ferry under General French be assigned to his command, and having been curtly refused by General Halleck, resigned. General Meade, of the Fifth Corps, who had been with the Army of the Potomac from its organization, commencing his career in it as commander of a brigade of the Pennsylvania Reserves, was, on the 28th, appointed to the command of the army, which continued its march northward, east of the South Mountain, moving in three columns, —the left wing, under General Reynolds, being preceded by Buford's division of cavalry.

On the night of the 29th, Buford discovered the camp-fires of the enemy between Monterey and Fairfield, and upon reporting it to Reynolds, at Emmittsburg, early on the 30th was ordered to move to Gettysburg. He, with two brigades of cavalry, entered the town after noon as Pettigrew's brigade of Confederate infantry was approaching on the Chambersburg Road with a wagon-train for the purpose of getting supplies, especially shoes, in the town. Upon the arrival of Buford, Pettigrew withdrew towards Cashtown, and the Federal cavalry went into camp on the Chambersburg Pike west of the town.

General Buford at once noticed the number

of roads concentrating in the town, and also believed he was confronting the advance of Lee's army, and that Gettysburg was to be the scene of a great battle. He said to Colonel Devin, "In the morning they will come booming on, three lines deep, and we will have to fight like devils to hold this position."

On this day, the 30th, Kilpatrick's Federal cavalry division, moving in advance of the centre of Meade's army, encountered Stuart's cavalry in the town of Hanover, some sixteen miles east of Gettysburg, as it was endeavoring to join Lee, and after a sharp contest, in which the 5th New York and 18th Pennsylvania were principally engaged, Stuart withdrew. As Gregg's Federal cavalry division was moving in advance of the right wing of the army still farther to the east, Stuart was compelled to move towards the Susquehanna and then to Carlisle, where, after a ride of one hundred and twenty-five miles since the morning of the 30th, he arrived on the afternoon of the 1st, only to find that the Confederate infantry had hastily withdrawn from there and gone towards Gettysburg. After a long, circuitous, and hard march the Confederate cavalry joined its army during the battle, having been rendered practically useless during the advance into Pennsylvania.

In the mean time, General Lee, having been

deprived of the aid of Stuart's cavalry in keeping him informed of the movements of the Federal army, was surprised on the 28th, at Chambersburg, to learn by a scout that it had not only crossed the Potomac, but was in pursuit and being manœuvred so as to endanger his army. He ordered Longstreet and Hill to move from the vicinity of Chambersburg, recalled Ewell from his threatened attack upon Harrisburg, and Early from that upon Columbia, upon the Susquehanna, and hastily directed a concentration of his army east of the South Mountain.

The two great armies, the mighty antagonists that had met and fought upon so many fields, were thus approaching each other for the stupendous and memorable contest at Gettysburg.

THE BATTLE.

THE FORCES ENGAGED.—WHAT STATES THEY REPRESENTED.

There were, according to the Field Return of June 30, "present for duty, equipped," in the Army of the Potomac, 83,900 infantry and artillery, including the Sixth Corps of 14,516, but a small portion of which was actively engaged in the battle, and 10,800 cavalry, while from the best information obtainable the Confederate army at the same time had upon the field and engaged about 70,000 infantry and artillery and 10,000 cavalry, so that the opposing forces were approximately equal.

The Federal army was composed of seven corps of infantry and one of cavalry, while the Confederate army had but three corps of infantry and a division of cavalry. There were nineteen Federal divisions of infantry as against but nine Confederate divisions, but all the subdivisions of the latter army were much larger than those of the former. For illustration, the largest Federal corps was the Sixth, with 14,516, and the smallest was the Twelfth, with 8193, while Rodes's Confederate division, by the Field

Return of June 30, had present for duty 8042, and the smallest division in that army was 7000 strong. The one division of Confederate cavalry was, numerically, almost as strong as the Federal corps of cavalry of three divisions. The Confederate regiments were on an average forty per cent. larger than those of the Federal army, and some of them were twice as large. The Confederate war department pursued the wise policy of putting its new forces into old veteran regiments, thus keeping them recruited, instead of organizing new regiments, as was done in the North. This great difference in the strength of divisions, brigades, and regiments in the two armies should be borne in mind when we come to consider them as they contended with one another.

It is remarkable that every loyal State east of the Mississippi except one,—Kentucky,—together with Minnesota, west of the river, and every one of the Confederate States, was represented by troops upon the field of Gettysburg.

There were present in the Federal or Union army 246 regiments of infantry, 34 of cavalry, and 68 batteries of artillery, and in the Confederate army, 171 regiments of infantry, 26 of cavalry, and 68 batteries of artillery.

They were divided among the States as follows:

THE BATTLE.

In the Federal army, of infantry, Connecticut had 5 regiments; Delaware, 2; Illinois, 1; Indiana, 5; Maine, 10; Maryland, 3; Massachusetts, 18; Michigan, 7; Minnesota, 1; New Hampshire, 3; New Jersey, 12; New York, 67; Ohio, 13; Pennsylvania, 68; Rhode Island, 1; Vermont, 10; Wisconsin, 6; West Virginia, 1. There were also 11 regiments of United States Regulars and 2 of United States Sharp-shooters. Of cavalry, Pennsylvania had 9 regiments; New York, 7; Michigan, 4; Illinois, 2; Indiana, 1; Maine, 1; Massachusetts, 1; Vermont, 1; New Jersey, 1; Maryland, 1; Ohio, 1, and a squadron; West Virginia, 1, and a squadron; United States Regulars, 4. Of artillery, Connecticut had 3 batteries; Maine, 3; Maryland, 1; Massachusetts, 4; Michigan, 1; New Hampshire, 1; New Jersey, 2; New York, 15; Ohio, 4; Pennsylvania, 5; Rhode Island, 5; West Virginia, 1; and United States Regulars, 23.

In the Confederate army, of infantry, Virginia had 41 regiments; Georgia, 36; North Carolina, 34; Alabama, 17; South Carolina, 11; Mississippi, 11; Louisiana, 10; Tennessee, 3; Florida, 3; Texas, 3; Arkansas, 1; and Maryland, 1. Of cavalry, Virginia had 19 regiments; South Carolina, 3; North Carolina, 2; Georgia, 2. Of artillery, Virginia had 39 batteries; Louisiana, 7; Georgia, 6; South Carolina, 5; North

Carolina, 4; Maryland, 4; Alabama, 2; and Mississippi, 1.

It should be remembered that with the exception of the cavalry, which carried breech-loading carbines, all the troops in both armies were armed with muzzle-loading rifles and muskets, and that the artillery was of muzzle-loading guns. Before the close of the war many infantry regiments were armed with breech-loading rifles, but this had not been done at the time of Gettysburg. In considering the battles of the Rebellion, the character of the arms as compared with those of to-day is often entirely overlooked.

FIRST DAY'S BATTLE, JULY 1.

GENERAL BUFORD, having arrived on the 30th with two brigades of his cavalry, went into camp on McPherson's farm, just beyond the western limits of the town. His position was upon a ridge sloping west to Willoughby Run. Vedettes and pickets were thrown out as far as Marsh Creek, three miles to the west, as also to the north, and the roads were carefully patrolled.

In the mist of the early morning of Wednesday, July 1, the cavalry pickets posted on the Chambersburg Pike at the bridge crossing Marsh Creek discovered the advance of the enemy, being the head of Heth's Confederate division, which had moved from its camp at Cashtown, about four miles farther west, at five o'clock. One of the pickets rode to the reserve with the information and the other rode across the bridge to reconnoitre. He was hailed by the advance-guard of the enemy, but, wheeling his horse, galloped back over the bridge and down behind the wall of the abutment, and from that position fired upon the enemy the first shot of the battle.

Apprised of the position of the Federal pickets, the Confederates halted and prepared for a cautious advance. Archer's Tennessee brigade was deployed on the right of the pike, and Davis's Mississippi on the left, a strong line of skirmishers was thrown out in advance of both brigades, Marye's Virginia artillery, posted on Lohr's Hill, opened fire, and the advance commenced.

On the other hand, additional squadrons of the 8th Illinois galloped to the support of that on picket on that portion of the line which did most of the skirmishing. These dismounted cavalry skirmishers with their carbines kept up an incessant fire upon the enemy, and by concealing themselves in the tall grass or behind fences and bushes, and by acting so boldly as to indicate strong support, so harassed and delayed the enemy that nearly two hours were consumed in advancing from Marsh Creek to Willoughby Run, though their artillery had kept up a fire successively from Lohr's, Whistler's, and School-House Ridges.

About eight o'clock the Confederates reached the little stream and encountered Gamble's brigade,—8th New York, 8th Illinois, two squadrons of the 12th Illinois, and three squadrons of the 3d Indiana Cavalry,—which Buford had advanced, in line of battle, dismounted, to the creek. Calef's horse artillery, Battery A, 2d United States, of six 3-inch rifle-guns, was in position, with two sections on the pike and the other in rear of the 8th New York, the left regiment. Farther to the right was Devin's brigade of cavalry,—6th and 9th New York, 17th Pennsylvania, and two companies of the 3d West Virginia,—holding the several roads from the north and guarding against movements from that direction.

For nearly two hours more did this little force—fighting the strong infantry brigades of Archer and Davis, supported by Pegram's battalion of five batteries of artillery posted at short range on Herr's Hill—hold the enemy in check.

General Buford, in his report, says,—

"The two lines soon became hotly engaged, we having the advantage of position, the enemy of numbers. Gamble's brigade held its own for more than two hours. Calef's battery fought upon this field as is seldom witnessed. At one time the enemy had upon it a concentric fire of twelve guns at short range, but Calef worked his guns deliberately and with wonderful effect upon the enemy. The brigade maintained this unequal contest until the First Division of the First Corps came up to its assistance, and then most reluctantly did it give up the front, a portion of the 3d Indiana continuing to fight with the troops that relieved them. Devin's brigade had its hands full. The enemy advanced upon it by four roads, and on each was checked until the infantry arrived to relieve it."

A little after nine o'clock General Reynolds, riding at furious speed, arrived upon the field in advance of the First Corps, and was merrily accosted by his old companion Buford. Together they rode along the line, encouraging the troopers in the unequal struggle, while a staff-officer was sent to hurry up Wadsworth's division of the First Corps, which, leaving the Emmittsburg Road, on which it was marching, double-quicked across the fields and arrived in rear of the line held by the cavalry shortly before ten o'clock.

Reynolds at once posted the leading brigade, Cutler's, across the Chambersburg Pike. On the right of the pike and north of the cut of, at that time, an abandoned railroad, which runs almost parallel with the pike, in the order named, from right to left, were the 76th New York, 56th Pennsylvania, 147th New York, and left of the pike were the 14th Brooklyn and the 95th New York Infantry, the 7th Indiana of the brigade being on duty with the trains in the rear. As the right regiments moved into position and relieved the cavalry they were confronted by the 42d and 2d Mississippi and 55th North Carolina Infantry, of Davis's brigade, the 11th Mississippi being detached.

In naming the regiments opposing each other, they will be named in the order of their forma-

FIRST DAY'S BATTLE. 37

tion from right to left, and it should be borne in mind that the right regiment of one brigade will ordinarily face the left one of the opposing brigade.

The 56th Pennsylvania was the first to move into line, and as it did so it immediately opened fire upon the 2d Mississippi. The other two regiments north of the railroad cut at once did the same, and Davis's advance was halted. Hall's Maine battery galloped up and relieved Calef's. On the left, Meredith's brigade—2d and 7th Wisconsin, 19th Indiana, and 24th Michigan Infantry, the 6th Wisconsin being in reserve in rear near the seminary—advanced upon McPherson's woods, now known as Reynolds's Grove, just as the cavalry was being forced out of it. Opposed to it was Archer's brigade,—1st Tennessee, 13th and 5th Alabama, 14th and 7th Tennessee Infantry,—which had crossed Willoughby Run and was moving up through the woods. Meredith's brigade at once charged, the 2d Wisconsin entering the woods, where it fought at close quarters, while the 7th Wisconsin, 19th Indiana, and 24th Michigan, farther to the left, swept down to and across the creek and up the slope beyond, taking the 1st Tennessee in flank and the rest of the line partially in the rear while the 2d Wisconsin fought it in front, compelling Archer and a number of men to surrender and the rest to break in confusion. The three Federal regiments were then withdrawn across the creek into the woods and the brigade line reformed and shortened, the 7th going to right of the 2d Wisconsin and the 24th Michigan to right of the 19th Indiana.

General Reynolds had returned to the left of the line as the 2d Wisconsin was charging into the woods, and while riding forward, and near the edge of the woods, was struck in the head by a bullet and almost instantly killed. This noble Pennsylvanian, who, like Meade, had commanded a brigade of the Pennsylvania Reserves, and who had risen to the command of the First Corps, one of the idolized chieftains of the army, was doomed to fall, at the head of his troops, upon the soil of his native State.

General Doubleday succeeded to the command of the corps. North of the railroad cut the 42d and 2d Mississippi advanced against the 76th New York, 56th Pennsylvania, and 147th New York, in front, while the 55th North Carolina, overlapping their right, wheeled and took them in flank. The two right regiments were driven back, while the 147th was almost surrounded, and Hall's Maine battery, on its left, lost a gun. The 14th Brooklyn and 95th New York, south of the pike, being threatened in rear, were hastily withdrawn a short distance and formed a new line facing the cut, while the 6th Wisconsin, in reserve near the seminary, double-quicked to their support, and, throwing two companies into the cut, took in flank the Confederates who had taken shelter in it. Exposed to front and flank fires, Davis was compelled to retreat with great loss, the prisoners including a large portion of the Mississippi regiments, with the colors of the 2d. The 147th New York was relieved from its dangerous position and the gun taken recaptured.

It was now eleven o'clock, and Heth reformed his line. Archer's brigade was moved farther to the right, where it was held in check by Gamble's cavalry brigade. The remnant of Davis's brigade was withdrawn to its former position, still north of the pike. On its right, occupying the ground Archer had, was placed Brockenbrough's Virginia brigade, while on the right of the latter was Pettigrew's North Carolina brigade. Pegram's battalion of five batteries was reinforced by the eight batteries of Garnett's and McIntosh's battalions, and all these continued the fire upon the Federal line.

Upon the Federal side, Doubleday's Pennsylvania division of the First Corps had arrived, with the remaining four batteries of the corps. Biddle's brigade, the 151st Pennsylvania being left in reserve near the seminary, was posted on the left of the woods occupied by Meredith's in the following order: 142d Pennsylvania, 20th New York, and 121st Pennsylvania Infantry, Cooper's Pennsylvania battery being between the 142d and 20th. The brigade was opposed to the 52d, 47th, and 11th, and the right of the 26th North Carolina Infantry, of Pettigrew's brigade, the left of the 26th facing the woods. Stone's Pennsylvania brigade—143d, 149th, and 150th Infantry—went into position beyond McPherson's barn, on the right of Meredith's brigade, and confronted at first the remnant of Davis's Mississippi brigade and the 47th and 55th Virginia, of Brockenbrough's, the 22d and 47th of the latter facing Meredith's brigade in the woods. Reynolds's New York battery took position in rear of McPherson's woods and orchard, and Stewart's United States and Stevens's Maine batteries in the rear on the slope near the seminary. Calef's United States again relieved Hall's Maine on the pike. After another determined attempt upon the part of the Confederates to carry the line held by the First Corps, and after another hour of heavy musketry, the corps still retained its position against fearful odds.

A little after one o'clock, as Pender's division of Hill's corps was about to reinforce Heth's in front, a new danger threatened the flank and

FIRST DAY'S BATTLE. 41

rear of the First Corps. Devin's cavalry discovered the approach of Rodes's large division of five brigades of infantry of Ewell's corps coming from the north. It was moving along Oak Ridge, which is the northern prolongation of Seminary Ridge, held by the Federals.

Fortunately, Robinson's division of the First Corps had reached the field some time before, and was lying in the grove near the seminary. Baxter's brigade moved rapidly to the Mummasburg Road and formed along it in this order: 90th Pennsylvania, 12th Massachusetts, 88th Pennsylvania, 83d New York, 97th New York, and 11th Pennsylvania Infantry, just as O'Neal's Alabama brigade was advancing to it. Baxter's command had just encountered the Alabama brigade when it had to change front to the left to meet an attack by Iverson's North Carolina brigade,—12th, 23d, 20th, and 5th Infantry. Taking position behind a stone wall along the crest of the hill, it poured destructive volleys into the North Carolinians and then charged them, while the right regiments of Cutler's brigade, which had been withdrawn to the ridge, swung around upon their flank. Iverson lost 500 killed and wounded, 1000 prisoners, and 3 stands of colors, the 88th Pennsylvania taking those of the 23d North Carolina and the 26th Alabama, the 97th New York those of the 20th

North Carolina, thus making the third success for the day for the troops of the First Corps.

O'Neal's brigade was now advancing against the right, when the 90th Pennsylvania was put in position along the Mummasburg Road at right angles to the rest of the brigade, and Paul's brigade of the division—13th Massachusetts, 104th New York, 16th Maine, 107th Pennsylvania, and 94th New York Infantry—moved to the support of Baxter's, extending and strengthening its line, a portion of the line being nearly parallel with the Mummasburg Road and the rest at right angles with it along the ridge. O'Neal's Alabama brigade—12th, 26th, 6th, and 5th Infantry—attacked the right and was driven back in confusion. Ramseur's North Carolina brigade—14th, 30th, 2d, and 4th Infantry—repeatedly attacked the front, but without success.

Another of Rodes's brigades, Daniel's North Carolina, moved past the front of Robinson's division, and while the 53d Regiment of the brigade, with the 3d Alabama, of O'Neal's, which had been detached from its brigade, and the 12th North Carolina, of Iverson's, attacked the 76th New York, 56th Pennsylvania, and 147th New York, of Cutler's brigade, on the left of Robinson, Daniel's other regiments—32d, 45th, 2d (battalion), and the 43d North

FIRST DAY'S BATTLE. 43

Carolina Infantry—moved farther to the right around to the railroad cut and attacked the 143d and 149th Pennsylvania, of Stone's brigade, which had been withdrawn from their first position and placed along the Chambersburg Pike to meet this attack. These regiments were mostly from the lumber regions of Pennsylvania, and were expert riflemen, and the volleys with which they greeted Daniel's men were said by Confederate officers to be the most destructive they ever witnessed.

With Rodes's division was Carter's battalion of artillery of four batteries, which took position upon Oak Ridge and added their destructive fire to those of Hill's corps. Still, though exposed to this fire of some sixty guns and attacked by eleven brigades, the First Corps of six brigades and six batteries held its ground until its rear was threatened by the repulse of the Eleventh Corps.

In the mean time, General Howard had arrived and succeeded to the command. His corps, the Eleventh, now commanded by Schurz, had also come up, and Schurz's and Barlow's divisions moved rapidly through the town and formed upon the open level ground north of it, while Steinwehr's division with Weidrick's New York battery remained in reserve upon East Cemetery Hill, south of the town. It was intended that the two divisions should advance and prolong the line held by Robinson's division along Oak Ridge. But after nearly an hour of manœuvring, these troops were put in line of battle, in the open low fields, where, without shelter of any kind, they were exposed to a very short-range fire of Carter's and Page's Virginia and Reese's Alabama batteries, posted on the ridge they were to occupy, and to that of the 5th Alabama Sharp-shooters. At about 2.30 o'clock, while still exposed to this fire, Von Amsberg's brigade of Schurz's division,—61st Ohio, 82d Illinois, 74th Pennsylvania, 45th and 157th New York Infantry,—on the right of the Mummasburg Road, gallantly advanced and encountered Doles's Georgia brigade of Rodes's division,—21st, 44th, 4th, and 14th Infantry. Portions of O'Neal's Alabama brigade reinforced Doles's, and Krzyzanowski's brigade— 58th New York, 26th Wisconsin, 119th New York, 75th Pennsylvania, and 82d Ohio Infantry—moved to the right and in support of Von Amsberg's, while Dilger's and Heckman's Ohio and Wheeler's New York batteries engaged those of the enemy. About the same time Barlow's division rapidly advanced to the right and took position on higher ground, between the Carlisle and Harrisburg Roads.

Barlow's command consisted of Von Gilsa's

FIRST DAY'S BATTLE. 45

brigade,—54th New York and 153d Pennsylvania Infantry (the 41st and 68th New York being detached),—Ames's brigade,—17th Connecticut, 25th, 75th, and 107th Ohio Infantry,—and Wilkeson's United States Battery. These regiments were threatening the flank and rear of Rodes's division when, at three o'clock, Early's division, coming east from Heidlersberg, appeared upon their flank, and while the batteries of Jones's battalion of artillery enfiladed the Eleventh Corps line, Gordon's Georgia brigade—60th, 31st, 13th, 61st, 38th, and 26th Infantry—suddenly emerged from beyond Rock Creek and attacked Barlow's division, which made a desperate resistance and then fell back to the Almshouse, where around the buildings it maintained itself until General Barlow had fallen severely wounded and Hays's Louisiana brigade, on the left of Gordon, was moving upon its rear, when it retreated to Cemetery Hill. In the mean while, Schurz's division had been compelled to fall back to the cross-road running from the Mummasburg Road to the Carlisle Road, where in the open ground it continued to fight until its right was turned, when it was driven through the town, several of the regiments, however, keeping their formation and retreating in order.

Hays's Louisiana and Hoke's North Carolina

brigades, of Early's division, which were moving to cut off the retreat of the Eleventh Corps, were delayed by Devin's cavalry brigade until Coster's brigade of Steinwehr's division double-quicked from East Cemetery Hill to the northeast of the town to aid in covering the retreat. The 73d Pennsylvania threw up a barricade across the Harrisburg Road at the entrance to the town, while the 27th Pennsylvania and 134th and 154th New York Infantry moved out and pluckily encountered the enemy, being confronted by Hays's Louisiana brigade,—5th, 6th, 7th, 8th, and 9th Infantry,—and Hoke's North Carolina brigade,—6th, 21st, and 57th Infantry. Fighting until they had lost half their numbers, while Devin's cavalry continued to harass the enemy on the flank, these regiments held their positions until the corps reached Cemetery Hill, with the loss of more than a thousand prisoners, most of whom were taken in the streets through which the corps crowded in confusion.

The withdrawal of the Eleventh Corps endangered the First. Robinson's division, assailed in front and flank, fighting desperately, the 16th Maine being almost sacrificed in covering the movements, fell back along Oak Ridge to near the seminary, after which, with the rest of the corps, it withdrew to Cemetery Hill, being the last troops to leave the field.

FIRST DAY'S BATTLE. 47

Returning to the left of the line, Meredith's brigade still held McPherson's woods, with Stone's brigade on its right on the pike and Biddle's on its left in the open field. While the fighting had been going on on the right, Brockenbrough's Virginia brigade had again assaulted the woods and had again been repulsed. Pettigrew's had also made a desperate attack upon Biddle's brigade. The 52d North Carolina, overlapping the line, had attacked the 121st Pennsylvania on the left in flank, compelling it to change front, and the 47th and 11th North Carolina encountered the 20th New York and 142d Pennsylvania, while at the same time the 26th North Carolina, fighting its way up by the woods, was penetrating a gap between the 142d Pennsylvania and the 19th Indiana, of Meredith's brigade, the left of which had been forced back. At this juncture the 151st Pennsylvania, which was in reserve near the seminary, rushed to the front and met the 26th North Carolina in one of the bloodiest struggles that took place on the field, as will be noticed when the losses of these regiments are stated. The Federal line was, however, still held.

Pender's division of Hill's corps now also advanced to the attack. Pettigrew's was relieved by Perrin's South Carolina brigade,—1st, 14th, 13th, and 12th Infantry,—and Brockenbrough's was relieved by Scales's North Carolina brigade,—16th, 22d, 34th, 13th, and 38th Infantry,—while on the right of Perrin's was Lane's North Carolina brigade,—7th, 37th, 28th, 18th, and 33d Infantry,—Thomas's Georgia brigade being kept in reserve. These three brigades at once renewed the attack upon the two small Federal brigades of Meredith and Biddle. Lane's was, however, halted by the fire which Gamble's brigade of dismounted cavalry poured into its flank at short carbine range, while a mounted regiment threatened it with a charge in front. Scales's and Perrin's fresh troops continued to advance, and after an heroic resistance the decimated commands of Meredith and Biddle were forced, step by step, from the positions they had held for so many hours to the open grove near the seminary, where they continued the battle.

Stone's Pennsylvania brigade still held its position. An attempt had been made to flank the 143d and 149th on the pike, but the 150th on the left changed front forward and repulsed the flanking force. Daniel's North Carolina and the remnant of Davis's Mississippi brigades succeeded in crossing the railroad-cut, and met the 143d and 149th face to face, while the left regiments of Brockenbrough's Virginia brigade attacked the 150th from the west; but still the brigade held its ground until almost surrounded, Scales's brigade having passed its rear, when it withdrew in perfect order to the position taken up by the other brigades and continued fighting.

This was a new brigade, and this was really its first battle. General Doubleday says of it,—

> "It came upon the field shouting, 'We have come to stay!' and it kept the promise. Every regiment of the brigade changed front forward and two changed front to the rear while closely engaged. The most eminent military writers regard the first movement as difficult and the latter as almost impossible to be executed under fire."

It was with the 150th that old John Burns, a citizen of the town, fought with his squirrel rifle until, by the advice of Colonel Wistar, he went into the woods and joined the 7th Wisconsin.

From their new position these brigades of Stone, Meredith, and Biddle maintained the fight, while the corps artillery poured grape and canister into the double lines of battle advancing upon their front and flank, the execution of Stewart's Battery B, 4th United States, upon Scales's brigade being fearful. Scales says his line was broken up, and only squads here and there indicated where regiments had stood.

There was but one field-officer left in this brigade.

At length, at four o'clock, the First Corps, after contending for six hours against more than twice its numbers, was, by the withdrawal of the Eleventh Corps, compelled to withdraw to Cemetery Hill, taking back all its artillery except a single caisson, the horses of which had been killed. It lost but one flag, that of the 150th Pennsylvania, whose guard having all been killed or wounded, the bearer, Corporal Gutelius, being wounded, sat down in the town to rest and was killed. This flag was presented to Jefferson Davis, and was found among his baggage when he was captured.

Keeping more to the west, the First Corps avoided the streets, which were crowded with the troops of the broken Eleventh Corps, and retired in good order to Cemetery Hill, Gamble's brigade of cavalry covering its retreat, as Devin's had that of the Eleventh.

General Meade was back at Taneytown when he received news of General Reynolds's death and a message from Buford urging him to send some one to take command. He had in the mean time directed General Hancock to turn over the command of the Second Corps to General Gibbon and proceed to Gettysburg.

FIRST DAY'S BATTLE.

Hancock arrived just as the Eleventh Corps reached Cemetery Hill. He at once restored order and inspired confidence. The batteries were placed so as to sweep the approaches to the hill, he personally putting Stewart's upon the Baltimore Pike. The Eleventh Corps was posted along Cemetery Hill, while Wadsworth's division of the First went into position on its right on Culp's Hill, and Robinson's and Doubleday's prolonged the line to the left of the Eleventh. Farther to the left, towards Round Top, was Buford's cavalry. About five o'clock General Sickles arrived from Emmittsburg with portions of the Third Corps, and extended the line nearly to Round Top. An hour later, General Slocum came up the Baltimore Pike with the Twelfth Corps, Williams's division going into position on the right of Wadsworth's, on Culp's and Spangler's Hills, and Geary's on the extreme left, on the slope of Round Top. Slocum, outranking Hancock, assumed command until the arrival of General Meade, about eleven o'clock. During the night the Second Corps reached the field and went into position on the left centre, between the First and Third.

Fortunately, the enemy had failed to take advantage of its success and attack the position until the arrival of these fresh troops had made it secure, and the battle of the first day was ended.

Having related where the several commands fought on that day, it may be interesting to consider how they fought, as shown by the losses they suffered.

In order to anticipate criticism and questioning of the correctness of the figures here given, it should be understood that the losses in the Federal regiments are taken from the official reports. Of course, subsequent information shows that these figures should be revised. Many of those reported missing, it was afterwards learned, were either killed or wounded, and on an average a fourth of the missing should be added to the killed or wounded. In inscriptions upon many of the monuments these corrections have been made, the Memorial Association being furnished with the names of the killed and wounded in affidavits of those competent to make them. But, to save confusion, the figures will be taken from the official reports, and the reader can bear in mind that in most instances a fourth of the missing should be added to the killed and wounded, in many cases the percentage being even higher. This will be just to all the commands. As to the Confederate reports, unfortunately, little reliance can be placed in their accuracy, the losses being generally understated. For instance, they report a loss at Gettysburg of captured or missing of 5150, while the record of prisoners of war in the office of the Adjutant-General at Washington bears the names of 12,227 captured at Gettysburg from July 1 to 5. Again, for Iverson's brigade, there is a report of 308 captured or missing, while Robinson's division captured over 1000 of that brigade in one charge. There is not much doubt that this understatement of losses upon the part of the Confederates was not only sanctioned but required by their war department and the commander of their army, as is shown by the following general order:

"GENERAL LEE'S ORDERS, NO. 63.
"HEAD-QUARTERS OF ARMY OF NORTHERN
"VIRGINIA, May 14, 1863.

"The practice which prevails in the army of including in the list of casualties those cases of slight injuries which do not incapacitate the recipients for duty is calculated to mislead our friends and encourage our enemies by giving false impressions as to the extent of our losses.

"The loss sustained by brigade or regiment is by no means an indication of the services performed or perils encountered, as experience shows that those who attack rapidly, vigorously, and effectually generally suffer the least. It is therefore ordered that in the future the reports of the wounded shall include only those whose injuries, in the opinion of medical officers, render them unfit for duty. It has also been observed that the published reports of casualties are in some instances unaccompanied by a statement of the number of men taken into action. The Commanding General deems it unnecessary to do more than direct the attention of the officers to the impropriety of thus furnishing the enemy with the means of computing our strength, in order to insure the immediate suppression of this pernicious and useless custom.

"By command of General Lee,
"W. H. TAYLOR,
"*Assistant Adjutant-General.*"

It is to be regretted that this policy of understating the losses upon the Confederate side was pursued, and that they cannot be given with exactness, for it would not only be interesting but a fitting tribute to the bravery of the troops.

The same modesty, however, was not always shown in reporting successes. Especially was this so with Brockenbrough's Virginia brigade, which is reported by General Heth as having captured two stands of colors, "the names of those who did it and the regiments to which the flags belonged, unfortunately, not being given," he says. There was a good reason for this failure to give particulars, for the only Federal flag taken on that line was that of the 149th Pennsylvania, which was placed to the left of that regiment at the railroad cut to deceive and entice the enemy, and which was captured by men of Davis's Mississippi brigade after all the guard had fallen. It, however, was recaptured in a charge by the 150th Pennsylvania. The colors of the latter regiment were taken in the town by men of Daniel's North Carolina brigade, in the manner before stated. Again, care was not observed even in making the reports of losses that were made, as shown in Lane's brigade, whose losses in the battle are stated in the official report as 389 and in another of August 13 as 660.

Then, in considering the losses of Archer's, Davis's, Pettigrew's, Scales's, and Lane's brigades, it must be remembered that they participated in Longstreet's assault, July 3, and that their reported losses include those for both days, as do those of O'Neal's and Daniel's include the losses in their fight at Culp's Hill on the 3d.

From the interesting statistics compiled by Colonel Fox in his "Regimental Losses," and the revised reports of the War Department, it would appear that there were about three killed or mortally wounded to seven otherwise wounded.

Commencing on the left, where the battle was opened by the First Corps, the losses were,—

REYNOLDS'S GROVE AND VICINITY.

FEDERAL LOSSES.

Cutler's Brigade.

Regiment.	Killed and wounded.	Missing.	Total loss.	Engaged.
56th Penna.	74	56	130	252
76th N. Y.	164	70	234	378
14th Brooklyn	118	99	217	..
95th N. Y.	69	46	115	..
147th N. Y.	177	92	269	380
Total	602	363	965	..

In only a few instances is the number engaged reported.

Subsequent reports show that of the ninety-two missing in the 147th New York, 40 were found to have been killed or severely wounded.

This was the last battle for the gallant 14th Brooklyn, its time expiring during the month.

Meredith's Brigade.

Regiment.	Killed and wounded.	Missing.	Total loss.	Engaged.
2d Wis.	182	51	233	302
6th Wis.	146	22	168	..
7th Wis.	126	52	178	..
19th Ind.	160	50	210	228
24th Mich.	272	91	363	496
Total	886	266	1152	..

The 24th Michigan was a new regiment, this being its first battle. It suffered the greatest numerical, but not the greatest *pro rata*, loss of any Federal regiment in the battle. It had

7 color-bearers killed and all the guard killed or wounded.

Stone's Brigade.

Regiment.	Killed and wounded.	Missing.	Total loss.	Engaged.
143d Penna.	162	91	253	465
149th Penna.	225	111	336	450
150th Penna.	187	77	264	397
Total	574	279	853	1312

This, as before stated, was the first battle for this splendid brigade, and it here commenced its brilliant record.

Biddle's Brigade.

Regiment.	Killed and wounded.	Missing.	Total loss.	Engaged.
20th N. Y.	146	24	170	287
121st Penna.	118	61	179	306
142d Penna.	141	70	211	362
151st Penna.	237	100	337	467
Total	642	255	897	1422

The 151st Pennsylvania was one of the two Pennsylvania nine months' regiments engaged in the battle, and whose time expired in a few days. In it were several companies recruited from academies, one company being exclusively composed of boys from the academy in Juniata County, of which Colonel McFarland, who here lost his leg, was the principal, and in the regiment were over a hundred who had been school-teachers.

It contended for most of the time with the 26th North Carolina, which lost 584 out of 800 engaged, and also for a time with the 12th South Carolina. The manner in which it fought is not only shown by its loss, twenty-five of the missing, as it was afterwards learned, being among the killed, but General Heth, in his report, speaking of the line held by this regiment, says the "dead of the enemy marked its line of battle with the accuracy of a line at a dress parade."

Artillery Brigade.

Battery.	Killed and wounded.
Hall's Me.	18
Stevens's Me.	23
Reynolds's N. Y.	17
Cooper's Penna.	11
Stewart's U. S.	36
Total	105

Gamble's Cavalry Brigade.

Regiment.	Killed and wounded.	Missing.
8th Ill.	6	1
12th Ill.	14	6
3d Ind.	27	5
8th N. Y.	24	16
Caley's U. S. Battery	12	..
Total	83	28

CONFEDERATE LOSSES.

The losses of the enemy facing these troops during the day, as reported, were,—

FIRST DAY'S BATTLE.

Davis's Mississippi Brigade.

Regiment.	Killed and wounded.
2d Miss.	232
42d Miss.	265
55th N. C.	198
Total	695

There are no missing reported for the brigade, though the greater part of the first two regiments was captured. A portion of the other losses was suffered on the 3d.

Archer's Tennessee Brigade.

The 13th Alabama, 5th Alabama, 12th Tennessee, 7th Tennessee, and 14th Tennessee report a loss of 160 killed and wounded and 517 missing, 75 of which were captured on the 1st, the rest being lost on the 3d.

Brockenbrough's Virginia Brigade.

The 40th, 47th, 55th, and 22d (Battalions) reported a total loss of killed and wounded of 148.

Pettigrew's North Carolina Brigade.

Regiment.	Killed and wounded.
11th N. C.	209
26th N. C.	588
47th N. C.	161
52d N. C.	147
Total	1105

The loss of the 26th should be 584, and of the remaining 216, 130 were lost on the 3d, its total loss in the battle being 588 killed and wounded and 126 missing out of 800 engaged. One company, 3 officers and 84 men, lost all but one.

A company in the 11th went into the fight with 3 officers and 35 men and lost 2 officers and 31 men, the captain and 4 men going into the fight on the 3d and 3 of them being killed or wounded.

This brigade lost over 500 additional on the 3d.

Scales's North Carolina Brigade.

Regiment.	Killed and wounded.
13th N. C.	126
16th N. C.	66
22d N. C.	89
34th N. C.	64
38th N. C.	79
Total	424

Missing, 110.

The missing and probably 100 of the others were lost on the 3d.

Perrin's South Carolina Brigade.

Regiment.	Killed and wounded.
1st S. C.	95
1st S. C. Rifles	11
12th S. C.	132
13th S. C.	130
14th S. C.	209
Total	577

FIRST DAY'S BATTLE.

Lane's North Carolina brigade suffered but slight loss on the first day, probably not over 120, it being engaged but slightly. Most of its reported loss occurred on the 3d, the total being 660.

Daniel's North Carolina Brigade.

Regiment.	Killed and wounded.
32d N. C.	142
43d N. C.	147
45th N. C.	219
53d N. C.	117
2d N. C. Battalion	153
Total	778

Missing, 116.

The loss of this brigade on the first day was approximately 750.

Pegram's, McIntosh's, and Garnett's artillery reported 84 killed and wounded and 16 missing.

The total Federal losses in the vicinity of Reynolds's Grove in the brigades of Cutler, Meredith, Stone, and Biddle, constituting the divisions of Wadsworth and Doubleday (temporarily under the command of Rowley), and including those of the corps artillery and Gamble's cavalry, were 2880 killed and wounded and 1191 missing, while those of the eight Confederate brigades opposing them were, according to their imperfect reports, 3971 killed and wounded and 317 missing.

OAK RIDGE.

FEDERAL LOSSES.

Baxter's Brigade.

Regiment.	Killed and wounded.	Missing.	Total loss.	Engaged.
11th Penna.	70	62	132	292
88th Penna.	59	51	110	296
90th Penna.	50	44	94	208
83d N. Y.	24	58	82	..
97th N. Y.	48	78	126	..
12th Mass.	57	59	116	..
Total	308	352	660	..

Paul's Brigade.

Regiment.	Killed and wounded.	Missing.	Total loss.	Engaged.
13th Mass.	84	101	185	..
94th N. Y.	78	175	253	..
104th N. Y.	102	92	194	..
107th Penna.	67	98	165	255
16th Me.	68	164	232	298
Total	399	630	1029	..

CONFEDERATE LOSSES.

The losses of the enemy opposing these two brigades were,—

O'Neal's Alabama Brigade.

Regiment.	Killed and wounded.
3d Ala.	91
6th Ala.	131
12th Ala.	83
26th Ala.	130
Total	435

Missing, 193.

Iverson's North Carolina Brigade.

Regiment.	Killed and wounded.
5th N. C.	143
12th N. C.	56
20th N. C.	122
23d N. C.	134
Total	455

Missing, 308.

Ramseur's North Carolina Brigade.

Regiment.	Killed and wounded.	Missing.	Total.
2d N. C.	31	1	32
4th N. C.	32	24	56
14th N. C.	42	2	44
30th N. C.	40	5	45
Total	145	32	177

A portion of the loss of O'Neal's brigade was incurred at Culp's Hill on the morning of the 3d. It is known that Iverson lost in prisoners over 1000, and at one time he reported his loss in killed and wounded at 500.

The total losses of the brigades of Baxter and Paul, Robinson's division, First Corps, on Oak Ridge were 707 killed and wounded and 982 missing, and those of the troops opposing them were 955 killed and wounded and at least 1400 missing.

The total losses of the First Corps this day were 3587 killed and wounded and 2173 missing, while those of the enemy confronting it were 4926 killed and wounded and 1717 missing.

ELEVENTH CORPS, LINE.

It is a great injustice to the troops of the Eleventh Corps to suppose, as is often done, that they did not fight with bravery on July 1, and nothing more eloquently tells of the courage they exhibited while exposed in the open level ground to the fire of eighteen guns than the statement of their losses.

FEDERAL LOSSES.

Von Amsberg's Brigade.

Regiment.	Killed and wounded.	Missing.	Total loss.	Engaged.
82d Ill.	23	89	112	. .
45th N. Y.	45	168	213	. .
157th N. Y.	193	114	307	. .
61st Ohio	42	12	54	. .
74th Penna.	50	70	120	381
Total	353	453	806	. .

Krzyzanowski's Brigade.

Regiment.	Killed and wounded.	Missing.	Total loss.	Engaged.
119th N. Y.	81	59	140	. .
82d N. Y.	102	89	191	. . .
26th Wis.	155	62	217	. .
75th Penna.	128	3	131	208
Total	466	213	679	. .

Von Gilsa's Brigade.

Regiment.	Killed and wounded.	Missing.	Total.
54th N. Y.	54	48	102
153d Penna.	165	46	211
Total	219	94	313

FIRST DAY'S BATTLE. 65

Ames's Brigade.

Regiment.	Killed and wounded.	Missing.	Total loss.	Engaged.
17th Conn.	101	96	197	386
25th Ohio	109	75	184	350
75th Ohio	90	96	186	..
107th Ohio	134	77	211	..
Total	434	344	778	..

Coster's Brigade.

Regiment.	Killed and wounded.	Missing.	Total loss.
27th Penna.	34	77	111
134th N. Y.	193	59	252
154th N. Y.	22	178	200
Total	249	314	563

Corps Artillery.

	Killed and wounded.	Missing.
Wheeler's N. Y. Battery	8	3
Dilger's Ohio Battery	13	.
Heckman's Ohio Battery	13	2
Wilkeson's U. S. Battery	13	4
Total	47	9

CONFEDERATE LOSSES.

The losses of the enemy opposing the Eleventh Corps were,—

Doles's Georgia Brigade.

Regiment.	Killed and wounded.	Missing.	Total loss.
4th Ga.	38	7	45
12th Ga.	39	10	49
21st Ga.	12	7	19
44th Ga.	9	58	67
5th Ala. (O'Neal's Brigade)	209	..	209
Total	307	82	389

A part of the loss of this brigade was caused by the flank fire of the right regiments of Paul's brigade of the First Corps.

Gordon's Georgia Brigade.

Regiment.	Killed and wounded.	Missing.	Total loss.
13th Ga.	103	..	103
26th Ga.	6	5	11
31st Ga.	43	..	43
38th Ga.	63	29	92
60th Ga.	33	5	38
61st Ga.	93	..	93
Total	341	39	380

Carter's artillery, killed and wounded, 8.

Hays's Louisiana brigade suffered considerable loss in the attack upon Coster's, but the greater part of its loss occurred on the evening of the 2d, there being nothing to show that on the 1st.

The total losses of the Eleventh Corps on this day, in less than two hours, were 1768 killed and wounded and 1427 missing. Those of the enemy, as reported, were 656 killed and wounded and 121 missing.

The casualties in the Eleventh Corps were in a great measure caused by the terrific artillery fire of Carter's battalion of eighteen guns posted on Oak Ridge, but a short distance in front.

The Federal losses for the day in the two

FIRST DAY'S BATTLE. 67

corps were 5355 killed and wounded and 3600 missing. The Confederate losses were 5682 killed and wounded and 1838 missing, nearly all of which, as has been noted, were suffered in front of the First Corps during the six hours it was engaged.

Among the casualties were General Reynolds, killed; Generals Meredith and Stone, Colonel Wistar, who succeeded Stone in command of the brigade, General Paul, shot through both eyes, Colonels Leonard, Root, and Coulter, who succeeded to the command of Paul's brigade, and General Barlow, wounded.

Of the 28 regiments of the First Corps engaged this day, there were 11 of Pennsylvania, 9 of New York, 3 of Wisconsin, 2 of Massachusetts, 1 of Indiana, 1 of Michigan, and 1 of Maine. Of the 48 regiments opposing them there were 28 of North Carolina, 6 of Alabama, 5 of South Carolina, 4 of Virginia, 3 of Tennessee, and 2 of Mississippi.

Of the 20 regiments of the Eleventh Corps engaged, there were 7 of New York, 5 of Ohio, 5 of Pennsylvania, 1 of Connecticut, 1 of Illinois, 1 of Wisconsin; and of the 19 regiments opposing them, 10 were of Georgia, 5 of Louisiana, 3 of North Carolina, and 1 of Alabama.

SECOND DAY'S BATTLE, JULY 2.

ON the morning of Thursday, July 2, the position of the Federal troops, which remained nearly the same during the remainder of the battle, was as follows:

Slocum's Twelfth Corps had the right, Williams's division occupying an irregular line, running from Rock Creek by way of Spangler's Spring to Culp's Hill, and Geary's division being posted on the hill, having been moved from its former position near Round Top. Wadsworth's division of the First Corps held the line between Culp's Hill and Cemetery Hill. At the foot of Cemetery Hill was Barlow's division of the Eleventh Corps, now commanded by Ames; on the hill, across the pike, was the division of Schurz, of the same corps, and on the left of it was that of Steinwehr. On the left of Steinwehr was Robinson's division of the First Corps (the corps now being commanded by Newton), extending across the Taneytown Road as far as Zeigler's Grove, while Doubleday's division of the same corps was in reserve in rear. On the left of Zeigler's Grove was Hancock's Second Corps, the divisions of Hays,

Gibbon, and Caldwell, then Sickles's Third Corps, the divisions of Humphreys and Birney. Later in the day, the Fifth Corps, under Sykes, which had marched all night from Hanover and arrived in the early morning, near where Rock Creek crosses the Baltimore Pike, occupied the ground on and about Round Top, on the left of the Third Corps. The Sixth Corps, under Sedgwick, which came up late in the afternoon of this day after a continuous march of thirty-two miles, was posted in the rear as a reserve, and portions of it were moved to different points of the field, as circumstances demanded. On the left was Buford's cavalry.

The Federal line from Cemetery Hill to Round Top faced nearly west, but from Cemetery Hill to the extreme right it faced almost in the opposite direction, being nearly semicircular in shape, the two flanks not being two miles distant from each other. The Confederate line was nearly the same shape, but of course, being the outer line, was much longer. On the right of it, in front of Round Top, were the divisions of Hood and McLaws, of Longstreet's corps. On their left, extending along Seminary Ridge, were the divisions of Anderson and Pender, of Hill's corps, on the left of which, extending around and through the town, was Rodes's division of Ewell's corps, then Early's and Johnson's divisions of the same corps, the latter reaching to Benner's Hill, on Rock Creek. Heth's division of Hill's corps was in reserve in the rear some distance, near where the Springs Hotel now stands. Pickett's division of Longstreet's corps was back towards Chambersburg, guarding trains.

Meade's head-quarters was on the Taneytown Road, a short distance in the rear of the Second Corps.

Lee's head-quarters was in the brick house, on the Chambersburg Road, in the rear of and near the seminary.

Wednesday night and Thursday forenoon passed in comparative silence, there being but little firing. But the troops had not been idle. Here and there rifle-pits were thrown up and defences made of the fences and stone walls, salients and lunettes constructed, artillery placed in position, ammunition and supplies brought up, and all preparations made for the impending contest.

By some mistake, Buford's two brigades of cavalry had been ordered to Westminster before Merritt's regular brigade or that of Farnsworth, of Kilpatrick's division, had arrived to take their places, and there had been thus left no protection on the flank.

To discover what force confronted him, Gen-

SECOND DAY'S BATTLE. 71

eral Sickles ordered Berdan's 1st United States Sharp-shooters and the 3d Maine Infantry on a reconnoissance into the woods, a mile or more beyond the Emmittsburg Road, where they met Wilcox's brigade,—8th, 9th, 10th, 11th, and 14th Alabama Infantry,—and were compelled to fall back.

Convinced that a strong force of the enemy was in front, Sickles moved the Third Corps to what he thought a better position. Birney's division was thrown out on a line almost perpendicular to Cemetery Hill, reaching from the Peach Orchard on the right towards Little Round Top, while Humphreys's division was advanced to the Emmittsburg Road, at a right angle to Birney's. The left of the line nearest to Round Top was held by Ward's brigade, in the woods beyond Devil's Den, the right of it reaching into the "Wheat-Field;" De Trobriand's came next, extending the line through the field and woods in the direction of the Peach Orchard, at the intersection of the Emmittsburg and Millerstown Roads, which was held by Graham's brigade, part of which faced south and the balance west along the Emmittsburg Road. On the right of Graham, extending along the road about half a mile from Sherfy's house to near Codori's house, were the brigades of Brewster and Carr, of Humphreys's division. Burling's brigade was in the rear of De Trobriand and Ward, and was afterwards divided and sent to reinforce different parts of the line. The batteries of the corps were well posted, Turnbull's F, 3d United States, was near Humphreys's right; on its left was Seely's K, 4th United States, while Randolph's E, 1st Rhode Island, was behind the Sherfy house, Clark's New Jersey on the road running towards Round Top, Smith's New York on the knoll above Devil's Den, in front of Round Top, and Winslow's New York in the Wheat-Field, to the right.

Lee had perceived this projection of Meade's left and took advantage of it. He prepared to turn that flank, and hoped to take his line in reverse and drive it from its strong position. He directed Longstreet to make the attempt, while Ewell should attack Meade's right and Hill threaten his centre, so as to prevent reinforcements being sent to the left. Longstreet moved under cover of heavy fire of his guns on Seminary Ridge and at other points. He sent his right division under Hood to strike De Trobriand and Ward on the left.

At about four o'clock Hood's division advanced, and, driving back the 2d United States Sharp-shooters upon the skirmish line, the 1st Texas and 3d Arkansas Infantry, of Robertson's Texas brigade, advanced upon Smith's battery, on the knoll above Devil's Den, and were encountered by the left of Ward's brigade,—99th Pennsylvania and 4th Maine Infantry,—while Anderson's Georgia brigade— 59th, 11th, 9th, 7th, and 8th Infantry—attacked the right of Ward's,—20th Indiana, 86th and 124th New York Infantry (the 3d Maine and 1st United States Sharp-shooters of this brigade being detached at the Peach Orchard). A desperate struggle ensued; the 1st Texas at one time almost seized the battery; but the enemy, being attacked in flank by De Trobriand, was repulsed. The left of Anderson's brigade —9th, 7th, and 8th Infantry—then attacked De Trobriand's brigade,—110th Pennsylvania, 5th Michigan, and 17th Maine Infantry—and was also repulsed. Robertson and Anderson were now reinforced by Benning's brigade,— 15th, 17th, 20th, and 2d Georgia Infantry,—and the three brigades made a desperate assault upon those of De Trobriand and Ward, which, though greatly outnumbered, held their ground, aided by Smith's and Winslow's New York batteries.

In the mean time, Law's brigade,—15th, 47th, 4th, 44th, and 48th Alabama Infantry,—with the 4th and 5th Texas, of Robertson's brigade, the two latter regiments following Law by a misunderstanding of orders, moved forward, over as rough ground as was ever passed over by troops, to seize Round Top, and were, after skirmishing with the 2d United States Sharpshooters, met by the 4th Maine, 40th New York, and 6th New Jersey Infantry, the latter being of Burling's brigade, which had been hurried into position to oppose them. Though making brave resistance, these regiments were forced back, and the position of Round Top and Ward's left endangered.

De Trobriand's brigade again repulsed that of Anderson, who was severely wounded, but Ward's, having been reduced in reinforcing the troops trying to protect Round Top, was again assailed by Robertson's and Benning's brigades.

Kershaw's brigade of McLaws's division,— 15th, 7th, 3d, 2d, and 8th South Carolina,— coming up, also threatened the right of De Trobriand's brigade, now composed of but three regiments.

Cabell's Confederate battalion of Carlton's Georgia, Fraser's Georgia, McCarthy's Virginia, and Manley's North Carolina batteries, and Alexander's battalion of Jordan's Virginia, Woolfolk's Virginia, Moody's Louisiana, Rhett's South Carolina, Taylor's Virginia, and Parker's Virginia batteries, in all about sixty guns, had taken position on Warfield Ridge, and were

SECOND DAY'S BATTLE. 75

directing their fire upon the Third Corps, and especially upon the troops at the Peach Orchard and along the Emmittsburg Road, while Latham's and Reilly's North Carolina batteries, posted beyond the Emmittsburg Road, directed their fire upon Devil's Den and Round Top. Upon the Federal side, Ames's New York, Thompson's Pennsylvania, and Hart's New York batteries had been sent to the Peach Orchard, and Phillips's and Bigelow's Massachusetts were put in position on the cross-road to the left of the orchard.

In the mean time, Sykes had been ordered up with the Fifth Corps, which had been resting in the rear, and Tilton's and Sweitzer's brigades of Barnes's division went into position on the right and rear of De Trobriand's brigade. Kershaw's right regiments,—15th, 7th, and 3d South Carolina,—facing east, attacked the 118th Pennsylvania, 18th and 22d Massachusetts, and 1st Michigan Infantry, of Tilton's brigade, on the right of De Trobriand's, while his left regiments,—3d (battalion), 2d, and 8th,—facing north, attacked the 3d Maine, 3d Michigan, and 141st Pennsylvania Infantry at the Peach Orchard. Tilton's brigade, being unprotected on the right, retired, exposing the right of De Trobriand, and compelling Sweitzer's brigade—32d Massachusetts, 62d Pennsylvania, and 4th Michigan Infantry (the

9th Massachusetts being on picket duty)—to fall back, notwithstanding the stubborn resistance it made.

During this time, General Warren, chief engineer on Meade's staff, had ascended Little Round Top, and not only saw the importance of holding it, but saw the columns of the enemy under Law, of Hood's division, advancing to seize it, driving before them the regiments at its feet. He hastened to the road where Ayres's division of the Fifth Corps was passing to the front, detached the 140th New York Infantry from Weed's brigade, and hurried it up the steep hill.

Before the 140th reached its position, Vincent's brigade of Barnes's division, which had been sent to hold Round Top, arrived upon the summit and went into position upon a ledge just below, the 16th Michigan Infantry on the right, the 44th New York and 83d Pennsylvania in the centre, and the 20th Maine on the left. Hood's troops were already charging up the hill, and a desperate encounter ensued. At last, Law, believing he could not force the front, attempted a flank movement upon the 16th Michigan with the 48th and the 44th Alabama Infantry, while the 4th Alabama, 5th and 4th Texas attacked the 16th Michigan, 44th New York, and 83d Pennsylvania in front. At

SECOND DAY'S BATTLE.

the same time the 47th Alabama engaged the 20th Maine farther to the left in front, and the 15th Alabama endeavored to turn its left. The movement upon the flank of the 16th Michigan was proving successful, when O'Rorke reached the right of the 16th with his 140th New York. The enemy were within a few feet of the top, and O'Rorke had no time to form, but charged his regiment down the opposite slope. Hazlett's Battery D, 5th United States, had, by great effort, scaled the heights and opened upon the Confederates.

The youthful O'Rorke, who had but two years before left West Point, was among the killed.

For nearly an hour the terrible conflict went on upon the crest of Little Round Top, the fighting continuing desperate, especially on the front of the 83d Pennsylvania and the 20th Maine, where at times the enemy broke through, and hand-to-hand encounters occurred. At last a charge of the 20th, when its ammunition was exhausted, led by Colonel Chamberlain, drove the Confederates from that part of the hill. The balance of Weed's brigade—91st and 155th Pennsylvania, and 146th New York—had come up and taken position on Vincent's right, and the rocky summit of the Federal left was secured, but at the cost of the lives of Generals Vincent and Weed, Colonel O'Rorke, Lieutenant Hazlett, and many others. General Vincent was killed while urging on his men. He had just been promoted from the colonelcy of the 83d Pennsylvania, by which regiment, and by his whole brigade, he was greatly beloved, being a cultured and gallant young officer.

General Weed was slain at his former battery, Hazlett's, on the summit of Little Round Top. Seeing his commander fall, Lieutenant Hazlett hastened to his side. The general seemed desirous of telling something, and while Hazlett was bending over him the bullet of a sharp-shooter killed the lieutenant, and he fell upon the body of his dead comrade. The Confederate General Hood was also wounded here.

Beyond Devil's Den, along the line of Birney's division, the struggle still continued. Robertson's 1st Texas and 3d Arkansas, Benning's 15th, 17th, 20th, and 4th Georgia, and the 59th and 11th Georgia of Anderson's renewed the attack upon Ward's brigade,—20th Indiana, 86th and 124th New York, and 99th Pennsylvania,—and drove it, with Smith's and Winslow's batteries, the former losing three guns, from the ground, young Colonel Ellis, of the 124th New York, being among the killed.

De Trobriand's three regiments—110th Pennsylvania, 17th Maine, and 5th Michigan (the 3d

SECOND DAY'S BATTLE. 79

Michigan being at the Peach Orchard and the 40th New York having been sent to the left of Ward)—had been reinforced by the 8th New Jersey and 115th Pennsylvania, of Burling's brigade. Benning's brigade at once assailed De Trobriand's thin line on the left flank, while Anderson's attacked it in front and Kershaw's threatened it from the right. The 2d South Carolina attempted to take Clark's New Jersey battery, to the right, but the 141st Pennsylvania, of Graham's brigade, lying in the road to the left of the Peach Orchard, poured into the regiment such destructive volleys that it was almost destroyed.

But the remnant of Birney's troops on the left was almost surrounded, though still fighting, when Caldwell's First Division of the Second Corps, which Hancock sent to the assistance of the Third Corps, arrived and moved into the Wheat-Field, which was to be afterwards known as the "whirlpool" of the battle. This was Hancock's old division, the largest in the Army of the Potomac, and one of the best. It lost more men in killed and wounded during the war than any other division.

Cross's brigade—61st New York, 81st and 148th Pennsylvania, and 5th New Hampshire Infantry—at once advanced to the left of De Trobriand, driving Anderson's Georgia brigade back upon Semmes's Georgia brigade of McLaws's division, which had just come into position to its left and rear. Birney led what remained of De Trobriand's command forward with cheers to the support of Cross. Semmes's 53d, 51st, 10th, and 50th Georgia in turn charged Cross, and a desperate fight ensued, in which Colonel Cross was killed. He was colonel of the famous 5th New Hampshire, a most fearless officer, idolized by his men. In a letter written before the battle of Chancellorsville he said, "Having received nine wounds in the present war, and three in other wars, I'm not afraid of rebel bullets." He lived a few hours after receiving his fatal wound. His last words were, "I did hope I would live to see peace, and our country restored. I have done my duty. I think the boys will miss me. All my effects I give to my mother. Oh, welcome, death! Say farewell to all."

At the same time, the Irish (Kelly's) Brigade, —116th Pennsylvania (4 companies), the 28th Massachusetts, and the 63d, 69th, and 88th New York Infantry (each of the three latter regiments consolidated into but two companies),— having knelt in the open field beyond the road and received absolution from the chaplain, with wild cheers charged across the field to the right of De Trobriand's line, just to the rear of the

SECOND DAY'S BATTLE.

position that had been occupied by Tilton, and met the 7th and 3d South Carolina, of Kershaw's, and the 50th Georgia, of Semmes's brigade, and after several volleys at a distance of thirty paces drove them back. Wofford's Georgia brigade of McLaw's division—16th, 18th, and 24th Infantry, and Cobb's and Phillips's Legions—now advanced to the left of Kershaw, and was met by Caldwell's Third Brigade, Zook's,—140th Pennsylvania, 52d and 66th New York Infantry,—with the 57th New York in support. At the same time, the Fourth Brigade, Brooke's,—145th Pennsylvania, 27th Connecticut, 53d Pennsylvania, 66th New York, and 2d Delaware Infantry,—charged across the Wheat-Field to the support of Cross, and breaking through Anderson's Georgia brigade and then through the right regiments of Semmes's,—53d, 51st, and 10th Georgia,—continued on across the little stream and to the high ground several hundred yards beyond, where alone it attempted to hold the ground gained. Sweitzer, with the 4th Michigan, 62d Pennsylvania, and 32d Massachusetts Infantry (of the Fifth Corps), also charged to support Brooke, and reached the wall at the farther side of the Wheat-Field. But Zook had been killed and his brigade outflanked on the right, compelling the other troops to withdraw, leaving Brooke's and Sweitzer's commands isolated and almost surrounded. Still, in a desperate struggle, they fought their way back over the Wheat-Field. General Brooke was wounded, and Colonel Jeffords, of the 4th Michigan, was run through by a bayonet while struggling over the colors of his regiment.

As Birney's and Caldwell's commands, each with a loss of over 1200 and three out of four brigade commanders in Caldwell's division, were being forced from the field, Ayres's division of United States Regulars, of the Fifth Corps, moved into action on the left. It was formed in two lines, the first being Burbank's brigade, —2d, 7th, 10th, 11th, and 17th Infantry,—and the second, Day's brigade,—3d, 4th, 6th, 12th, and 14th Infantry,—the regiments each averaging from five to six companies.

The withdrawal of Caldwell's division uncovered Ayres's flank, and his brave regulars were soon attacked by the brigades of Benning, Anderson, Kershaw, and Wofford, but the magnificent division, with its thorough discipline, fought its way through the forces that almost surrounded it and took position on the right of Weed's brigade, upon Little Round Top, having lost 950 out of 2000.

Emboldened by their continued successes, the Confederates with wild yells now swarmed into the intermediate low ground between the timber and Round Top. On they rushed for the possession of the hill, but they suddenly halted, for before them they saw the solid line of troops that had been hurried up from other portions of the field. Then McCandless's brigade of Crawford's division of Pennsylvania Reserves—6th, 11th, 1st, and 2d Infantry, and Bucktail Rifles—dashed forward with cheers, Crawford carrying the flag of the 1st, over the low marshy ground in front. At the same time, Wheaton's brigade of the Sixth Corps—62d New York, 139th, 93d, and 98th Pennsylvania Infantry (the 102d Pennsylvania being on duty with the trains)—advanced on the right of the Reserves. The Confederates fought with determination, but they received a destructive volley, and were driven to the stone wall at the top of the knoll. Here another effort was made to retain this position, but they were compelled to withdraw to the Wheat-Field beyond, and the Reserves held the wall. Here Colonel Fred. Taylor, of the Pennsylvania Bucktail Rifles, was shot through the heart while leading his men forward. It was now nearly dark, and the battle was ended upon this part of the line.

In the mean time the 3d Maine and 3d Michigan Infantry, in the Peach Orchard out at the angle of the line at the Emmittsburg and Millerstown (now Wheat-Field) Roads, had been attacked by the 3d Battalion, and 2d and 8th South Carolina Regiments of Kershaw's brigade from the south, while Barksdale's Mississippi brigade of McLaws's division,—21st, 17th, 13th, and 18th Infantry,—advancing from the west, attacked Graham's Pennsylvania brigade of Birney's division,—63d, 105th, 57th, 114th, 68th, and 141st Pennsylvania Infantry,—the first five facing west and the 141st south.

The 2d New Hampshire Infantry, of Burling's brigade, which had had roll-call upon the field under fire, a little distance in the rear, and but eight found to be absent, was ordered into the orchard between the 68th and 141st, and the 7th New Jersey of the same brigade was ordered forward to support the batteries. While Randolph's Rhode Island, Clark's New Jersey, Ames's New York, Thompson's Pennsylvania, and Hart's New York batteries poured grape and canister into the advancing Confederates, and most of the Confederate batteries in front battered the Peach Orchard and vicinity, a desperate struggle took place between the Mississippians and the Pennsylvania and New Hampshire troops, in which the former lost 747, the Pennsylvanians 739, and the New Hampshire men 193. With their left flank and rear exposed by the withdrawal of the troops from the Wheat-Field, the Federal troops were forced to

SECOND DAY'S BATTLE. 85

abandon the position, thus uncovering the left of Humphreys's division on their right, along the Emmittsburg Road. General Graham was wounded and captured.

General Sickles, while fearlessly exposing himself beyond the Trostle House, was wounded, losing a leg, and General Birney succeeded to the command of the Third Corps.

Humphreys had maintained his position along the Emmittsburg Road with little trouble, though his line was exposed to a severe front and enfilading artillery fire. But as Barksdale's Mississippi brigade, followed by Alexander's battalion of six batteries, now swept around his left, the brigades of Wilcox, Perry, and Wright, of Anderson's division of Hill's Corps, moved against his front, while on their left those of Mahone and Posey, of the same division, and the whole of Pender's division, prepared for an advance against the Federal line. The 1st Massachusetts Infantry, of Carr's brigade, and the 5th New Jersey, of Burling's, on the skirmish line, were driven in. The left of Wilcox's Alabama brigade—11th, 8th, and 9th Infantry—was met by the 26th Pennsylvania, 1st and 11th Massachusetts Infantry, the right of Carr, and the fire of Turnbull's United States battery, while Perry's Florida brigade—5th, 2d, and 8th Infantry—moved upon the right flank of the

26th. Wilcox's right regiments, the 10th and 14th Alabama, and the left regiments of Barksdale, the 13th and 18th Mississippi Infantry, encountered Seely's United States battery, supported by the 5th New Jersey and the other regiments of Carr,—16th Massachusetts, 11th New Jersey, and 12th New Hampshire (the 84th Pennsylvania being on duty with the trains),—the 73d New York (4th Excelsior), of Humphreys's other brigade, and the 105th Pennsylvania, of Graham's brigade, the latter regiment, though separated from its brigade, still fighting on the left. Barksdale's right regiments, the 21st and 17th Mississippi Infantry, moving upon the left flank, met the other regiments of the New York Excelsior Brigade, Brewster's,—70th, 71st, 72d, 74th, and 120th Infantry,—which were also exposed to the fire of Alexander's batteries. Farther to the right of the division, Wright's Georgia brigade was at the same time moving past the flank.

Humphreys, with but two brigades,—all of Burling's except the 5th New Jersey having been sent to the support of Birney,—and with his flanks now exposed, seeing the splendid lines of the three brigades of Anderson coming to attack him, wanted to go forward to meet them, but Birney ordered him to fall back upon a line with the Second Corps. No finer manœu-

SECOND DAY'S BATTLE. 87

vring, it is said, was ever witnessed on a battlefield under such terrible fire. His regiments, massed in double columns, executed a backward march with great precision, undisturbed by the volleys poured into them, halting at points indicated to form line of battle and open fire upon the advancing enemy. He reached his position in splendid order, after having lost 1506 of his division killed and wounded, including 11 of his staff, and only 163 missing, most of whom were among the killed.

In the mean time, Hancock had been intrusted with the command of this part of the line. Into the gap which separated it from the left around Round Top thirty pieces of artillery, under Major McGilvery, had been hurried, being so posted that the centre faced the Trostle House, and Willard's brigade of Hays's division of the Second Corps took position in the centre of the gap. Reinforcements were also ordered from the First, Sixth, and Twelfth Corps.

Willard's fine brigade—11th, 126th, 125th, and 39th New York Infantry—moved out to cover the left of Humphreys, and met the 21st, 17th, 13th, and 18th Mississippi, of Barksdale's brigade. With both flanks exposed, Willard's brigade suffered terribly, losing over 700, among the killed being General Willard, who fell among the dead that surrounded him.

Barksdale's brigade, with its brave leader riding ahead of it, rushed forward in a gallant charge upon Humphreys; but Barksdale was mortally wounded and fell into the hands of the Federals, while his splendid brigade was driven back.

Wilcox's Alabama and Perry's Florida brigades, upon Barksdale's left, now again attacked Humphreys's two small brigades, that had already lost more than half their numbers, —Brewster's (Excelsior) and Carr's. The 11th Alabama, supported by the 10th and 14th, was passing around the left flank of Humphreys when the 1st Minnesota Infantry, of Gibbon's division, Second Corps, which regiment had been moved to that part of the field, was ordered by Hancock to charge the Alabamians, and the regiment made its renowned charge, losing in it 201 of 263 engaged.

Doubleday's and a portion of Robinson's divisions of the First Corps were now brought forward by General Newton and placed on Humphreys's left.

The Confederate brigades of Barksdale, Wilcox, and Perry fought desperately, losing one-third their number in killed and wounded, but were repulsed and driven beyond the Emmittsburg Road.

Farther to the left, Lockwood's brigade of

two regiments—150th New York and 1st Maryland Infantry (Potomac Home Brigade)—crossed Plum Creek and attacked the left of Wofford's Georgia brigade.

The 19th Massachusetts and 42d New York Infantry, of Gibbon's division, had been ordered to the support of Humphreys's right, but were outflanked and suffered severely.

While the brigades of Barksdale, Wilcox, and Perry were assailing Humphreys's position, Wright's Georgia brigade—3d, 22d, 48th Infantry, and 2d Battalion—had passed farther to his right, where they encountered the 15th Massachusetts and 82d New York Infantry, of the Second Corps, which regiments had been ordered forward to the Emmittsburg Road. These two regiments fought until the 15th lost 148 and the 82d 123, and both the regimental commanders had fallen, when they fell back to their former positions. The Georgians, alone, with no supports upon either flank, gallantly advanced in the face of musketry and the fire of Ransom's United States and Brown's Rhode Island batteries, over almost the same ground that Pickett's division were to move the following day, and bravely attacked the line held by Gibbon's division, taking Brown's Rhode Island battery, and then encountering the 69th Pennsylvania, 59th New York, 7th Michigan, and 19th

Maine Infantry. Unaided, the brave brigade maintained its position up to within a hundred feet of the wall held by the Federal troops. The 71st, 72d, and 106th Pennsylvania Infantry, advancing to the support of the first line, the Confederates were driven back, and, being charged by the three last regiments and the 19th Maine, were driven beyond the Emmittsburg Road, with a loss of many prisoners, including several officers and two flags, Brown's battery being also recaptured. The assault made by Wright's brigade displayed courage and intrepidity unsurpassed in the battle. General Lee, Hill, and the division commander, Anderson, together were eye-witnesses of it, and yet nothing was done to support it, neither Mahone's or Posey's brigades, of Anderson's, on the left of Wright's, nor Pender's division being ordered to advance. It is said that General Pender was about to give the order to advance to his division when he was mortally wounded by a shell.

At twilight the Confederates gave up the attack on the Federal left and retired. The Federal position had been greatly strengthened by the arrival of fresh troops, the balance of the Sixth Corps being in reserve in the rear of Little Round Top.

The 20th Maine, of Vincent's brigade of the

SECOND DAY'S BATTLE.

Fifth Corps, and Fisher's brigade of the Pennsylvania Reserves, of the same corps,—5th, 9th, 10th, and 12th Infantry,—had taken possession of Big Round Top, capturing a small force of the enemy occupying it.

During the latter part of the struggle on the left, in the evening, simultaneous and fierce assaults were made on the extreme right and right centre. On the right, at Culp's Hill, Williams's division of the Twelfth Corps and Candy's and Kane's brigades of Geary's division had been hastily withdrawn to support the left when it was so badly threatened, leaving only Greene's brigade of the latter division— 60th, 78th, 102d, 137th, and 149th New York Infantry—to hold the long line there. About half-past six this brigade was attacked by Johnson's division of Ewell's corps. On the right of the brigade the works were held only by a skirmish line, and they were captured by Steuart's brigade—1st Maryland, 1st and 3d North Carolina, 10th, 23d, and 37th Virginia Infantry—and Walker's (Stonewall) brigade,—4th, 5th, 27th, and 3d Virginia Infantry. The right of Greene's line, the 137th New York, was thrown back at right angles to the left, in order to meet the attack on the right, but at the same time his left was furiously assaulted by Jones's brigade,— 25th, 42d, 48th, and 59th Virginia Infantry,—supported by Williams's brigade,—2d, 10th, 14th, and 15th Louisiana Infantry. Wadsworth, to assist Greene, extended his line to the right, and though so fearfully outnumbered, the Federal troops held their position, being well protected by breastworks and the large boulders.

Kane's brigade of Geary's division,—29th, 109th, and 111th Pennsylvania Infantry,—on its way to resume its position in the works, came in contact with Steuart's and Walker's brigades, the advance of which was thus checked, and about midnight the fighting ceased for the night, except slight skirmishing.

The Confederates, in the darkness, did not know how close they were to the Baltimore Pike in the rear of the Federal position, or to the trains and reserve artillery which were parked but a short distance from the position they had reached, and which they might have secured or endangered had they continued their advance after taking the works. They might have inflicted incalculable damage had they advanced to the pike, but they thought they were being entrapped, because of the little resistance they met with at the abandoned works.

In the mean time, during the attacks on the left and right, a most daring attempt was made against the right centre to carry East Cemetery Hill, that part of the hill opposite the entrance to the National Cemetery. Hays's brigade—5th, 6th, 7th, 8th, and 9th Louisiana Infantry—and Hoke's brigade—6th, 21st, and 57th North Carolina Infantry—formed quietly in the edge of the town and advanced across the low ground in magnificent style, as if to attack Culp's Hill, until opposite Cemetery Hill, when they suddenly changed direction to the right and dashed towards Cemetery Hill. Along the stone wall, near the foot of the hill, lay Ames's division of the Eleventh Corps. On the right was Von Gilsa's brigade,—41st New York, 153d Pennsylvania, 68th and 54th New York Infantry,—and on the left Harris's brigade,—17th Connecticut, 75th, 25th, and 107th Ohio Infantry. The 17th Connecticut had been in line between the 75th and 25th Ohio, but had been withdrawn and placed on the right of the division, leaving a gap in the line between the 75th and the 25th Ohio.

Penetrating this gap and crowding back Harris's brigade and the left of Von Gilsa's, the brave Confederates advanced up the hill, under cover of the darkness and smoke, and the charging columns were soon rushing among the batteries on the crest, the 6th North Carolina and 9th Louisiana leading the assault. Weidrick's I, 1st New York Battery, was north of the wall, towards the town; on the south of the wall, was Ricketts's F, 1st Pennsylvania, on its right being Reynolds's L, 1st New York, and in its rear, on the road, Stewart's B, 4th United States. Their guns were depressed as much as possible and fired grape and canister, but they could not stay the enemy.

Weidrick's battery was captured entire, and the left gun of Ricketts's was spiked while the gunners were fighting around it. This battery had received orders not to limber up under any circumstances, but to fight to the last, and it obeyed the order. A fierce hand-to-hand fight ensued, the young cannoneers, fighting with pistols, hand-spikes, and rammers, crying, "Death rather than surrender our guns on our own soil." The battery guidon was planted in one of the lunettes, and a Confederate officer seized it, when he was shot dead by young Riggin, its bearer, who himself was instantly killed, and fell with his flag in his hands. An officer of the 7th Louisiana was brained with a hand-spike by a young gunner, and a sergeant of the same regiment was severely wounded with a stone by Lieutenant Brockway. In the mean time, General Ames had rallied the left of Harris's brigade—25th, 75th, and 107th Ohio—behind the wall, near the crest of the hill, the 17th Connecticut continuing the fight at the foot, farther to the right. The color-bearer of the

107th Ohio mounted the wall and waved his flag, when he fell dead; the flag was seized by Adjutant Young, who immediately afterwards rushed into the 8th Louisiana, shot its color-bearer, seized its flag, and, severely wounded, fell with it inside his own lines. The hand-to-hand fight about the guns continued until reinforcements, hurried from the left of the cemetery, arrived. Carroll's brigade of Hays's division of the Second Corps, the 4th Ohio, 7th West Virginia, and 14th Indiana, charged to the right of Ricketts's, while to its left the 73d Pennsylvania, of Steinwehr's division, Eleventh Corps, double-quicking out of the cemetery, charged upon those who had taken Weidrick's battery. Schurz led the 58th and 119th New York, of his division, also to its support. The Confederate troops who had made this daring attack were driven from the hill after they had lost nearly two-thirds of their number.

To the left of the pike, Rodes's division advanced against that part of Cemetery Hill held by Schurz and Steinwehr. The right of his line not being supported by Pender's division, as arranged, soon came to a halt, while the left moved forward against the position held by the 27th Pennsylvania, 55th and 73d Ohio, and 136th New York, but was repulsed with a loss of a stand of colors.

The ground of the fierce and sanguinary fighting on East Cemetery Hill remains almost unchanged. The redans and lunettes are still preserved, with cannon to mark the position of the batteries.

The struggle of the second day was now ended, having during the day extended along nearly the whole line.

Towards evening Gregg's cavalry division, having arrived from Hanover, had gone into position on the right flank, and his skirmishers had had a brisk engagement with two regiments of Ewell's corps, which had attempted to dislodge them. Kilpatrick's cavalry division had also a sharp fight with a portion of Stuart's cavalry near Hunterstown about sundown.

LOSSES FOR THE DAY.

Commencing on the left of the line, the losses on this day, as reported, were as follows:

ROUND TOP.

FEDERAL LOSSES.

Vincent's Brigade.

Regiment.	Killed and wounded.	Missing.	Total loss.	Engaged.
20th Me.	120	5	125	386
16th Mich.	57	5	62	218
44th N. Y.	108	3	111	..
83d Penna.	55	..	55	208
Total	340	13	353	..

Weed's Brigade.

Regiment.	Killed and wounded.	Missing.	Total loss.
140th N. Y.	125	18	143
146th N. Y.	28	..	28
91st Penna.	19	..	19
155th Penna.	19	..	19
Total	191	18	209
Hazlett's U. S. Battery	13	..	13

Federal losses, 544 killed and wounded and 31 missing; total, 575.

CONFEDERATE LOSSES.

Law's Alabama Brigade.

Regiment.	Killed and wounded.	Missing.	Total loss.
4th Ala.	87	..	87
15th Ala.	161	..	161
44th Ala.	94	..	94
47th Ala.	40	..	40
48th Ala.	102	..	102
Total	484	146	484 = 630

Robertson's Texas Brigade.

Regiment.	Killed and wounded.	Missing.	Total loss.
4th Texas	87	..	87
5th Texas	109	..	109
Total	196	..	196

Confederate losses, 680 killed and wounded and 146 missing; total, 826.

WHEAT-FIELD, INCLUDING STRIP OF WOODS ON SIDES AND DEVIL'S DEN.

FEDERAL LOSSES.

Ward's Brigade (Third Corps).

Regiment.	Killed and wounded.	Missing.	Total loss.	Engaged.
20th Ind.	146	10	156	268
86th N. Y.	62	4	66	..
124th N. Y.	85	5	90	238
99th Penna.	99	11	110	339
4th Me.	70	74	144	..
2d U. S. Sharp-shooters	28	15	43	..
Total	490	119	609	..

De Trobriand's Brigade (Third Corps).

Regiment.	Killed and wounded.	Missing.	Total loss.	Engaged.
5th Mich.	105	4	109	..
17th Me.	130	3	133	..
40th N. Y.	143	7	150	..
110th Penna.	53	..	53	152
Total	431	14	445	..

Burling's Brigade (Third Corps).

Regiment.	Killed and wounded.	Missing.	Total loss.
6th N. J.	33	8	41
8th N. J.	45	2	47
115th Pa.	18	3	21
Total	96	13	109

Tilton's Brigade (Fifth Corps).

Regiment.	Killed and wounded.	Missing.	Total loss.
118th Penna.	22	3	25
18th Mass.	24	3	27
1st Mich.	38	4	42
22d Mass.	30	1	31
Total	114	11	135

SECOND DAY'S BATTLE.

Sweitzer's Brigade (*Fifth Corps*).

Regiment.	Killed and wounded.	Missing.	Total loss.	Engaged.
62d Penna.	135	40	175	426
4th Mich.	89	76	165	342
32d Mass.	75	5	80	..
Total	299	121	420	..

Cross's Brigade (*Second Corps*).

Regiment.	Killed and wounded.	Missing.	Total loss.	Missing.
5th N. H.	80	..	80	177
61st N. Y.	62	..	62	..
81st Penna.	54	8	62	175
148th Penna.	120	5	125	460
Total	316	13	329	..

Kelly's Brigade (*Second Corps*).

Regiment.	Killed and wounded.	Missing.	Total loss.	Engaged.
28th Mass.	65	35	100	224
63d N. Y. (2 cos.)	15	8	23	75
69th N. Y. (2 cos.)	19	6	25	..
88th N. Y. (2 cos.)	24	4	28	90
116th Penna. (4 cos.)	13	9	22	66
Total	136	62	198	..

Zook's Brigade (*Second Corps*).

Regiment.	Killed and wounded.	Missing.	Total loss.	Engaged.
140th Penna.	181	60	241	540
52d N. Y.	28	10	38	..
57th N. Y.	32	2	34	..
66th N. Y.	35	9	44	..
Total	276	81	357	..

Brooke's Brigade (Second Corps).

Regiment.	Killed and wounded	Missing.	Total loss.	Engaged.
27th Conn. (2 cos.)	33	4	37	74
2d Del.	72	12	84	..
64th N. Y.	79	19	98	204
53d Penna.	74	6	80	124
145th Penna.	76	8	84	228
Total	334	49	383	..

AYRES'S DIVISION (FIFTH CORPS).
Burbank's Brigade.

Regiment.	Killed and wounded.	Missing.	Total loss.	Engaged.
2d U. S. (6 cos.)	61	6	67	..
7th U. S. (4 cos.)	57	2	59	116
10th U. S. (3 cos.)	48	3	51	93
11th U. S. (6 cos.)	111	9	120	..
17th U. S. (7 cos.)	143	7	150	260
Total	420	27	447	..

Day's Brigade.

Regiment.	Killed and wounded.	Missing.	Total loss.
3d U. S. (6 cos.)	72	1	73
4th U. S. (4 cos.)	40	..	40
6th U. S. (5 cos.)	44	..	44
12th U. S. (8 cos.)	79	13	92
14th U. S. (8 cos.)	128	4	132
Total	363	18	381

Pennsylvania Reserves (Fifth Corps).

Regiment.	Killed and wounded.	Missing.	Total loss.	Engaged.
1st Penna.	46	..	46	444
2d Penna.	38	..	38	273
6th Penna.	24	..	24	380
11th Penna.	41	..	41	392
Bucktail Rifles	46	2	48	349
Total	195	2	197	1838

SECOND DAY'S BATTLE.

Wheaton's Brigade (Sixth Corps).

Regiment.	Killed and wounded.	Missing.	Total loss.
62d N. Y.	12	..	12
93d Penna.	10	..	10
98th Penna.	11	..	11
139th Penna.	20	..	20
Total	53	..	53

Artillery.

Battery.	Killed and wounded.	Missing.	Total loss.
Smith's N. Y.	12	1	13
Winslow's N. Y.	10	8	18
Bigelow's Mass.	26	2	28 and 60 horses.
Phillips's Mass.	21	..	21 and 40 horses.
Total	69	11	80

Federal losses in Wheat-Field, 3592 killed and wounded and 541 missing; total, 4133.

CONFEDERATE LOSSES.

Robertson's Texas Brigade.

Regiment.	Killed and wounded.
1st Texas	93
3d Ark.	142
Total	235

Anderson's Georgia Brigade.

Regiment.	Killed and wounded.	Missing.	Total loss.
7th Ga.	15	..	..
8th Ga.	139	..	..
9th Ga.	189	..	..
11th Ga.	204	..	..
59th Ga.	116	..	..
Total	663	54	717

Benning's Georgia Brigade.

Regiment.	Killed and wounded.	Missing.	Total loss.
2d Ga.	91	..	..
15th Ga.	171	..	..
17th Ga.	90	..	..
20th Ga.	121	122	..
Total	473	122	595

Wofford's Georgia Brigade.

Regiment.	Killed and wounded.	Missing.
16th Ga.	61	..
18th Ga.	19	..
24th Ga.	36	..
Cobb's (Ga.) Legion	22	..
Phillips's (Ga.) Legion	28	..
Total	166	112

The total losses reported for this brigade, however, are 334, which is greater than that shown by the regimental reports.

Semmes's Georgia Brigade.

Regiment.	Killed and wounded.	Missing.
10th Ga.	86	..
50th Ga.	78	..
51st Ga.	55	..
53d Ga.	87	..
Total	306	91

The total loss for the brigade is reported as 430.

SECOND DAY'S BATTLE.

Kershaw's South Carolina Brigade.

Regiment.	Killed and wounded.	Missing.	Total loss.
3d S. C.	81	2	83
7th S. C.	103	7	110
15th S. C.	119	18	137
Total	303	27	330

Confederate losses, 2416 killed and wounded and 406 missing; total, 2822.

The casualties among officers were very severe on both sides upon this part of the field.

Among those upon the Federal side killed or wounded, in addition to the Brigade Commanders Cross, Zook, and Brooke, were the colonel, lieutenant-colonel, and major of the 124th New York, the colonels of the 86th New York, 20th Indiana, 4th Maine, 5th Michigan, 110th, 140th, and 145th Pennsylvania, and 4th Michigan, and the major of the 62d Pennsylvania.

The loss of field-officers in the Confederate regiments was also severe, but is not officially reported.

Among the regiments deserving special mention here is the 17th Maine, which went into the field with most of the men bare-footed from hard marching and without having had rations for twenty-four hours, yet fought until 133 of its number had fallen.

PEACH ORCHARD.

FEDERAL LOSSES.

Regiment.	Killed and wounded.	Missing.	Total loss.	Engaged.
3d Me. (Ward's brig.)	77	45	122	210
3d Mich. (De Trobriand's brigade)	38	7	45	..
Total	115	52	167	..

Graham's Brigade.

Regiment.	Killed and wounded.	Missing.	Total loss.	Engaged.
57th Penna.	57	58	115	207
63d Penna.	30	4	34	296
68th Penna.	139	13	152	320
105th Penna.	123	9	132	274
114th Penna.	94	60	154	312
141st Penna.	128	21	149	202
Total	571	165	736	1611

Burling's Brigade.

Regiment.	Killed and wounded.	Missing.	Total loss.	Engaged.
2d N. H.	157	36	193	330
7th N. J.	101	13	114	..
Total	258	49	307	..

Artillery.

Battery.	Killed and wounded.	Missing.	Total loss.
Clark's N. J.	17	5	22
Thompson's Penna.	24	4	28
Ames's N. Y.	7	2	9
Hart's N. Y.	16	..	16
Total	64	11	75

Federal losses, 1008 killed and wounded and 277 missing; total, 1285.

CONFEDERATE LOSSES.

Kershaw's South Carolina Brigade.

Regiment.	Killed and wounded.	Missing.	Total loss.
2d S. C.	152	2	154
8th S. C.	100	. .	100
3d S. C. Battalion	43	3	46
Total	295	5	300

Barksdale's Mississippi Brigade.

Regiment.	Killed and wounded.	Missing.	Total loss.
13th Miss.	165	. .	. .
17th Miss.	200	. .	. .
18th Miss.	100	. .	. .
21st Miss.	103	. .	. .
Total	568	92	660

This brigade, however, reported a loss of 655 killed and wounded and 92 missing, which is probably more correct.

Confederate losses, 950 killed and wounded and 97 missing; total, 1047.

The casualties of the opposing forces were nearly equal. A portion of those in Barksdale's brigade, however, was suffered when that brigade afterwards encountered the Excelsior and Willard's New York brigades. Upon the other hand, most of those in the 105th Pennsylvania occurred as the regiment fought its way back with Humphreys's division, it halting in line and fighting in eight different positions, changing front to rear, while under fire, four times.

EMMITTSBURG ROAD, INCLUDING GROUND TO REAR OVER WHICH HUMPHREYS'S DIVISION FOUGHT.

FEDERAL LOSSES.

Carr's Brigade.

Regiment.	Killed and wounded.	Missing.	Total loss.	Engaged.
1st Mass.	99	21	120	..
11th Mass.	119	10	129	..
16th Mass.	68	13	81	..
12th N. H.	81	11	92	..
11th N. J.	141	12	153	275
26th Penna.	206	7	213	365
Total	714	74	788	..
5th N. J. (Burling's)	78	16	94	..

Excelsior (Brewster's) Brigade.

Regiment.	Killed and wounded.	Missing.	Total loss.	Engaged.
70th N. Y.	113	4	117	..
71st N. Y.	78	13	91	243
72d N. Y.	86	28	114	305
73d N. Y.	154	8	162	..
74th N. Y.	86	3	89	..
120th N. Y.	184	19	203	..
Total	701	75	776	..

Harrow's Brigade (Second Corps).

Regiment.	Killed and wounded.	Missing.	Total loss.	Engaged.
1st Minn.	201	..	201	263
15th Mass.	120	28	148	239
82d N. Y.	108	15	123	461
Total	429	43	472	963

The loss of the 15th Massachusetts includes loss on the 3d. The 1st Minnesota on the 3d

SECOND DAY'S BATTLE.

lost 24 of the 62 remaining on the 2d, and the 82d New York lost 69 on that day.

Willard's Brigade.

Regiment.	Killed and wounded.	Missing.	Total loss.	Engaged.
39th N. Y.	95	. .	95	. .
111th N. Y.	235	14	249	400
125th N. Y.	130	9	139	. .
126th N. Y.	221	10	231	402
Total	681	33	714	. .

The losses reported include those for the 2d and 3d, and, judging by what troops in the same line suffered on the 3d, this brigade probably lost 200 on that day.

Artillery.

Battery.	Killed and wounded.	Missing.	Total loss.
Randolph's R. I.	29	1	30 and 40 horses.
Turnbull's U. S.	23	1	24 . .
Seeley's U. S.	21	4	25 and 28 horses.
Watson's U. S.	20	2	22 . .
Total	93	8	101

Federal losses, 2496 killed and wounded and 249 missing; total, 2745.

CONFEDERATE LOSSES.

Wilcox's Alabama Brigade.

Regiment.	Killed and wounded.	Missing.	Total loss.
8th Ala.	161	. .	161
9th Ala.	58	. .	. .
10th Ala.	104	. .	. .
11th Ala.	75	. .	. .
14th Ala.	48	257	. .
Total	446	. .	. .

This brigade reports a loss, however, of 520 killed and wounded and 257 missing, which is nearer correct, but it also includes loss, suffered on the 3d, of 204 not reported by regiments.

Perry's Florida Brigade.

Regiment.	Killed and wounded.	Missing.	Total loss.
2d Fla.	81	..	..
5th Fla.	75	..	..
8th Fla.	94	..	..
Total	250	205	455

One hundred and fifty-five of the above were lost on the 3d, not reported by regiments, but included in the missing.

Wright's Brigade.

Regiment.	Killed and wounded.	Missing.	Total loss.
3d Ga.	100	..	..
22d Ga.	96	..	..
48th Ga.	90	..	..
2d Battalion	49	..	..
Total	335	333	668

The casualties in Barksdale's brigade have been given with those at Peach Orchard, though probably half of them, 370, were suffered upon this line.

Confederate artillery engaged during the day reported losses for the 2d and 3d as follows:

	Killed and wounded.	Missing.	Total loss.
Cabell's battalion	37	..	37
Alexander's battalion	133	6	139
Henry's battalion	27	..	27
Lane's battalion	24	6	30
Total	221	12	233

Confederate losses, 1326 killed and wounded and 652 missing; total, 1978.

Among the field-officers killed or wounded on the Federal side upon this part of the line were General Willard and the commanders of the 5th, 7th, and 11th New Jersey, 72d New York, 1st Minnesota, 15th and 20th Massachusetts, and 82d New York, and the major of the 26th Pennsylvania.

The casualties in Humphreys's division were caused to a great extent by the fire of Alexander's battalion of six batteries of artillery, which followed in the wake of Barksdale's brigade, and were worked with terrible effect.

The losses of the other regiments engaged in repulsing the assault of Wright's brigade upon Cemetery Hill are not given, as they were but slight, and will be included in the heavy losses which all those regiments incurred on the 3d.

EAST CEMETERY HILL.

FEDERAL LOSSES.

The reports do not show what casualties the 17th Connecticut, 25th, 75th, and 107th Ohio, of Harris's brigade, or the 68th New York and 153d Pennsylvania, of Von Gilsa's, suffered in the attack upon East Cemetery Hill, as their reports include the losses on the 1st, but they can be approximated from those of the following regiments not engaged on the 1st.

Von Gilsa's Brigade.

Regiment.	Killed and wounded.	Missing.	Total loss.
41st N. Y.	73	2	75
54th N. Y.	54	48	102
Total	127	50	177
73d Penna.	34	..	34

Carroll's Brigade.

Regiment.	Killed and wounded.	Missing.	Total loss.
4th Ohio	26	5	31
14th Ind.	31	..	31
17th W. Va.	46	1	47
Total	103	6	109
33d Mass.	45	..	..
Weiderick's N. Y. battery	13	..	..
Ricketts's Penna. battery	23	..	..

Federal losses reported, 345 killed and wounded and 56 missing; total, 401.

SECOND DAY'S BATTLE.

CONFEDERATE LOSSES.
Hays's Brigade.

Regiment.	Killed and wounded.	Missing.	Total loss.
5th La.	36	13	49
6th La.	39	21	60
7th La.	51	6	57
8th La.	62	13	75
9th La.	49	23	72
Total	237	76	313

Avery's (Hoke's) Brigade.

Regiment.	Killed and wounded.	Missing.	Total loss.
6th N. C.	151	21	172
21st N. C.	74	37	111
57th N. C.	26	36	62
Total	251	94	345

Confederate losses, 488 killed and wounded and 170 missing; total, 658.

It will be noted that, while this assault is called that of the "Louisiana Tigers," the three North Carolina regiments lost more than the five Louisiana regiments, according to the reports.

RECAPITULATION OF LOSSES FOR THE DAY.
FEDERAL.

	Killed and wounded.	Missing.	Total loss.
Round Top	544	31	575
Wheat-Field	3592	541	4133
Peach Orchard	1008	277	1285
Emmittsburg Road	2396	249	2745
East Cemetery Hill	345	56	401
Total	7885	1154	9139

CONFEDERATE LOSSES.

	Killed and wounded.	Missing.	Total loss.
Round Top	686	146	832
Wheat-Field	2416	406	2822
Peach Orchard	950	97	1047
Emmittsburg Road	1326	652	1978
East Cemetery Hill	488	170	658
Total	5806	1471	7337

THIRD DAY'S BATTLE, JULY 3.

THE battle opened on the third day at four o'clock in the morning, on the right, on Culp's Hill, where Johnson's division had effected a lodgement the night before. Here, as has been related, the enemy had been encountered the night before by Kane's brigade of Geary's division (Twelfth Corps) upon its return from the left, the advance of which had been surprised to find their works occupied by the enemy, who opened fire upon them. Owing to the nature of the ground and the darkness, the Federal troops were compelled to lie upon their arms and await the coming of morning.

In the mean time, Pickett's division of Longstreet's corps had arrived from Chambersburg and taken position opposite the Federal centre, between Anderson's and Heth's divisions of Hill's corps. O'Neal's and Daniel's brigades of Rodes's division had moved out of town, around to their left, to reinforce Johnson in his new position, as had also Smith's brigade of Early's division.

Upon the Federal side, Kane's and Candy's brigades of Geary's division had joined Greene's brigade of the same division in the works defended so well the night before by Greene's men. The 6th Wisconsin, 14th Brooklyn, and 147th New York Infantry, of Wadsworth's division, First Corps, and 82d Illinois, 45th New York, and 61st Ohio Infantry, of the Eleventh Corps, had gone to Greene's assistance and did good service, but returned to their own commands upon the arrival of Candy and Kane. Williams's division of the Twelfth Corps had also returned from the left, where it had gone the evening before, and taken position near Spangler's Spring. Lockwood's independent brigade—1st Maryland (Eastern Shore), 1st Maryland (Potomac Home Brigade), and 150th New York Infantry—had joined the corps.

Colonel Best had his corps artillery—Muhlenberg's F, 4th United States, Kinzie's K, 5th United States, Knap's Pennsylvania, Winegar's New York, and Rigby's Maryland batteries—in splendid position upon Powers's Hill, upon the pike in the rear of the cemetery, and upon McAllister's Hill, and it opened a furious fire upon the enemy, with a range of only 600 or 800 yards.

Williams's division, now commanded by Ruger (Williams being in command of the Twelfth Corps and Slocum that of the right

THIRD DAY'S BATTLE. 115

wing), moved forward on the right. McDougall's brigade—145th New York, 5th Connecticut, 46th Pennsylvania, 3d Maryland, 123d New York, and 20th Connecticut Infantry—advanced against the enemy's left, composed of the 10th and 23d Virginia and 1st North Carolina Infantry of Steuart's brigade. In the mean time the Confederates attacked Geary's division. On the right of their line were Williams's brigade—1st, 2d, 10th, 14th, and 15th Louisiana Infantry—and Jones's brigade—42d, 48th, 21st, 44th, 50th, and 25th Virginia Infantry. Williams's two right regiments attacked Cutler's brigade of the First Corps, on the left of Greene, —56th Pennsylvania, 76th, 147th New York, and 14th Brooklyn Infantry,—while the others, with those of Jones, attacked Greene's brigade, —137th, 149th, 102d, 78th, and 60th New York Infantry.

In the centre, the 3d North Carolina, 1st Maryland, and 37th Virginia, of Steuart's brigade, supported by the 32d, 43d, and 45th North Carolina Infantry, of Daniel's brigade, attacked Kane's brigade,—109th, 29th, and 11th Pennsylvania,—which brigade was fighting inside of and almost at right angles to the works, and the Confederates were repulsed. The 147th Pennsylvania and 5th Ohio Infantry, of Candy's brigade, on the right of and at an angle to

Kane's, aided in the repulse by the enfilading fire they were enabled to pour into the attacking columns. Farther to the left, Jones's Virginia and Williams's Louisiana brigades renewed the attack upon Greene's brigade, being reinforced by O'Neal's Alabama brigade. At the same time, Greene was reinforced by the rest of Candy's brigade,—7th, 29th, and 66th Ohio, and 28th Pennsylvania Infantry,—and the attack was repulsed.

Walker's Virginia brigade reinforced Daniel's and Steuart's, and Lockwood's brigade reinforced Greene and Candy, followed shortly by Shaler's brigade of the Sixth Corps,—23d and 82d Pennsylvania, and 65th, 67th, and 122d New York Infantry.

Some distance to the right, Colgrove's brigade of Ruger's division—2d Massachusetts, 27th Indiana, 3d Wisconsin, 13th New Jersey, and 107th New York Infantry—had resumed almost the same position it occupied the day before, and was upon the left flank of the Confederate line held by Walker's Virginia brigade. In rear of Walker's, and at right angles to it, facing Colgrove's brigade, was the 49th Virginia Infantry, of Smith's brigade, with the 52d Virginia immediately in rear of it, and the 31st Virginia some distance in rear of the 52d. Separating Smith's and Colgrove's lines was a

THIRD DAY'S BATTLE.

little meadow, little more than a hundred yards in width. Across this meadow the 2d Massachusetts and 27th Indiana Infantry were ordered to charge against Smith's line, which was on a slight elevation in the woods north of the meadow. They started across the meadow with cheers, the 2d Massachusetts being somewhat in advance; but the 2d Virginia Infantry, of Walker's brigade, unseen, was in the woods to their left, on the west side of the meadow, and as they reached the open ground they met a furious fire from Smith's two regiments, and the 2d Virginia, facing about, poured deadly volleys into the flank of the 2d Massachusetts. The regiments were driven back before they had crossed the meadow, the 2d with a loss of 136 and the 27th with a loss of 110. The Confederates attempted to follow these two regiments, but were met by the fire of the 3d Wisconsin and 13th New Jersey Infantry.

For six hours the terrible struggle continued along the line of the Twelfth Corps. The volleys of musketry were deafening. Nearly all the woods in which the battle raged have since died, showing how terrific was the fire.

The Confederates, after several attempts to take the works held by Greene's brigade and to drive Kane's from the position it held on the right of Greene, at 10.25 massed in column by regiments and made a last bold effort to break through the Federal lines, the attack falling principally upon Kane's brigade, but it was repulsed with severe loss, and under the combined attack of the six brigades of the Twelfth Corps the seven brigades of the Confederates were driven beyond Rock Creek, with a loss of nearly 2000 killed and wounded and 3 stands of colors.

At eleven o'clock the battle ceased on the right. The Federal line was now almost as it was at noon the day before, before the Third Corps moved out to the Emmittsburg Road and the Wheat-Field, except that the Fifth Corps extended the line on the left, occupying Little, and Big Round Tops.

On the right, at Culp's Hill, was the Twelfth Corps, on its left Wadsworth's division of the First; then the Eleventh upon Cemetery Hill, on its left Robinson's division of the First; then Hays's (except Carroll's brigade, still on Cemetery Hill with the Eleventh) and Gibbon's divisions of the Second; then Doubleday's division of the First, including Stannard's Vermont brigade, which had joined it the evening of the 1st; then Caldwell's division of the Second, in support of McGilvery's artillery; then the Fifth. The Sixth Corps was distributed to strengthen different parts of the line. Wheaton's brigade,

THIRD DAY'S BATTLE.

now commanded by Nevin,—93d, 98th, 102d, and 139th Pennsylvania, and 62d New York Infantry,—still lay to the right and front of Little Round Top. To its left and rear was Bartlett's brigade, of Wright's division,—5th Maine, 121st New York, 95th and 96th Pennsylvania Infantry,—while to its right and rear was Torbert's New Jersey brigade of the same division,—1st, 2d, 3d, and 15th New Jersey Infantry. In rear of Bartlett's was Eustis's brigade, of Wheaton's division,—7th, 10th, 37th Massachusetts, and 2d Rhode Island Infantry. Russell's brigade, of Wright's division,—6th Maine, 5th Wisconsin, 49th and 119th Pennsylvania Infantry,—and Grant's Vermont brigade,—2d, 3d, 4th, 5th, and 6th Infantry,—of Howe's division, were posted on the extreme left, to the rear of Big Round Top, to guard against an anticipated flank movement from that direction. Neill's brigade, of Howe's division,—7th Maine, 61st Pennsylvania, 33d, 43d, 49th, and 77th New York Infantry,—was sent to the extreme right, on Wolf's Hill, beyond Rock Creek, while Shaler's brigade, as we have noticed, went to the support of the Twelfth Corps. Stewart's United States, Weidrick's New York, Ricketts's Pennsylvania, and Reynolds's New York batteries still occupied Cemetery Hill. Bancroft's 4th United States, Dilger's 1st Ohio, Taft's

New York, Eakin's 1st United States, Wheeler's 13th New York, Huntington's Ohio, Hill's 1st West Virginia, and Edgell's New Hampshire batteries, under Major Osborne, were placed in the cemetery. On the left of the cemetery, near Zeigler's Grove, were Woodruff's United States, Arnold's Rhode Island, Cushing's United States, Brown's Rhode Island, and Rorty's New York batteries, under Captain Hazzard. Next to these, on the left, were Fitzhugh's New York, Parsons's New Jersey, Daniel's Michigan, Thomas's United States, Thompson's Pennsylvania, Phillips's Massachusetts, Sterling's Connecticut, Hart's New York, Cooper's Pennsylvania, Dow's Maine, and Ames's New York batteries, under Major McGilvery. On the extreme left were Gibbs's Ohio and Hazlett's United States batteries, the latter now commanded by Lieutenant Rittenhouse.

The Confederate army was also practically in the same position as it was on the evening of the 2d, Hood's division being on the extreme right. Benning's brigade held the ground about Devil's Den, which it had captured from Ward, Robertson's and Law's lay to its right, at the foot of Big Round Top, while Anderson's brigade extended the line westward from Round Top across the Emmittsburg Road. McLaws's division occupied the ground held the day before by Humphreys's, Kershaw being at the Peach Orchard and Wofford on the west side of the Wheat-Field, Pickett's division lying to the left of McLaws's, west of the Emmittsburg Road. Hill's corps was still in the centre and Ewell's on the left. Their artillery was well posted. Along the high ground on the Emmittsburg Road were Alexander's battalion of 8 batteries; Eshleman's Washington, of 4; Deering's, of 4; Cabell's, of 4; and Pogue's, of 4. To the left, on Seminary Ridge, were Garnett's, of 4; Lane's, of 3; Pegram's, of 5; McIntosh's, of 4; and Carter's, of 4.

Smith's brigade, of Steinwehr's division, 55th and 73d Ohio and 136th New York Infantry, lay on the west side of Cemetery Hill, along the Taneytown Road, since noon of the 1st until the close of the battle, and, though not otherwise engaged, its skirmishers were constantly on the line, and the brigade lost heavily, the 55th losing 49, the 73d 145, and the 136th 109. The 33d Massachusetts of this brigade was detached, being between Cemetery Hill and Culp's Hill with Stevens's Maine battery, losing 45. A third of a mile in front of Hays's division were the Bliss house and barn, which afforded an excellent cover for the Confederate sharp-shooters, who kept up an annoying fire. In the afternoon of the 2d the 12th New Jersey, with companies of the 1st Delaware and 106th Pennsylvania Infantry, charged the barn, encountering the 16th and 49th Mississippi Infantry, of Posey's brigade, and capturing about 100 prisoners. On the morning of the 3d the 12th New Jersey again charged the buildings, driving out those occupying it. Soon afterwards the 14th Connecticut again charged and, by direction of General Smyth, burned the buildings.

THE FINAL ASSAULT UPON CEMETERY RIDGE.

Preparations were at once made for what proved to be the last tremendous and deadly encounter. Meade had strengthened the position held by the First and Second Corps on Cemetery Hill by reserve lines of Infantry, and battery after battery had formed in park until eighty guns were trained upon Seminary Ridge. Upon the other side, Lee had massed seventy-five long-range guns upon the slight eminence held by Humphreys's division the day before; and sixty-three on Seminary Ridge. These guns were supported by other batteries in position.

There were two hours of comparative silence, until one o'clock P.M., when the signal gun was fired from Seminary Ridge by the Washington Artillery of New Orleans, and there was opened between the one hundred and thirty-eight Confederate guns and the eighty Federal guns the heaviest and most terrible artillery fire ever witnessed upon any battle-field in this country, if upon any in the world. It opened so suddenly that men were torn to pieces before they could rise from the ground upon which they had been lolling; some were stricken down with cigars in their mouths; one young soldier was killed with the portrait of his sister in his hand. The earth was thrown in clouds; splinters flew from fences and rocks; mingled with the roar of the artillery were the groans of wounded men and the fierce neighing of mangled horses. For two hours the air was filled with projectiles of every kind, hurled from two hundred guns; but the Federal troops stood the fire without wavering.

In the mean time the fresh troops of Pickett's Confederate division had been massed under cover of the slight ridge running between Seminary Ridge and the Emmittsburg Road, in rear of the artillery, while Pettigrew's division (formerly Heth's, who was wounded on the first day) was massed to their rear and left behind Seminary Ridge.

In the rear of the right of Pickett were the brigades of Wilcox and Perry, with that of Wright in reserve. In the rear of the right of

Pettigrew were the brigades of Scales and Lane, of Pender's division, commanded by Trimble, Pender having been killed the evening before.

When the artillery ceased firing, upon Chief of Artillery General Hunt's order, General Warren having informed him by signal from Round Top that under the smoke in the valley the enemy were forming for an attack, these troops moved from behind their cover and advanced majestically across the fields towards Cemetery Hill, Pickett's division on the right, Pettigrew's to its left and rear, *en echelon*, supported by Scales's and Lane's brigades. Kemper's brigade, of Pickett's division, was on the right, —24th, 11th, 1st, 7th, and 3d Virginia Infantry; on its left was Garnett's,—8th, 18th, 19th, 28th, and 50th Virginia Infantry,—while Armistead's —14th, 9th, 53d, 57th, and 38th Virginia Infantry—was in the rear, moving rapidly to take position on their left.

On the left of Pickett were the four brigades of Pettigrew's division: first, Frye's (Archer being a prisoner),—1st, 7th, and 14th Tennessee, 5th and 13th Alabama Infantry; then Marshall's (formerly Pettigrew's),—11th, 26th, 47th, and 52d North Carolina Infantry; Davis's,—2d, 11th, and 42d Mississippi and 55th North Carolina Infantry; and Brockenbrough's,—22d, 23d, 40th,

THIRD DAY'S BATTLE.

47th, and 55th Virginia Infantry. In the rear of Frye's and Marshall's brigades were Lowrance's (formerly Scales's)—1st, 16th, 22d, 34th, 13th, and 38th North Carolina Infantry—and Lane's,—33d, 18th, 7th, 28th, and 37th North Carolina Infantry,—these two brigades being under Trimble. Together, the assaulting party numbered about 14,000. The point of direction was the small "copse" of trees to the left of Zeigler's Grove, held by Gibbon's division of the Second Corps. After advancing some distance, the three brigades of Pickett's division made a half-wheel to the left, in order to move towards the objective point.

McGilvery's forty guns on the left, with those of the two batteries on Round Top, opened a terrible fire upon them, partly taking them in flank, and soon afterwards Hazzard's and Osborne's batteries opened upon them, the former with grape and canister, when their line was near enough.

Into their steady ranks were poured solid shot, spherical case, shrapnel, shell, and canister. Great gaps were torn in their lines, but they closed up each time and moved bravely on against the deadly storm. They reached the Emmittsburg Road within five hundred feet of the Federal line, posted behind the stone walls. As Kemper's brigade on the right of Pickett's division executed the wheel, its front and flank were exposed to the fire of the 20th New York and 151st Pennsylvania Infantry, of Doubleday's division, and to that of Stannard's brigade, —13th, 14th, and 16th Vermont Infantry,—of the same division, which regiments were on the left of Gibbon's division, and as the assaulting columns moved on towards the copse of trees, the two first-named regiments, moving in the same direction, continued firing, while the 13th and 16th Vermont, by direction of General Hancock, changed front forward on first company and opened directly upon Kemper's flank, nearly destroying the 24th and 11th Virginia Regiments, and causing his brigade to crowd to the left. Armistead's brigade moved rapidly in between Kemper's and Garnett's, and together they charged to the projection and angle of the wall held by Webb's Philadelphia brigade,— 69th, 71st, and 72d, and two companies of the 106th Pennsylvania Infantry (the balance of the 106th having been sent the evening before to support batteries on Cemetery Hill). As the division neared the wall it was joined on its left by Frye's Tennessee brigade, of Pettigrew's line, and at the same time Lowrance's North Carolina brigade rushed from the rear and joined Frye's and Garnett's at the angle of the wall. The two guns of Cushing's battery at the wall were silenced, and the left of the 71st Pennsylvania was withdrawn to a line with the right, at the wall to the rear. Through this gap the Confederates crossed the wall. Garnett had been killed and Kemper wounded. The other guns of Cushing's Battery A, 4th United States, were posted near the clump of trees near by. Armistead, putting his hat on his sword, dashed forward towards the battery, followed by a portion of his command, and fell dead by the side of Cushing, near the "copse" of woods, which was the extreme point reached by the Confederates in this charge.

As the right flank of the 69th Pennsylvania was passed, the two right companies were thrown back at an angle to the wall, firing into the enemy that had crossed it. At the same time, to the left of the regiment, there was a gap in the wall which had been made for the passage of a battery the day before. Through this gap the enemy also passed, but the regiment held its position. Cowan's New York battery galloped up and opened with double charges of canister, at twenty paces, upon the enemy who had passed the left of the 69th.

The 72d and the two companies of the 106th Pennsylvania moved from their position in the second line to the right and rear of the 69th, and opened upon the enemy crowding over the wall.

To the left of Webb's, Hall's brigade,—19th and 20th Massachusetts, 42d and 59th New York, and 7th Michigan Infantry,—after firing at short range upon the enemy in its front, made a half-wheel to the rear and attacked the enemy in flank. Harrow's brigade—1st Minnesota, 15th Massachusetts, 19th Maine, and 82d New York Infantry—moved from the left and also attacked Pickett in flank. General Hancock, riding to the very front, was wounded, and, lying upon the front line in a reclining position, with the blood gushing from a wound in the groin, directed the battle.

Farther to the right, Marshall's brigade,—11th, 26th, 47th, and 52d North Carolina,—Davis's,—2d, 11th, and 42d Mississippi, and 55th North Carolina,—and Lane's,—7th, 18th, 28th, 33d, and 37th North Carolina,—were fighting with Smyth's brigade of Hays's division of the Second Corps,—12th New Jersey, 1st Delaware, 14th Connecticut, and 108th New York Infantry,—and Sherrill's (formerly Willard's),—39th, 11th, 125th, and 126th New York Infantry. The two little brigades of Hays's division poured fearful volleys into the brave foe, which compelled some of them to crowd to their right upon Pickett, while others fled or surrendered. Woodruff's battery, in the grove to the right, moved forward and swept the enemy with canister. The 8th Ohio, on the skirmish line to the right, changed front forward on left company, and opened fire upon the flank.

Meanwhile, to the left, at the angle of the wall, the several regiments mentioned advanced and poured into the yelling and desperate assailants a converging deadly fire, and the attack was ended. When the smoke lifted, the three brigades of Pickett's division were annihilated. Nearly half of those who survived the death which they so bravely faced were prisoners. The division lost all three of its brigadiers, Garnett and Armistead being killed, and Kemper severely wounded and a prisoner. It lost every field-officer of its fifteen regiments, except one lieutenant-colonel, and two-thirds of its line officers were either killed or wounded, and but about 2000 out of 4900 men returned to their line. It lost twelve out of fifteen battle-flags.

Pettigrew's and Trimble's divisions had also been repulsed with a loss of about 2000, and fifteen stands of colors. Troops had been hurried from the First, Third, and Sixth Corps to aid in repulsing the attack, but it had ended before they arrived.

The left of the charging column, under Pettigrew and Trimble, suffered as severely as the right, under Pickett.

Great injustice has been done these troops

by the prevailing erroneous impression that they failed to advance with those of Pickett. *Such is not the fact.* As they were formed behind Seminary Ridge, they had over thirteen hundred yards to march under the terrible fire to which they were exposed, while Pickett's division, being formed under cover of the intermediate ridge, had but nine hundred yards to march under fire. At the first the assaulting columns advanced *en echelon*, but when they reached the Emmittsburg Road they were on a line, and together they crossed the road. The left of Pettigrew's command becoming first exposed to the fearful enfilading fire upon their left flank from the 8th Ohio and other regiments of Hays's division, and of Woodruff's battery and other troops, the men on that portion of the line (Brockenbrough's brigade) either broke to the rear or threw themselves on the ground for protection. But Pettigrew's other brigades,— Frye's, Davis's, and Marshall's,—with the brigades of Lowrance and Lane, under Trimble, advanced with Pickett up to the stone wall, and there fought desperately. This is substantiated by the fact that the colors of the 1st and 14th Tennessee and 13th and 5th Alabama were captured at the angle of the wall, and eleven others were picked up between the Emmittsburg Road and the stone wall, in front of Hays's

THIRD DAY'S BATTLE.

division. Pettigrew and Trimble, with three of their brigade commanders, Frye, Marshall, and Lowrance, were wounded. Davis's brigade lost all its field-officers, Marshall's all but one, and Frye's five out of seven.

As the assaulting columns reached the wall, Wilcox's Alabama and Perry's Florida brigades to the right, marching according to orders, but having become separated from Pickett, had resumed the march towards the left, advancing from the top of the crest, from behind which Pickett had emerged, directly towards McGilvery's batteries and the Third Corps, but, being received with a severe fire by Stannard's Vermonters, who had changed front again, and exposed to a heavy artillery fire, and seeing the commands of Pickett, Pettigrew, and Trimble repulsed, they withdrew under cover of the hill.

Thus ended this reckless and ever-renowned effort to carry Cemetery Hill by direct assault in the face of a hundred cannon and of the Federal army. The bravery displayed by the troops engaged in it will be ever admired by all those who have a pride in American courage. The point which the charging columns reached is well known as the "high-water-mark of the Rebellion," as from the time of that repulse until the close of the war the hopes of its leaders waned, and reverses attended the courageous and determined efforts of its armies. It lies to the west of the Taneytown Road, and the field and its surroundings remain almost unchanged.

The prominent Confederate officers killed or wounded in this struggle have already been named. Upon the Federal side, Hancock, Gibbon, and Webb were wounded, all of them having been in the thickest of the battle.

But why call this Pickett's charge? In this assault there were engaged 42 Confederate regiments. In Pickett's division there were 15 Virginia regiments. In Pettigrew's and Trimble's there were 15 North Carolina, 3 Mississippi, 3 Tennessee, 2 Alabama, and 4 Virginia, the latter being Brockenbrough's brigade. In addition to the artillery fire, they encountered 9 regiments of New York, 5 of Pennsylvania, 3 of Massachusetts, 3 of Vermont, 1 of Michigan, 1 of Maine, 1 of Minnesota, 1 of New Jersey, 1 of Connecticut, 1 of Ohio, 1 of Delaware,—27 in all.

The troops of Trimble's and Pettigrew's divisions behaved as gallantly as those of Pickett. Some prominent writers, even historians like Swinton and Lossing, have said that the left of the line did not advance as was expected, and that it was because the troops were not of the same "fine quality" as those upon the right;

that they were "raw, undisciplined," etc. Yet but two days before these same soldiers of Pettigrew and Trimble had fought around Reynolds's Grove for six hours, in a struggle with the First Corps that is unsurpassed for bravery and endurance, and where so many of their number had fallen. There were, in fact, no better troops in the Confederate army than they. Is history repeating itself? If the event is correctly recorded, there were at Thermopylæ 300 Spartans, 700 Thespians, and 300 Thebans. It is said the latter went over to the enemy, but the Thespians died, to a man, "at the pass" with the Spartans. Yet for twenty-three centuries epic song and story have well preserved the memory of the Spartans, while the devoted Thespians are forgotten.

All honor to the Spartan Virginians who, with well-dressed ranks and in splendid array, moved so gallantly, so steadily, so dauntlessly across that death-swept field, but honor, too, the Thespian North Carolinians and other troops who, too, marched and fought there that day. The valor of the one will not be dimmed by according justice to the other.

This assault was a reckless and useless waste of valor and life. Had those making it succeeded in breaking the Federal line, their success could only have been temporary, as they must have succumbed to the immense number of troops, who, without weakening the line elsewhere, were hurrying to the point of attack.

The Memorial Association, with appropriations especially made by the States for that purpose, has erected at the copse of trees a very unique and artistic memorial, and upon the open pages of an immense bronze volume are recorded the incidents of this historic assault, with the names of all the commands that participated in it on both sides.

GREGG'S CAVALRY FIGHT ON THE RIGHT FLANK.

It was part of General Lee's plan to send Stuart's cavalry with portions of Ewell's corps during the assault upon the centre of the Federal army around its right flank, with the intention of gaining its rear, and thus cause consternation among the troops at the very time of the attack in front.

Out on the Bonnaughtown or Hanover road, some three miles to the right and in advance of the Federal infantry, was the cavalry division of General D. McM. Gregg. With this division, and for the time acting under General Gregg, was Custer's splendid Michigan brigade, of Kilpatrick's division.

Gregg's division consisted of McIntosh's bri-

THIRD DAY'S BATTLE. 135

gade,—3d Pennsylvania, 1st New Jersey, and 1st Maryland Cavalry,—Randoll's Light Battery E, 1st United States (the 1st Pennsylvania Cavalry being upon duty at Meade's headquarters with the 2d Pennsylvania, and the 1st Massachusetts being with the Sixth Corps), and J. Irvin Gregg's brigade,—16th Pennsylvania, 1st Maine, and 10th New York Cavalry (the 4th Pennsylvania having been ordered to report to General Pleasonton in rear of the centre). Huey's brigade of this division—2d and 4th New York, 6th Ohio, and 8th Pennsylvania Cavalry—had been sent to Westminster to protect the trains. Custer's brigade was composed of the 1st, 5th, 6th, and 7th Michigan Cavalry and Pennington's Light Battery M, 2d United States.

During the heavy cannonading, General Stuart, leaving some sharp-shooters in front to engage the attention of the Federal cavalry, moved swiftly to the left under cover of the woods, with the brigades of Hampton, Fitzhugh Lee, W. H. F. Lee, and Jenkins, and Breathed's and Griffin's Maryland and McGregor's Virginia Light Batteries. When he debouched from the woods, to his surprise he found that Gregg had been on the alert and was in his front. Having failed to elude his adversary, Stuart now determined to force his way, and there ensued upon those fields one of the best and most closely fought cavalry engagements of the war.

Custer's brigade had just left its position to return and rejoin its division on the left flank, and McIntosh's had taken its place, the 1st New Jersey and a part of the 3d Pennsylvania being on the skirmish line. McIntosh, convinced that the enemy was in his front, determined to develop it, and advanced his skirmish line to near Rummell's barn, when the engagement opened. The Confederate line was held by a portion of Hampton's and Fitzhugh Lee's brigades.

Gregg immediately ordered Custer back with his brigade, the 1st Maryland was placed on the right to guard that flank, and Irvin Gregg's brigade was also ordered up at a trot. Stuart at the same time brought forward, on his right, Jenkins's brigade,—14th, 15th, 16th, 17th, 34th, and 35th Virginia Mounted Infantry. The 6th Michigan went into position to meet it on the left of the 3d Pennsylvania. In the mean time, Randol's and Pennington's batteries opened fire upon those of the enemy on the hill back of Rummell's house. The enemy now attempted to turn the right of the Federal line, but was repulsed by a gallant charge of a squadron of the 3d Pennsylvania. The 1st New Jersey's and 3d Pennsylvania's ammunition was nearly exhausted, when the 5th Michigan was sent to relieve them; but at the same time W. H. F. Lee's brigade (commanded by Chambliss)—7th, 10th, 13th, and 15th Virginia, and 2d North Carolina Cavalry—came to the support of the Confederate line. The 3d Pennsylvania returned to the line, with the 1st New Jersey, and fought dismounted along the fence until every cartridge of carbine and pistol was gone. At the same time Jenkins's brigade was repulsed by the 6th Michigan with its repeating rifles. Fitzhugh Lee's brigade—1st, 2d, 3d, 4th, and 5th Virginia Cavalry—now reinforced the Confederate left. The 1st Virginia charged in splendid style against Gregg's right centre, and was met in a counter-charge by the 7th Michigan, in close column of squadrons. They met at a fence, where, face to face, they fought in a desperate manner. The Confederates were reinforced; when the 5th Michigan went to the assistance of the 7th, which was falling back, the 1st New Jersey and 3d Pennsylvania opened on the flanks of the 1st Virginia and the rest of Fitzhugh Lee's brigade, and they were driven back.

As a last desperate effort, Hampton's brigade,—1st and 2d South Carolina, Cobb's and Phillips's (Georgia) and Jeff. Davis's (South Carolina) Legions, and 1st North Carolina Cavalry,—in close column of squadrons, with sabres drawn, charged in magnificent style upon the Federal batteries, which poured into it percussion shell and canister.

Gregg hurled against them the 1st Michigan, under Custer. Upon both sides every horse was on the jump and every trooper wildly yelling; the lines clashed together with a terrific shock. The enemy's charge was checked; but Hampton was immediately reinforced by Fitzhugh Lee's brigade, and the fight was renewed. Gregg mounted all his men as quickly as possible, and McIntosh, with his staff and orderlies, joined in the charge. The fighting was at the closest quarters. Hampton was wounded with a sabre by a charge of a squadron of the 1st New Jersey, and Captain Newhall, of the 3d Pennsylvania, was wounded with the spear of a flag-staff, tearing open his mouth. In a frenzied manner the fighting went on. Then Captain Miller's squadron of the 3d Pennsylvania charged from the right and went through the Confederate line, cutting a portion of it off and driving it past Rummell's, close up to Breathed's Confederate battery, which limbered up and left the field. At last the Confederates wavered, then turned and fled from the field. Many Federals, charging too far ahead, were swept along as prisoners by the retreating enemy.

Gregg and his division had well maintained

THIRD DAY'S BATTLE.

the reputation they had for steadiness and discipline. Irvin Gregg's brigade did not participate, as it was engaged in preventing a movement by Confederate infantry upon the right of the Federal infantry, and arrived to the support of the cavalry after the fight was over.

The Federal cavalry, though so greatly outnumbered,—being but seven regiments against Stuart's twenty,—fought as if inspired by a knowledge of the fearful consequences that might follow its defeat, and as if the safety of the army was in its keeping, and there, isolated from the rest of the army, the troopers fought and won their battle. For hours the booming of light artillery and the roar of carbines were mingled with the crack of pistol and the clash of sabre. Each assault of Stuart was hurled back, and charge was met with counter-charge, until, defeated and whipped, the famous Confederate cavalry leader was compelled to withdraw his badly crippled squadrons and abandon his attempts to reach the flanks of the Federal army. The fighting was nearly all at close quarters, and the sabre and pistol were freely used. In one spot there were found, after the battle, a Federal and a Confederate cavalryman lying head to head, each stretched at full length, with his sabre firmly clasped, and each with his head split open, showing how simultaneously they had dealt each other death-blows as they dashed together.

THE CAVALRY CHARGE UPON THE LEFT.

Upon the left of the Federal line there was also a great cavalry charge this day, and the Confederates were kept busy protecting their right flank. About noon Kilpatrick, with Farnsworth's brigade of his own division—5th New York, 18th Pennsylvania, 1st Vermont, and 1st West Virginia Cavalry—and Merritt's Regular brigade, of Buford's division,—1st, 2d, 5th, and 6th United States, and 6th Pennsylvania Cavalry,—crossed Plum Creek to the left of Round Top and endeavored to strike the supply trains of the enemy.

Farnsworth, at the head of his brigade, bravely charged the infantry posted behind the stone walls. With the 1st Vermont and a portion of the 1st West Virginia, he broke through the line of the 1st Texas Infantry, and at a furious gallop passed along the rear of the Confederate line until he met the fire of the 4th Alabama Infantry, which had been hurried back from the line to meet him, when he boldly wheeled his brave command and galloped westward straight for Bachman's South Carolina battery upon the slope of the hill near the Emmittsburg Road, riding up so close to the mouth of the guns that a captain of the 1st West Virginia fell in under the guns with his horse, which had been shot. Exposed now to the fire of the 9th Georgia Infantry, which had double-quicked to the support of the battery, the intrepid leader again wheeled and attempted to ride along the Confederate rear, meeting this time the fire of the 15th Alabama Infantry, which had quickly moved back from Law's line to stay his daring advance. Once more he wheeled and attempted to break back through the line of the Texans, but, being surrounded, he was killed and his brave command scattered, some of them even escaping up Big Round Top, leading their horses.

Farther out on the Emmittsburg Road, Merritt's United States Regular Cavalry, in an effort to reach the trains, was engaged in heavy skirmishing for over three hours with Anderson's 7th, 8th, 9th, 11th, and 59th Georgia Infantry. The movements were successful in detaining a large force of the enemy's infantry on that part of the field to watch them.

In the mean time, in front of Little Round Top, a rebel battery was causing considerable damage, and McCandless's brigade of Pennsylvania Reserves was ordered to attempt its capture. Leaving the 6th Infantry to engage Wofford's Georgia brigade in front, McCandless moved, with the 1st, 2d, and 11th Infantry and Bucktail Rifles, to his left, and then advanced with the Bucktails as skirmishers. The brigade, having drawn the fire of Benning's brigade,— 2d, 15th, 17th, and 20th Georgia Infantry,— threw itself upon the ground until the volleys had passed over it, and then, springing to its feet, charged the enemy until it had reached a position in rear of the battery, when it quickly changed direction and swept over the battery, capturing it, with two hundred prisoners and a stand of colors.

CASUALTIES FOR THE DAY.

CULP'S HILL.

FEDERAL LOSSES.

GEARY'S DIVISION (TWELFTH CORPS).

Greene's Brigade.

Regiment.	Killed and wounded.	Missing.	Total loss.
60th N. Y.	52	..	52
78th N. Y.	27	3	30
102d N. Y.	21	8	29
137th N. Y.	127	10	137
149th N. Y.	52	3	55
Total	279	24	303

THIRD DAY'S BATTLE.

Candy's Brigade.

Regiment.	Killed and wounded.	Missing.	Total loss.
5th Ohio	18	. .	18
7th Ohio	18	. .	18
29th Ohio	38	. .	38
60th Ohio	17	. .	17
28th Penna.	24	3	27
147th Penna.	20	. .	20
Total	135	3	138

Kane's Brigade.

Regiment.	Killed and wounded.	Missing.	Total loss.	Engaged.
29th Penna.	58	8	66	488
109th Penna.	9	1	10	149
111th Penna.	22	. .	22	259
Total	89	9	98	896

RUGER'S DIVISION (TWELFTH CORPS).

Lockwood's Brigade.

Regiment.	Killed and wounded.	Missing.	Total loss.
1st Md.	103	1	104
1st Md., E. S.	23	2	25
150th N. Y.	30	15	45
Total	156	18	174

Colgrove's Brigade.

Regiment.	Killed and wounded.	Missing.	Total loss.
2d Mass.	132	4	136
27th Ind.	109	1	110
13th N. J.	21	. .	21
3d Wis.	10	. .	10
107th N. Y.	2	. .	2
Total	274	5	279

McDougall's Brigade.

Regiment.	Killed and wounded.	Missing.	Total loss.
5th Conn.	2	5	7
20th Conn.	27	1	28
3d Md.	8	..	8
46th Penna.	12	1	13
123d N. Y.	13	1	14
145th N. Y.	10	..	10
Total	72	8	80

Shaler's Brigade (Sixth Corps).

Regiment.	Killed and wounded.	Missing.	Total loss.
23d Penna.	14	..	14
82d Penna.	6	..	6
65th N. Y.	9	..	9
67th N. Y.		1	1
122d N. Y.	42	2	44
Total	71	3	74
Corps artillery	9	..	9

CONFEDERATE LOSSES.

JOHNSON'S DIVISION.

Steuart's Brigade.

Regiment.	Killed and wounded.	Total loss.
1st Md.	144	144
1st N. C.	52	52
3d N. C.	156	156
10th Va.	21	21
23d Va.	18	18
37th Va.	54	54
Total	445	445

The brigade, however, reported a loss of 482 killed and wounded and 190 missing.

THIRD DAY'S BATTLE.

Williams's Brigade.

Regiment.	Killed and wounded.	Total loss.
1st La.	39	39
2d La.	62	62
10th La.	91	91
14th La.	65	65
15th La.	38	38
Total	295	295

Loss reported by brigade, 352 killed and wounded, 36 missing; total loss, 388.

Walker's Brigade.

Regiment.	Killed and wounded.	Total loss.
2d Va.	14	14
4th Va.	86	86
5th Va.	51	51
27th Va.	41	41
33d Va.	48	48
Total	240	240

Loss reported by brigade, 243 killed and wounded, 87 missing; total loss, 330.

Jones's Brigade.

Regiment.	Killed and wounded.	Missing.	Total loss.
21st Va.	50	. .	50
25th Va.	70	. .	70
42d Va.	56	. .	56
44th Va.	56	. .	56
48th Va.	76	. .	76
50th Va.	99	. .	99
	407	61	407 = 468

EARLY'S DIVISION.

Smith's Brigade.

Regiment.	Killed and wounded.	Missing.	Total loss.
31st Va.	20	7	27
40th Va.	90	10	100
52d Va.	15	..	15
Total	125	17	142

The losses of Daniel's and O'Neal's brigades are not reported separately for this day, and the others were understated.

	Killed and wounded.	Missing.	Total loss.
Total Federal losses	1085	70	1155
Total Confederate losses	1609	391	2000

The losses of the Federal troops here were comparatively light, because they were protected by breastworks and the large boulders, an advantage they seldom enjoyed during the war.

CEMETERY RIDGE.

FEDERAL LOSSES.

GIBBON'S DIVISION (SECOND CORPS).

Harrow's Brigade.

Regiment.	Killed and wounded.	Missing.	Total loss.	Engaged.
19th Me.	195	4	199	..
82d N. Y.	69	..	69	..
1st Minn.	24	..	24	62
Total	288	4	292	62

THIRD DAY'S BATTLE.

The loss of the 15th Massachusetts, of this brigade, in the two days was 148, most of it being on the 2d, where it has been given with that of the 82d New York, which that day lost 123, and the 1st Minnesota 201 of 263 engaged.

Webb's Philadelphia Brigade.

Regiment.	Killed and wounded.	Missing.	Total loss.	Engaged.
69th Penna.	122	7	129	329
71st Penna.	79	19	98	331
72d Penna.	189	2	191	458
106th Penna. (2 cos.)	63	4	67	..
Total.	453	32	485	1118

Hall's Brigade.

Regiment.	Killed and wounded.	Missing.	Total loss.
19th Mass.	70	7	77
20th Mass.	124	3	127
7th Mich.	65	..	65
42d N. Y.	70	4	74
59th N. Y. (4 cos.)	34	..	34
Total	363	14	377

Stannard's Brigade (First Corps).

Regiment.	Killed and wounded.	Missing.	Total loss.
13th Vt.	113	10	123
14th Vt.	86	21	107
16th Vt.	118	1	119
Total	317	32	349

The losses of the 20th New York, and the 151st Pennsylvania, of the First Corps, for this day are not reported, being given with the heavy losses they suffered on the 1st.

HAYS'S DIVISION (SECOND CORPS).

Smyth's Brigade.

Regiment.	Killed and wounded.	Missing.	Total loss.
14th Conn.	62	4	66
1st Del.	64	13	77
12th N. J.	106	9	115
108th N. Y.	102	..	102
10th N. Y. (4 cos.)	6	..	6
Total	340	26	366
8th Ohio (Carroll's brigade)	101	1	102

The 12th New Jersey withheld its fire until the enemy was within twenty yards of the wall, and then opened with buck and ball, causing great slaughter in Frye's and Lowrance's brigades.

Lieutenant William Smith, in command of the 1st Delaware, was found after the battle, dead, with his sword in one hand and a Confederate flag in the other.

The loss of Willard's brigade—39th, 111th, 125th, and 126th New York—for the two days was 714, 500 of which was probably incurred on the 2d in the encounter with Barksdale's brigade, and the balance of 200 on the 3d.

THIRD DAY'S BATTLE.

Artillery.

Battery.	Killed and wounded.	Missing.	Total loss.
Woodruff's U. S.	25	..	25
Cushing's U. S.	38	..	38
Arnold's R. I.	31	1	32
Brown's R. I.	26	2	28
Rorty's N. Y.	26	..	26
Cowan's N. Y.	12	..	12
Total	158	3	161

CONFEDERATE LOSSES.

PICKETT'S DIVISION.

Garnett's Brigade.

Regiment.	Killed and wounded.	Total loss.
8th Va.	54	54
18th Va.	87	87
19th Va.	44	44
28th Va.	77	77
56th Va.	62	62
Total	324	324

The brigade report, however, shows the loss to be 402 killed and wounded and 539 missing.

Armistead's Brigade.

Regiment.	Killed and wounded.	Missing.	Total loss.
9th Va.	71	..	71
14th Va.	108	..	108
38th Va.	170	..	170
53d Va.	104	..	104
57th Va.	121	..	121
Total	574	643	574=1217

Kemper's Brigade.

Regiment.	Killed and wounded.	Missing.	Total loss.
1st Va.	64	..	64
3d Va.	67	..	67
7th Va.	94	..	94
11th Va.	109	..	109
24th Va.	128	..	128
Total	462	317	462 = 779

Total for division, 1438 killed and wounded and 1499 missing.

PETTIGREW'S AND TRIMBLE'S DIVISIONS.

In view of the controversy as to the comparative casualties in Pickett's division, and in Pettigrew's and Trimble's, it would be very interesting if those of the latter two divisions upon this day had been separately reported, they having been so severely engaged on the 1st.

While they cannot be ascertained accurately, they can, however, be closely approximated.

Commencing with Archer's brigade, Colonel Frye, commanding it, said that as they neared the wall General Garnett, commanding Pickett's left brigade, called out to him that he was dressing on him (Frye), and that together they approached the wall. This brigade reports a loss of 517 missing, 75 of whom, the report says, were captured on the 1st with General Archer.

THIRD DAY'S BATTLE. 151

The balance, 442, must therefore have been lost on the 3d, and it can be fairly assumed that at least three-fourths of them were killed and wounded, if not more, for the brigade here lost 5 of 7 field-officers killed and wounded, and line-officers in proportion, and the men in the ranks were as much exposed.

In Pettigrew's brigade, the 26th North Carolina reported a loss of 126 missing, all of which must have been on the 3d, as the regiment remained in possession of the field on the 1st. It went into battle on the 3d with but 216, and had but 84 remaining when the regiment retired to its own line. Therefore 132 must have been lost in killed, wounded, and missing, and certainly the other three regiments,—11th, 47th, and 52d, the latter two being much larger,—having also gone across the Emmittsburg Road, and met the fire of Hays's division and Woodruff's battery, must have lost as heavily, making a brigade loss of 528, 300 of whom were killed and wounded. This is not an exaggerated estimate, inasmuch as the brigade lost here all its field-officers but one, and the report says regiments came out commanded by lieutenants.

But when we come to Davis's Mississippi brigade we have a more certain basis of calculation. The 11th Mississippi regiment, being on duty with the trains, was not engaged on the 1st, and its reported loss, 202, was all incurred on the 3d. The other three regiments, 2d and 42d Mississippi and 52d North Carolina, reported a loss of killed and wounded of 695 in the two days. A large portion of the 2d and 42d was captured on the 1st, but the remnants of these regiments, with the 55th North Carolina, a large regiment, together most likely equalled in strength on the 3d that of the 11th, and lost as heavily, making at least 400 for the brigade.

General Lane reported a loss of 660 killed and wounded, most of which he says "occurred on the 3d, his loss on the 1st being but slight," and if it is estimated at a third of the entire loss, there would be a loss of 440 for the 3d.

Scales's brigade lost 425 killed and wounded and 110 missing, the latter of whom must have all been lost on the 3d, as it retained possession of the field on the 1st. As the remnant of this brigade went up to the wall with Archer's, it is but fair to assume that of the 425 killed and wounded, at least 100 were lost on the 3d, making a total loss of 210 for the day.

Brockenbrough's brigade reported a loss of 148 for the two days, and most of this occurred on the 1st in front of Reynolds's Grove.

The losses, therefore, of these two divisions were approximately,—

THIRD DAY'S BATTLE. 153

	Killed and wounded.	Missing.	Total loss.
Archer's brigade	330	112	442
Pettigrew's brigade	300	228	528
Davis's brigade	244	160	404
Lane's brigade	264	176	440
Scales's brigade	125	85	210
Total	1263	761	2024

Wilcox's brigade, of Anderson's division, reported a loss of 204 killed and wounded on the 3d, and Perry's 155.

	Killed and wounded.	Missing.	Total loss.
Total Federal losses	2220	112	2332
Total Confederate losses	3060	2260	5320

There were engaged during the day upon Culp's Hill and Cemetery Ridge, upon the Federal side, 21 regiments of New York, 13 of Pennsylvania, 5 of Ohio, 4 of Massachusetts, 3 of Vermont, 3 of Connecticut, 3 of Maryland, 2 of New Jersey, 1 of Michigan, 1 of Minnesota, one of Delaware, 1 of Wisconsin, 1 of Indiana,— 59 in all; and upon the Confederate side, 36 of Virginia, 22 of North Carolina, 7 of Alabama, 5 of Louisiana, 3 of Mississippi, 3 of Tennessee, and 1 of Maryland,—77 in all, those of Virginia predominating this day, as those of North Carolina did on the 1st, and those of Georgia on the 2d.

CAVALRY LOSSES ON RIGHT FLANK.

GREGG'S FEDERAL COMMAND.

McIntosh's Brigade.

Regiment.	Killed and wounded.	Missing.	Total loss.
1st N. J.	7	..	7
3d Penna.	15	6	21
Total	22	6	28

Custer's Brigade.

Regiment.	Killed and wounded.	Missing.	Total loss.
1st Mich.	53	20	73
5th Mich.	38	18	56
6th Mich.	27	1	28
7th Mich.	61	39	100
Total	179	78	257

STUART'S CONFEDERATE DIVISION.

	Killed and wounded.	Missing.	Total loss.
Hampton's brigade	75	16	91
Fitzhugh Lee's brigade	21	29	50
W. H. F. Lee's brigade	29	12	41
Total	125	57	182

FEDERAL CAVALRY ON LEFT FLANK.

KILPATRICK'S COMMAND.

Farnsworth's Brigade.

Regiment.	Killed and wounded.	Missing.	Total loss.
1st Vt.	38	27	65
1st West Va.	8	4	12
18th Penna.	6	8	14
5th N. Y.	2	4	6
Total	54	43	97

Merritt's Regular Brigade.

Regiment.	Killed and wounded.	Missing.	Total loss.
6th Penna.	10	2	12
1st U. S.	12	3	15
2d U. S.	10	7	17
5th U. S.	4	1	5
6th U. S.	34	208	242
Total	70	221	291

The losses of the latter regiment occurred in desperate engagement during a reconnoissance near Fairfield.

The battle of Gettysburg, with its severe and desperate fighting and terrible slaughter and suffering, was over. The magnitude of the struggle was unsurpassed during the war. The result of the battle was a severe blow to the cause of the Rebellion. The defeat of Lee blasted the bright hopes of himself and other prominent leaders. He had invaded Pennsylvania with the intention of transferring to Northern soil the burden of the contending armies and to threaten Philadelphia, New York, and other principal cities. He had crossed the Potomac with what he considered an invincible army. With that army beaten, crippled, its discipline and morale seriously damaged, and its prestige gone, he was compelled to commence his weary retreat into Virginia.

General Meade was loath to believe that his adversary had commenced his retreat. Early on the 4th, Gregg's cavalry division was sent out on a reconnoissance, and discovered the Confederate army retreating in the most hurried manner. The pursuit was commenced by the Cavalry Corps under Pleasonton. A portion of it moved rapidly to Emmittsburg in the afternoon, and from there to Monterey Pass, which it reached after dark, and where it found Stuart's cavalry endeavoring to convoy a wagon-train, more than nine miles long, over the mountains. Amid the darkness and terrible thunder-storm of that night a fierce fight occurred between the two forces, and the Federal cavalry defeated Stuart's, capturing many prisoners and destroying almost the whole wagon-train as it madly dashed down the narrow mountain road in the darkness of the night.

The Federal cavalry the next day moved to Boonsboro' and then to Hagerstown, reaching there in advance of Lee's army. It opposed his advance with determination, but Lee moved on to Williamsport and Falling Waters, where he arrived with his army in a pitiable condition and without adequate means to cross the river.

Pleasonton's troopers for several days seriously harassed the enemy, but no general attack was made.

On the 13th of July an attack by the army was ordered for the 14th, but when the advance was made, next day, it was discovered that Lee had succeeded in transferring his army across the Potomac the night before. However, the cavalry, upon dashing upon the rearguard at Falling Waters, captured several hundred prisoners. General Pettigrew, who had been wounded at Gettysburg, was killed here. With some difficulty Lee moved his army to the banks of the Rapidan, and his disastrous campaign was over.

It is idle, perhaps, to speculate as to what might have been the result had General Meade been permitted by the authorities at Washington to carry out Hooker's plan, and send the 10,000 troops under French at Harper's Ferry up the Potomac, to destroy the bridges and the lines of communication of the Confederate army, instead of withdrawing them to Washington. In fact, there was a large number of troops in the defences of Washington that could have easily been spared to reinforce French, so that he could have successfully resisted the passage of the Potomac by Lee's army when it attempted to recross into Virginia.

Again, the thought suggests itself, What would have been the result had the 20,000 emergency troops of Pennsylvania and the

4000 or 5000 of other States, which were lying at Harrisburg and in the upper end of the Cumberland Valley, been moved during the battle to the passes of the South Mountain, and, throwing up works, opposed the return of the Confederate army over the mountain? The passes were much nearer to the western than to the eastern side of the mountain, and there was every facility for the construction of strong defensive works. It will not do to say that these troops were raw and undisciplined. For the answer to it will be the conduct at Gettysburg, as we have seen, of such new regiments as the 24th Michigan, 151st Pennsylvania, and those of Stone's Pennsylvania brigade, all of which there fought their first battle. What, too, of the 40,000 French and Prussian boys who fought and fell at Lutzen? Or a still better answer will be the record of the 125th, 128th, and 130th Pennsylvania Infantry, which, within a month after their muster-in, fought at Antietam so as to win the admiration of veteran regiments,—the 125th losing 146 killed and wounded; the 128th, 119; and the 130th, 178,—they being, as General French said, "undrilled but admirably equipped, and of the best material." So were these emergency troops well equipped, with Springfield rifles, and composed of intelligent men, whose spirit can be

THIRD DAY'S BATTLE.

best judged by the fact that, when they enlisted, they believed that they were the only troops who would stand between Lee's army and the Northern cities. Again, it must be remembered that a large portion of them had been in service and had been discharged for wounds or other causes. Among them, too, were the greater portion of the 16 regiments of Pennsylvania nine-months' troops who had recently been discharged,—men who fought at Antietam, as has just been stated, and who had also composed that splendid division which, under the intrepid Humphreys at Fredericksburg, had gallantly charged the wall on Marye's Heights, after they had seen such veteran divisions as those of Hancock, French, and Howard fail and the slopes covered with those who had fallen in the fruitless assaults.

Equipped and officered, and animated by the spirit that they were, these troops would certainly have offered determined and sturdy resistance to Lee's retreating army had they been in position in the mountain-passes.

With French's force destroying the communications and holding the fords, with the emergency troops on the mountain, with the cavalry and the fresh troops of the Sixth Corps thrown across its path east of the mountains, and the balance of the enthusiastic Army of the Potomac upon its rear and flank, what would have been the position of Lee's army with its depleted ammunition-chests and without supplies?

Might not that which happened two years afterwards at Appomattox have occurred in Pennsylvania, in the shadow of the South Mountain?

TOTAL CASUALTIES OF THE BATTLE.

	Killed and wounded.	Missing.	Total loss.
Federals	17,555	5435	22,990
Confederates (as reported)	15,298	5150	20,448

At least a fourth of the missing were among the killed and wounded. Of the latter, there were heretofore mentioned three killed to seven wounded, according to the revised reports of the War Department, and the interesting and highly instructive statistics compiled by Colonel Fox, of Albany, New York, in his valuable book, "Regimental Losses."

There were 12,227 wounded and unwounded Confederates captured, according to the list on file in the Adjutant-General's office in Washington.

Only two brigades of the eight of the Federal Sixth Corps were engaged, that of Nevin in front of Round Top and that of Shaler upon Culp's Hill.

Every Confederate regiment was actively engaged, except those of Mahone's Virginia,

THIRD DAY'S BATTLE. 161

Posey's Mississippi, and Thomas's Georgia brigades, which were only engaged as skirmishers.

Upon the map which precedes this narrative the positions of the troops are marked with approximate accuracy, so that an intelligent idea can be formed of the location of the lines of battle during the three days.

POINTS ON THE FIELD WHERE THE PRINCIPAL FIGHTING OCCURRED, IN THE ORDER OF ITS SEVERITY.

Federals.

	Killed and wounded.	Missing.	Total loss.
1. Wheat-Field	3592	541	4133
2. Reynolds's Grove	2880	1191	4071
3. Emmittsburg Road	2396	249	2645
4. Cemetery Ridge	2220	112	2332
5. Eleventh Corps Line	1768	1427	3195
6. Culp's Hill	1085	70	1155
7. Peach Orchard	1008	277	1285
8. Oak Ridge	707	982	1689
9. Round Top	544	31	575
10. East Cemetery Hill	345	56	401

Confederates.

	Killed and wounded.	Missing.	Total loss.
1. Wheat-Field	2416	406	2822
2. Reynolds's Grove	3971	317	4288
3. Emmittsburg Road	1326	652	1978
4. Cemetery Ridge	3030	3550	6580
5. Eleventh Corps Line	656	121	777
6. Culp's Hill	1609	391	2000
7. Peach Orchard	950	97	1047
8. Oak Ridge	955	1400	2355
9. Round Top	680	146	826
10. East Cemetery Hill	488	170	658

LOSSES BY DIVISIONS.

Federal.

Division.	Corps.	Killed and wounded.	Missing.
Humphreys's	Third	1865	227
Birney's	Third	1648	362
Gibbon's	Second	1541	93
Doubleday's	First	1505	591
Wadsworth's	First	1495	633
Hays's	Second	1225	66
Caldwell's	Second	1063	206
Ayres's	Fifth	966	63
Barnes's	Fifth	860	44
Schurz's	Eleventh	817	659
Barlow's	Eleventh	814	492
Robinson's	First	703	983
Steinwehr's	Eleventh	613	333
Geary's	Twelfth	503	36
Williams's	Twelfth	493	40
Crawford's	Fifth	210	3
	Sixth (not engaged)	212	30
	Cavalry	442	470

Confederate.

Division.	Corps.	Killed and wounded.	Missing.
Heth's	Hill's	2316	534
Rodes's	Ewell's	2149	704
McLaws's	Longstreet's	1851	327
Hood's	Longstreet's	1847	442
Pender's[1]	Hill's	1584	116
Johnson's	Ewell's	1498	375
Pickett's	Longstreet's	1389	1499
Anderson's	Hill's	1275	840
Early's	Ewell's	966	226
	Cavalry	176	64

---

[1] In Caldwell's "History of McGowan's South Carolina Brigade," the number of killed and wounded in Pender's division at Gettysburg is stated as 2982.

THIRD DAY'S BATTLE.

LOSSES BY STATES.

Federal States.

	Killed and wounded.	Missing.
New York	4953	1663
Pennsylvania	4443	1452
Massachusetts	1078	316
Ohio	895	376
Michigan	810	259
Maine	743	228
Wisconsin	618	188
New Jersey	609	71
Indiana	480	69
Vermont	358	59
New Hampshire	321	47
Connecticut	228	114
Minnesota	223	1
Delaware	136	25
Maryland	136	4
Rhode Island	92	5
West Virginia	54	13
Illinois	43	96
U. S. Regulars	1167	296

Confederate States.

	Killed and wounded.	Missing.
North Carolina	3286	718
Virginia	2872	1813
Georgia	2759	689
Alabama	1788	796
Mississippi	1445	92
South Carolina	1214	37
Lousiana	622	128
Texas	309	120
Florida	250	205
Maryland	149	..
Arkansas	142	..
Tennessee	87	300

With some prolixity, and with probable tediousness to the reader, the position of every regiment and battery in both armies actively engaged in the battle has been stated, together with the casualties it suffered and the names of the commands which fought with it and those which fought against it. The movements and positions of the several commands have been given as they have been established by the information gathered by the Memorial Association in the manner mentioned in the introduction. The losses are based entirely upon the official reports.

Every effort has been made by the Memorial Association to give proper credit to each command for what it did, to do injustice to none, of North or South.

The people of each State can be justly proud of its troops who fought at Gettysburg, and may well render unto them tributes of admiration and homage. And the people of our whole country can rejoice that there was nothing done by any to tarnish their record as soldiers. The two great armies of Americans, which, for those three memorable days, in the heat and glare of the July sun of 1863, met in determined, fierce, and deadly combat upon the field of Gettysburg, by their fidelity and gallantry, their fortitude and valor, carved the highest niche in the temple of martial fame and glory for the American soldier.

"All time will be the millennium of their glory." One was right and the other wrong. But, in the knowledge of the subsequent development, progress, peace, and prosperity of our united, common country, victor and vanquished now alike believe that in the Providence of God it was right and well that the issue at Gettysburg was determined as it was. And the people of all sections of our great republic, moved by the impulse of sincere and zealous loyalty, of fervent and exalted patriotism, may say, "All is well that ends well."

THE NATIONAL CEMETERY.

GETTYSBURG was the first cemetery in the country dedicated to the exclusive burial of soldiers, and was the first of our many national cemeteries.

A few days after the terrific battle, Governor A. G. Curtin, of Pennsylvania, hastened to the relief of the sick and wounded soldiers, visited the battle-field and the numerous hospitals in and around Gettysburg, for the purpose of perfecting the arrangements for alleviating the sufferings and ministering to the wants of the wounded and dying. He appointed David Wills, Esq., of Gettysburg, to act as his special agent there.

The governor, with that profound sympathy and that care and anxiety for the soldier which always characterized him, approved the design for a soldier's cemetery, and directed a correspondence to be entered into at once with the governors of the other States having soldiers buried on the battle-field. The governors of the different States, with great promptness, seconded the project, and the details of the arrangement were subsequently agreed upon. Grounds favorably situated were selected by the agent, and the governor directed him to purchase them for the State of Pennsylvania, for the specific purpose of the burial of the soldiers who fell in defence of the Union in the battle of Gettysburg, lots in this cemetery to be gratuitously tendered to each State having such dead on the field. The expenses of the removal of the dead, of the laying out, ornamenting, and enclosing the grounds, of erecting a lodge for a keeper, and of constructing a suitable monument to the memory of the dead, were to be borne by the several States, and assessed in proportion to their population, as indicated by their representation in Congress. The governor stipulated that the State of Pennsylvania would subsequently keep the grounds in order, and the buildings and fences in repair.

Seventeen acres of land on Cemetery Hill, at the apex of the triangular line of battle of the Union army, were purchased by Pennsylvania for this purpose. There were stone fences upon these grounds, which had been advantageously used by the infantry, and upon the elevated portions many batteries of artillery had been planted.

The following-named commissioners, appointed by the governors of the different States which had soldiers buried in the Soldiers' National Cemetery at Gettysburg, met in Harrisburg, Pennsylvania, on the 17th of December, 1863 : Hon. B. W. Norris, of Maine ; Hon. L. B. Mason, of New Hampshire ; Mr. Henry Edwards, of Massachusetts ; Mr. Alfred Coit, of Connecticut ; Hon. Levi Scobey, of New Jersey ; Mr. David Wills, of Pennsylvania ; Colonel James Worrall, of Pennsylvania ; Colonel John S. Berry, of Maryland ; Mr. L. W. Brown and Colonel Gordon Lofland, of Ohio ; Colonel John G. Stephenson, of Indiana ; Mr. W. Y. Selleck, of Wisconsin. Mr. David Wills, of Pennsylvania, was elected chairman of the meeting, and Mr. W. Y. Selleck, of Wisconsin, secretary.

After some discussion, a committee of four was appointed to prepare and put in appropriate shape the details of the plan in reference to the Soldiers' National Cemetery at Gettysburg. Colonel John G. Stephenson, of Indiana, Mr. Henry Edwards, of Massachusetts, Hon. Levi Scobey, of New Jersey, and Mr. David Wills, of Pennsylvania, constituting the committee, made the following report :

"WHEREAS, In accordance with an invitation from His Excellency, A. G. Curtin, Governor of Pennsylvania, the governors of the several States appointed commissioners, who met at Harrisburg, December 17, 1863, to represent the States in convention, for the purpose of making arrangements for finishing the Soldiers' National Cemetery; therefore, be it

"*Resolved*, By the said commissioners, that the following

be submitted to the different States interested in the Soldiers' National Cemetery, through their respective governors.

"*First*. That the Commonwealth of Pennsylvania shall hold the title to the land which she has purchased at Gettysburg for the Soldiers' National Cemetery, in trust for States having soldiers in said cemetery, in perpetuity, for the purpose to which it is now applied.

"*Second*. That the Legislature of the Commonwealth of Pennsylvania be requested to create a corporation to be managed by trustees, one to be appointed by each of the governors of the States of Maine, New Hampshire, Vermont, Massachusetts, Rhode Island, Connecticut, New York, New Jersey, Pennsylvania, Maryland, Delaware, West Virginia, Ohio, Indiana, Illinois, Michigan, Wisconsin, Minnesota, and of such other States as may hereafter desire to be represented in this corporation, which trustees shall at their first meeting be divided into three classes, the term of office of the first class to expire on the 1st day of January, 1865, the second class on the 1st day of January, 1866, and the third class on the 1st day of January, 1867, the vacancies thus occurring to be filled by the several governors, and the persons thus appointed to fill such vacancies to hold their office for the term of three years. This corporation shall have exclusive control of the Soldiers' National Cemetery.

"*Third*. The following is the estimated expenses of finishing the cemetery:

Enclosing grounds	$15,000.00
Burial expenses and superintending	6,000.00
Headstones	10,000.00
Laying out grounds and planting trees	5,000.00
Lodge	2,500.00
Monument	25,000.00
Total	$63,500.00

"*Fourth*.—That the several States be asked to appropriate a sum of money, to be determined by a division of the estimated expenses according to representation in Congress, to be expended in defraying the cost of removing and reinterring the dead, and finishing the cemetery, under directions of the cemetery corporation.

"*Fifth*.—When the cemetery shall have been finished, the grounds are to be kept in order, the house and enclosure in repair, out of a fund created by annual appropriations made by the States, which may be represented in the cemetery corporation, in proportion to their representation in Congress."

The report of the committee was unanimously adopted.

Letters from the governors of the following States, which were not represented by commissioners, were received, expressing their disposition to approve any reasonable action of the meeting in reference to the completion of the cemetery at Gettysburg,—viz., Hon. Horatio Seymour, New York; Hon. Austin Blair, Michigan; Hon. James Y. Smith, Rhode Island; Hon. William Cannon, Delaware; and Hon. Henry G. Swift, Minnesota.

The following committee was appointed by the chairman, with the view to procure designs for a monument to be erected in the cemetery: Hon. Levi Scobey, New Jersey; Hon. B. W. Morris, Maine: Mr. D. W. Brown, Ohio; Colonel J. G. Stephenson, Indiana, and Colonel John S. Berry, Maryland.

The plans and designs of the cemetery, as laid out and designed by Mr. William Saunders, were adopted.

"The Soldiers' National Cemetery" was incorporated by an Act of Legislature of Pennsylvania, approved March 25, 1864.

The cemetery is beautifully located upon the highest ground of Cemetery Ridge.

The enclosure around it consists of a very substantial, well-built stone wall, surmounted with heavy dressed coping stone. This wall extends along the east, north, and west sides of the grounds. The division fence between the Soldiers' National Cemetery and the local cemetery is of iron. The front fence and gate-way are of ornamental iron-work. The gate-way bears this inscription :

> "On Fame's eternal camping ground
>   Their silent tents are spread,
> While glory guards with solemn round
>   The bivouac of the dead."

The gate-lodge is a handsome stone building, two stories high. The grounds are beautifully graded and tastefully planted with trees and shrubs. The erection of the head-stones, costing over $20,000, and which took over a year to complete, is a most permanent and durable piece of work.

MR. SAUNDERS'S DESIGN FOR THE GROUNDS.

The eminent landscape gardener, Mr. William Saunders, of the Department of Agriculture, Washington, was employed to lay out the grounds. His remarks on the design were as follows :

" In constructing a design for the cemetery, the following considerations and details suggested themselves as objects of paramount importance :

"*First*. The great disparity that exists with reference to the space required for the interments of each State necessitates a discrimination as to position and extent, while the peculiar solemnity of the interest attached by each State to each interment allows of no distinction. Therefore, the arrangement must be of a kind that will obviate criticism as to position, and at the same time possess other equally important requirements and relations to the general design.

"*Second.* The principal expression of the improvement should be that produced by simple grandeur and propriety.

"*Third*. To arrange the roads, walks, trees, and shrubs, so as to answer every purpose required by utility, and realize a pleasing landscape and pleasure-ground effect, at the same time paying due regard to economy of construction, as well as to the future cost of maintenance and keeping the grounds.

"*Fourth*. To select an appropriate site for the monument.

" In order to secure the conditions embraced in the first

of the above propositions, a semicircular arrangement was adopted for the interments. By referring to the plan, the propriety of this mode will, I think, be conceded without further explanation. The ground appropriated to each State is part, as it were, of a common centre; the position of each lot, and, indeed, of each interment, is relatively of equal importance, the only difference being that of extent, as determined by the number of interments belonging to each State. The coffins are deposited side by side, in parallel trenches. A space of twelve feet is allowed to each parallel, about five feet of which form a grass path between each row of interments. The configuration of the ground surface is singularly appropriate at the point selected, falling away in a gradual and regular slope in every direction from the centre to the circumference, a feature alike pleasing and desirable. In order to secure regularity, the headstones are precisely alike throughout the entire area of lots, and are constructed so as not to detract from the effect and prominence of the monument. The head stones form a continuous line of granite blocks, rising nine inches above the ground, and showing a face or width of ten inches on their upper surface. The name, company, and regiment are carved in the granite, opposite each interment, thus securing a simple and expressive arrangement, combined with great permanence and durability.

"The prevailing expression of the cemetery should be that of *simple grandeur*. Simplicity is that element of beauty in a scene that leads gradually from one object to another in easy harmony, avoiding abrupt contrasts and unexpected features. Grandeur, in this application, is closely allied to solemnity. Solemnity is an attribute of the sublime. The sublime in scenery may be defined as continuity of extent, the repetition of objects in themselves simple and commonplace. We do not apply this epithet to the scanty tricklings of the brook, but rather to the collected waters of the ocean. To produce an expression of grandeur we must avoid intricacy and great variety of parts, more particularly must we refrain from introducing any intermixture or meretricious display of ornament.

"The disposition of trees and shrubs is such as will ultimately produce a considerable degree of landscape effect. Ample spaces of lawn are provided. These will form vistas, as seen from the drive, showing the monument and other prominent points. Any abridgement of these lawns by planting, further than is shown in the design, will tend to destroy the massive effect of the groupings, and in time would render the whole confused and intricate. As the trees spread and extend, the quiet beauty produced by these open spaces of lawn will yearly become more striking. Designs of this character require time for this development, and their ultimate harmony should not be impaired or sacrificed to immediate and temporary interest. Further, to secure proper breadth of scene, few walks or roads are introduced. A main roadway or drive of sufficient width courses around the grounds; a few paths or walks are also provided for facilitating the inspection of the interment lots. Roads and walks are exclusively objects of utility; their introduction can only be justified by direct necessity.

"The centre of the semicircle is reserved for the monument. An irregularly shaped belting of dwarf shrubbery borders and partially isolates it from the lots. It may be suggested that the style of the monument should be in keeping with the surrounding improvements, showing no effort to an exhibition of cost or ostentatious display on the one hand, and no apparent desire to avoid reasonable expense on the other.

"The gate-way and gate house should be also designed in the same spirit,—massive, solid, substantial, and tasteful.

"With regard to the future keeping of the ground, the walks should be smooth, hard, and clean, the grass kept short, and maintained as clean and neat as the best pleasure-ground in the country. No effort should be wanting to attain excellence in this respect.

"WILLIAM SAUNDERS.

"DEPARTMENT OF AGRICULTURE, WASHINGTON, D. C."

REPORT OF SAMUEL WEAVER, SUPERINTENDENT OF EXHUMING OF THE BODIES.

"GETTYSBURG, March 19, 1864.

"To DAVID WILLS, ESQ.,

"*Agent for A. G. Curtin, Governor of Pennsylvania:*

"SIR,—I herewith submit the following brief report of the results of my labors as the superintendent of the exhuming of the bodies of the Union soldiers that fell on the battle-field of Gettysburg.

"The contractor commenced the work of exhuming on Tuesday, the 27th of October last, and finished yesterday. The work has been protracted much beyond our original anticipations, by reason of the ground being frozen for a long time during the winter, thus entirely suspending the work, and also by the number of bodies exceeding our first calculations.

"The number taken up and removed to the Soldiers' National Cemetery is 3354, and to these add the number of the Massachusetts soldiers, taken up by the authorities of the city of Boston, by special contract, amounting to 158, making the total number of removals 3512. Of these, 979 were nameless, and without any marks or surroundings to designate the State from which they volunteered. The rest were, in most instances, marked with boards, on which the name, company, and regiment were written in pencil or cut by their comrades who buried them. In some instances the regiment to which the soldier belonged was discovered, and sometimes only the State from which he volunteered, and in these cases they were buried in their appropriate State lot.

"There was not a grave permitted to be opened or a body searched unless I was present. I saw every body taken out of its temporary resting-place, and all the pockets carefully searched; and where the grave was not marked I examined all the clothing and everything about the body to find the name. I then saw the body carefully placed in the coffin, and if there was a head-board, I required it to be at once nailed to the coffin. At the same time I wrote the name, company, and regiment of the soldier on the coffin, numbered the coffin, and entered in my book the same endorsement. This book was returned to your office every evening, to copy and compare with the daily return, made by the superintendent of the interments in the cemetery. In these scrutinizing searches the names of a number of lost soldiers were found. They were discovered in various ways, sometimes by the pocket-diaries, by letters, by names in Bible or Testament, by photographs, names in pocket-books, descriptive list, express receipts, medals, names on some part of the clothing, belt, or cartridge-box, etc.

"There were some articles of value found on the bodies—money, watches, jewelry, etc. I took all relics, as well as articles of value, from the bodies, packed them up, and labelled them, so that the friends can get them. There are many things valueless to others which would be of great interest to the friends. I herewith submit a list of names of persons and articles found upon them, and you will, no doubt, take means to get information to the friends by advertisement or otherwise, so that they may give notice where and to whom these things shall be forwarded. I have two hundred and eighty-seven such packages.

"The bodies were found in various stages of decomposition. On the battle-field of the first day the rebels obtained possession before our men were buried, and left most of the unburied from Wednesday until Monday following, when our men buried them. After this length of time they could not be identified. The consequence was that but few on the battle-field of July 1 were marked. They were generally covered with a small portion of earth dug up from alongside of the body. This left them much exposed to the heat, air, and rains, and when these bodies were taken up there was nothing remaining but the dry skeleton.

"Where bodies were in heavy clay soil or in marshy places they were in a good state of preservation. Where they were in sandy, porous soil they were entirely decomposed. Frequently our men were buried in trenches, a shallow ditch, in which they were laid side by side.

"Before we commenced our work the battle-field had been overrun by thousands of sorrowing friends in search of lost ones, and many of the graves were opened and but partially or carelessly closed.

"In searching for the remains of our fallen heroes we examined more than three thousand rebel graves. They were frequently buried in trenches, and there were instances of one hundred and fifty in a trench.

"It may be asked how we could distinguish the bodies of our own men from those of the rebels. This was generally very easily done. In the first place, as a general rule, the rebels never went into battle with the United States coat on. They sometimes took the pantaloons from our dead and wore them, but not the coat. The rebel clothing is made of cotton, and is of a gray or brown color. Occasionally I found one with a blue cotton jean roundabout on. The clothing of our men is of wool, and blue, so that if the body had on the coat of our uniform, it was a pretty sure indication that it was that of a Union soldier. But if the body were without a coat, then there were other infallible marks. The shoes of the rebels were differently made from those of our soldiers. If these failed, then the underclothing was the next part examined. The rebel cotton undershirt gave proof of the army to which it belonged. In no instance was a body allowed to be removed which had any portion of the rebel clothing on it. Taking all these things together, we never had much trouble in deciding, with infallible accuracy, whether the body was that of a Union soldier or a rebel. And I firmly believe that there has not been a single mistake made in the removal of the soldiers to the cemetery by taking the body of a rebel for a Union soldier.

"All which is respectfully submitted.

"SAMUEL WEAVER."

THE GRAVES.

The grounds are laid off in lots for each State, proportioned in size to the number of bodies identified as those of soldiers belonging to such State. There is also a lot set apart for the burial of the remains of those who belonged to the regular service. The graves of about one-third of the dead were unmarked, but these bodies are deposited in prominent and honorable positions at each end of the semicircular arrangement of the lots. The grounds naturally have a gradual slope in every direction from the centre of the semicircle to the circumference. Each lot is laid off in sections, with a space of five feet for a walk between each section. The outer section is lettered A, and so on in alphabetical order. As the observer stands in the centre of the semicircle, facing the circumference, the burials commence at the right hand of the section in each lot, and the graves are numbered numerically. A register was made of the number, name, regiment, and company of the occupant of each grave. Two feet of space is allotted to each, and they are laid with the heads towards the centre of the semicircle. At the head of the graves there is a stone wall, built up from the bottom as a foundation for the headstones, which are placed along the whole length of each section, and on which, opposite each grave, are engraved the name, regiment, and company of the deceased. These headstones are all alike in size, the design being wholly adapted to a symmetrical order, and one which combines simplicity and durability. No other marks are permitted to be erected.

A few of the States sent agents to Gettysburg to superintend the removal and burial of their dead, while most of them intrusted the arrangements for that purpose to the agent of the State of Pennsylvania. The Boston city authorities, in concert with the Governor of Massachusetts, sent an efficient committee to Gettysburg, who made the removals of the Massachusetts dead by their own special arrangements.

The State of Pennsylvania, in 1865, published in book form a complete list by States of all the burials, giving, where possible, names, companies, and regiments. The following is the number of burials by States:

Maine	104	Ohio	131
New Hampshire	49	Indiana	80
Vermont	61	Illinois	6
Massachusetts	159	Michigan	171
Rhode Island	12	Wisconsin	73
Connecticut	22	Minnesota	52
New York	866	U. S. Regulars	138
New Jersey	78	Unknown—Lot North	411
Pennsylvania	526	Unknown—Lot South	425
Delaware	15	Unknown—Lot Inner Circle	143
Maryland	22		
West Virginia	11	Total	3555

DEDICATION SERVICES.

The consecration of these cemetery grounds was, in due time, suggested by Governor Curtin. Hon. Edward Everett was invited to deliver the oration, and the 19th of November, 1863, was fixed upon as the day. To Major-General D. N. Couch, commanding the Department of the Susquehanna, was committed the arrangements. Birgfield's Brigade Band, of Philadelphia, was invited to furnish the music for the ceremonial of consecration, which was done gratuitously. The Presidential party was accompanied by the Marine Band from the Navy-Yard at Washington, and the military detachment was attended by the band from Fort McHenry, Baltimore.

The President of the United States was present and participated in the solemnities, delivering a brief dedicatory address. The occasion was further made memorable by the presence of large representations from the army and navy, the Secretary of State, the Ministers of France and Italy, the French admiral and other distinguished foreigners, and several members of Congress; also of the governors of a large number of the States, with their staffs, and a vast concourse of citizens from all the States.

Letters were received, in reply to invitations addressed to them, from Major-General Meade, Lieutenant-General Scott, Admiral Charles Stewart, and the Secretary of the Treasury, Hon. Salmon P. Chase, regretting their inability to be present and expressing their approval of the project.

Letter of General Meade.

"HEAD-QUARTERS ARMY OF THE POTOMAC,
"November 13, 1863.

"DAVID WILLS, ESQ.,

"*Agent for the Governor of Pennsylvania, etc.:*

"SIR,—I have the honor to acknowledge the invitation which, on behalf of the governors of Pennsylvania and other States interested, you extend to me, and the officers and men of my command, to be present on the 19th instant at the consecration of the burial-place of those who fell on the field of Gettysburg.

"It seems almost unnecessary for me to say that none can have a deeper interest in your good work than comrades in arms, bound in close ties of long association and mutual confidence and support with those to whom you are paying this last tribute of respect; nor could the presence of any be more appropriate than that of those who stood side by side in the struggle, shared the peril, and the vacant places in whose ranks bear sad testimony to the loss they have sustained. But this army has duties to perform which will not admit of its being represented on the occasion; and it only remains for me, in its name, with deep and grateful feelings, to thank you and those you represent for your tender care of its heroic dead, and for your patriotic zeal, which, in honoring the martyr, gives a fresh incentive to all who do battle for the maintenance of the integrity of the government.

"I am, very respectfully,
"Your obedient servant,
"GEORGE G. MEADE,
"*Major-General Commanding.*"

In the afternoon of the 18th the President and the distinguished personages accompanying him arrived at Gettysburg by a special train. In the course of the evening the President and Secretary of State were serenaded, and the following remarks were made by Mr. Seward, in response to the call:

"FELLOW-CITIZENS,—I am now sixty years old and upward; I have been in public life practically forty years of that time, and yet this is the first time that ever any people, or community, so near to the border of Maryland, was found willing to listen to my voice; and the reason was that I saw, forty years ago, that slavery was opening before this people a graveyard that was to be filled with brothers, falling in mutual political combat. I knew that the cause that was hurrying the Union into this dreadful strife was slavery; and when, during all the intervening period, I elevated my voice it was to warn the people to remove that cause, while they could, by constitutional means, and so avert the catastrophe of civil war, which has fallen upon the nation. I am thankful that you are willing to hear me at last. I thank God that I believe this strife is going to end in the removal of that evil, which ought to have been removed by deliberate councils and peaceful means. I thank my God for the hope that this is the last fratricidal war which will fall upon the country, which is vouchsafed to us by Heaven,—the richest, the broadest, the most beautiful, the most magnificent, and capable of a great destiny, that has ever been given to any part of the human race. And I thank Him for the hope that when that cause is removed, simply by the operation of abolishing it, as the origin and agent of the treason, that is without justification and without parallel, we shall henceforth be united, be only one country, having only one hope, one ambition, and one destiny. To-morrow, at least, we shall feel that we are not enemies, but that we are friends and brothers, that this Union is a reality, and we shall mourn together for the evil wrought by this rebellion. We are now near the graves of the misguided, whom we have consigned to their last resting-place, with pity for their errors, and with the same heart full of grief with which we mourn over a brother by whose hand, raised in defence of his government, that misguided brother perished.

"When we part to morrow night, let us remember that we owe it to our country and to mankind that this war shall have for its conclusion the establishing of the principal of democratic government, the simple principle that whatever party, whatever portion of the community, prevails by constitutional suffrage in an election, that party is to be respected and maintained in power until it shall give place, on another trial and another verdict, to a different portion of the people. If you do not do this, you are drifting at once and irresistibly to the very verge of universal, cheerless, and hopeless anarchy. But with that principle this government of ours, the purest, the best, the wisest, and the happiest in the world, must be, and, so far as we are concerned, practically will be, immortal. Fellow-citizens, good-night."

EXERCISES IN THE CEMETERY NOVEMBER 19, 1863.

Prayer of Rev. Dr. Stockton.

"O God, our Father, for the sake of Thy Son, our Saviour, inspire us with Thy Spirit, and sanctify us to the right fulfilment of the duties of this occasion.

"We come to dedicate this new historic centre as a national cemetery. If all departments of the one government which Thou hast ordained over our Union, and of the many governments which Thou hast subordinated to our Union, be here represented; if all classes, relations, and interests of our blended brotherhood of people stand severally and thoroughly apparent in Thy presence, we trust that it is because Thou hast called us, that Thy blessing awaits us, and that Thy designs may be embodied in practical results of incalculable and imperishable good.

"And so, with Thy holy Apostle, and with the Church of all lands and ages, we unite in the ascription, 'Blessed be God, even the Father of our Lord Jesus Christ, the Father of mercies, and the God of all comfort, who comforteth us in all our tribulation, that we may be able to comfort them which are in any trouble, by the comfort wherewith we ourselves are comforted of God.'

" In emulation of all angels, in fellowship with all saints, and in sympathy with all sufferers, in remembrance of all Thy works, in reverence of Thy ways, and in accordance with Thy word, we laud and magnify Thine infinite perfections, Thy creative glory, Thy redeeming grace, Thy providential goodness, and the progressively richer and fairer developments of Thy supreme, universal, and everlasting administration.

" In behalf of all humanity, whose ideal is divine, whose first memory is Thine image lost and whose last hope is Thine image restored, and especially of our own nation, whose history has been so favored, whose position is so peerless, whose mission is so sublime, and whose future is so attractive, we thank Thee for the unspeakable patience of Thy compassion and the exceeding greatness of Thy lovingkindness. In contemplation of Eden, Calvary, and Heaven, of Christ in the Garden, on the Cross, and on the Throne ; nay more, of Christ as coming again in all-subduing power and glory, we gratefully prolong our homage. By this altar of sacrifice, on this field of deliverance, on this mount of salvation, within the fiery and bloody line of these "munitions of rock," looking back to the dark days of fear and trembling and to the rapture and relief that came after, we multiply our thanksgivings and confess our obligations to renew and perfect our personal and social consecration to Thy service and glory.

" Oh, had it not been for God ! For lo ! our enemies, they came unresisted, multitudinous, mighty, flushed with victory and sure of success. They exulted on our mountains, they revelled in our valleys ; they feasted, they rested ; they slept, they waked, they grew stronger, prouder, bolder every day ; they spread abroad, they concentrated here ; they looked beyond this horizon to the stores of wealth, to the haunts of pleasure, and to the seats of power in our capital and chief cities. They prepared to cast a chain of slavery around the form of Freedom, binding life and death together forever. Their premature triumph was the mockery of God and man. One more victory, and all was theirs! But behind these hills was heard the feebler march of a smaller, but still pursuing host. Onward they hurried, day and night, for God and their country. Footsore and way-worn, hungry, thirsty, faint,—but not in heart, —they came to dare all, to bear all, and to do all that is possible to heroes. And Thou didst sustain them! At first they met the blast on the plain, and bent before it like the trees in a storm. But then, led by Thy hand to these hills, they took their stand upon the rocks and remained as firm and immovable as they. In vain were they assaulted. All art, all violence, all desperation, failed to dislodge them. Baffled, bruised, broken, their enemies recoiled, retired, and disappeared. Glory to God for this rescue! But, oh, the slain! In the freshness and fulness of their young and manly life, with such sweet memories of father and mother, brother and sister, wife and children, maiden and friends, they died for us. From the coasts beneath the Eastern star, from the shores of Northern lakes and rivers, from the flowers of Western prairies, and from the homes of the midway and border, they came here to die for us and for mankind. Alas, how little we can do for them! We come with the humility of prayer, with the pathetic eloquence of venerable wisdom, with the tender beauty of poetry, with the plaintive harmony of music, with the honest tribute of our Chief Magistrate, and with all this honorable attendance; but our best hope is in Thy blessing, O Lord, our God. O Father, bless us. Bless the bereaved, whether present or absent; bless our sick and wounded soldiers; bless all our rulers and people; bless our army and navy; bless the efforts for the suppression of the rebellion;

and bless all the associations of this day and place and scene forever. As the trees are not dead though their foliage is gone, so our heroes are not dead though their forms have fallen. In their proper personality they are all with Thee, and the spirit of their example is here. It fills the air, it fills our hearts. And, long as time shall last, it will hover in the skies and rest on this landscape, and the pilgrims of our own land and from all lands will thrill with its inspiration, and increase and confirm their devotion to liberty, religion, and God.

"Our Father which art in heaven, Hallowed be thy name. Thy kingdom come. Thy will be done in earth, as it is in heaven. Give us this day our daily bread. And forgive us our debts, as we forgive our debtors. And lead us not into temptation, but deliver us from evil : For thine is the kingdom, and the power, and the glory, forever. Amen."

EXTRACTS FROM THE ADDRESS OF HON. EDWARD EVERETT.

"Standing beneath this serene sky, overlooking these broad fields now reposing from the labors of the waning year, the mighty Alleghanies dimly towering before us, the graves of our brethren beneath our feet, it is with hesitation that I raise my poor voice to break the eloquent silence of God and Nature. But the duty to which you have called me must be performed ; grant me, I pray you, your indulgence and your sympathy.

"It was appointed by law in Athens that the obsequies of the citizens who fell in battle should be performed at the public expense, and in the most honorable manner. Their bones were carefully gathered up from the funeral pyre, where their bodies were consumed, and brought home to the city. There, for three days before the interment, they lay in state, beneath tents of honor, to receive the votive offerings of friends and relatives, flowers, weapons, precious ornaments, painted vases (wonders of art, which after two thousand years adorn the museums of modern Europe), the last tributes of surviving affection. Ten coffins of funeral cypress received the honorable deposit, one for each of the tribes of the city, and an eleventh in memory of the unrecognized, but not therefore unhonored, dead, and of those whose remains could not be recovered. On the fourth day the mournful procession was formed; mothers, wives, sisters, daughters, led the way, and to them it was permitted by the simplicity of ancient manners to utter aloud their lamentations for the beloved and lost; the male relatives and friends of the deceased followed; citizens and strangers closed the train. Thus marshalled, they moved to the place of interment in that famous Ceramicus, the most beautiful suburb of Athens, which had been adorned by Cimon, the son of Miltiades, with walks and fountains and columns, whose groves were filled with altars, shrines, and temples, whose gardens were kept forever green by the streams from the neighboring hills, and shaded with the trees sacred to Minerva and coeval with the foundation of the city, whose circuit enclosed

> "'the olive Grove of Academe,
> Plato's retirement, where the Attic bird
> Trilled his thick-warbled note the summer long,'

whose pathways gleamed with the monuments of the illustrious dead, the work of the most consummate masters that ever gave life to marble. There, beneath the overarching plane-trees, upon a lofty stage erected for the purpose, it was ordained that a funeral oration should be pronounced by some citizen of Athens, in the presence of the assembled multitude.

"Such were the tokens of respect required to be paid at

Athens to the memory of those who had fallen in the cause of their country. For those alone who fell at Marathon, a special honor was reserved. As the battle fought upon that immortal field was distinguished from all others in Grecian history, for its influence over the fortunes of Hellas,—as it depended upon the event of that day whether Greece should live, a glory and a light to all coming time, or should expire, like the meteor of a moment,—so the honors awarded to its martyr-heroes were such as were bestowed by Athens on no other occasion. They alone, of all her sons, were entombed upon the spot which they had forever rendered famous. Their names were inscribed upon ten pillars, erected upon the monumental tumulus which covered their ashes (where, after six hundred years, they were read by the traveller Pausanias), and although the columns, beneath the hand of time and barbaric violence, have long since disappeared, the venerable mound still marks the spot where they fought and fell,—

> " ' That battle-field where Persia's victim horde
> First bowed beneath the brunt of Hellas' sword.'

"And shall I, fellow-citizens, who, after an interval of twenty-three centuries, a youthful pilgrim from the world unknown to ancient Greece, have wandered over that illustrious plain, ready to put off the shoes from off my feet as one that stands on holy ground, who have gazed with respectful emotion on the mound which still protects the dust of those who rolled back the tide of Persian invasion and rescued the land of popular liberty, of letters, and of art from the ruthless foe, stand unmoved over the graves of our dear brethren who so lately, on three of those all-important days which decided a nation's history, days on whose issue it depended whether this august republican Union, founded by some of the wisest statesmen that ever lived, cemented with the blood of some of the purest patriots that ever died, should perish or endure, rolled back the tide of an invasion not less unprovoked, not less ruthless, than that which came to plant the dark banner of Asiatic despotism and slavery on the free soil of Greece? Heaven forbid! And could I prove so insensible to every prompting of patriotic duty and affection, not only would you, fellow-citizens, gathered, many of you, from distant States, who have come to take part in these pious offices of gratitude, you, respected fathers, brethren, matrons, sisters, who surround me, cry out for shame, but the forms of brave and patriotic men who fill these honored graves would heave with indignation beneath the sod.

"We have assembled, friends, fellow citizens, at the invitation of the executive of the great central State of Pennsylvania, seconded by the governors of seventeen other loyal States of the Union, to pay the last tribute of respect to the brave men who, in the hard-fought battles of the first, second, and third days of July last, laid down their lives for the country on these hills and the plains before us, and whose remains have been gathered into the cemetery which we consecrate this day. As my eye ranges over the fields whose sods were so lately moistened by the blood of gallant and loyal men, I feel as never before how truly it was said of old, that it is sweet and becoming to die for one's country. I feel as never before how justly, from the dawn of history to the present time, men have paid the homage of their gratitude and admiration to the memory of those who nobly sacrificed their lives that their fellow-men may live in safety and in honor. And if this tribute were ever due, when, to whom, could it be more justly paid than to those whose last resting-place we this day commend to the blessing of Heaven and of men?

* * * * * * * *

THE NATIONAL CEMETERY.

"I must leave to others, who can do it from personal observation, to describe the mournful spectacle presented by these hill sides and plains at the close of the terrible conflict. It was a saying of the Duke of Wellington, that, next to a defeat, the saddest thing was a victory. The horrors of the battle-field, after the contest is over, the sights and sounds of woe, let me throw a pall over the scene, which no words can adequately depict to those who have not witnessed it, on which no one who has witnessed it, and who has a heart in his bosom, can bear to dwell. One drop of balm alone, one drop of heavenly, life-giving balm, mingles in this bitter cup of misery. Scarcely has the cannon ceased to roar, when the brethren and sisters of Christian benevolence, ministers of compassion, angels of pity, hasten to the field and the hospital, to moisten the parched tongue, to bind the ghastly wounds, to soothe the parting agonies alike of friend and foe, and to catch the last whispered message of love from dying lips. 'Carry this miniature back to my dear wife, but do not take it from my bosom until I am gone.' 'Tell my little sister not to grieve for me; I am willing to die for my country.' 'Oh, that my mother were here!' When, since Aaron stood between the living and the dead, was there ever so gracious a ministry as this? It has been said that it is characteristic of Americans to treat women with a deference not paid to them in any other country. I will not undertake to say whether this is so ; but I will say that, since this terrible war has been waged, the women of the loyal States, if never before, have entitled themselves to our highest admiration and gratitude, alike those who at home, often with fingers unused to toil, often bowed beneath their own domestic cares, have performed an amount of daily labor not exceeded by those who work for their daily bread, and those who in the hospital and the tents of the Sanitary and Christian Commissions have rendered services which millions could not buy. Happily the labor and the service are their own reward. Thousands of matrons and thousands of maidens have experienced a delight in these homely toils and services, compared with which the pleasures of the ball-room and the opera-house are tame and unsatisfactory. This, on earth, is reward enough, but a richer is in store for them. Yes, brothers, sisters of charity, while you bind up the wounds of the poor sufferers, the humblest, perhaps, that have shed their blood for the country, forget not who it is that will hereafter say to you, ' Inasmuch as ye have done it unto one of the least of these my brethren, ye have done it unto me.'

*   *   *   *   *   *   *   *

"And now, friends, fellow-citizens of Gettysburg and Pennsylvania, and you from remoter States, let me again, as we part, invoke your benediction on these honored graves. You feel, though the occasion is mournful, that it is good to be here. You feel that it was greatly auspicious for the cause of the country that the men of the East and the men of the West, the men of nineteen sister States, stood side by side on the perilous ridges of the battle. You now feel it a new bond of union that they shall lie side by side till the clarion, louder than that which marshalled them to the combat, shall awake their slumbers. God bless the Union! it is dearer to us for the blood of brave men which has been shed in its defence. The spots on which they stood and fell; these pleasant heights; the fertile plain beneath them; the thriving village whose streets so lately rang with the strange din of war; the fields beyond the ridge, where the noble Reynolds held the advancing foe at bay, and while he gave up his own life, assured by his forethought and self-sacrifice the triumph of the two succeeding days; the little streams which wind through the hills, on whose banks in after-times the wondering ploughman will turn up, with the rude weapons of savage warfare, the fearful missiles of modern artillery; Seminary Ridge, the Peach Orchard, Cemetery, Culp's, and Wolf's Hills, Round Top, Little Round Top, humble names, henceforward dear and famous, no lapse of time, no distance of space, shall cause you to be forgotten. 'The whole earth,' said Pericles, as he stood over the remains of his fellow-citizens who had fallen in the first year of the Peloponnesian war,—' the whole earth is the sepulchre of illustrious men.' All time, he might have added, is the millennium of their glory. Surely I would do no injustice to the other noble achievements of the war, which have reflected such honor on both arms of the service, and have entitled the armies and the navy of the United States, their officers and men, to the warmest thanks and the richest rewards which a grateful people can pay. But they, I am sure, will join us in saying, as we bid farewell to the dust of these martyr-heroes, that wheresoever throughout the civilized world the accounts of this great warfare are read, and down to the latest period of recorded time, in the glorious annals of our common country, there will be no brighter page than that which relates the BATTLES OF GETTYSBURG."

ADDRESS OF PRESIDENT LINCOLN.

President Lincoln then delivered that immortal address, that masterpiece of English composition, which will ever rank him among the world's greatest orators:

"Fourscore and seven years ago our fathers brought forth upon this continent, a new nation, conceived in liberty, and dedicated to the proposition that all men are created equal.

"Now we are engaged in a great civil war, testing whether that nation, or any nation so conceived and so dedicated, can long endure. We are met on a great battle-field of that war. We have come to dedicate a portion of that field as a final resting-place for those who here gave their lives that that nation might live. It is altogether fitting and proper that we should do this.

"But, in a larger sense, we cannot dedicate,—we cannot consecrate—we cannot hallow—this ground. The brave men, living and dead, who struggled here, have consecrated it, far above our poor power to add or detract. The world will little note, nor long remember what we say here, but it can never forget what they did here. It is for us the living, rather, to be dedicated here to the unfinished work which they who fought here have thus far so nobly advanced. It is rather for us to be here dedicated to the great task remaining before us,—that from these honored dead we take increased devotion to that cause for which they here gave the last full measure of devotion—that we here highly resolve that these dead shall not have died in vain—that the nation, under God, shall have a new birth of freedom—and that the government of the people, by the people, for the people, shall not perish from the earth."

THE MONUMENT.

The design of the monument, as executed by Mr. J. G. Batterson, of Hartford, Connecticut, is intended to be purely historical, telling its own story with such simplicity that any discerning mind will readily comprehend its meaning and purpose.

The superstructure is sixty feet high, and consists of a massive pedestal, twenty-five feet square at the base, and is crowned with a colossal statue representing the Genius of Liberty. Standing upon a three-quarter globe, she raises with her right hand the victor's wreath of laurel, while with her left she gathers up the folds of our national flag under which the victory has been won. Projecting from the angles of the pedestal are four buttresses, supporting an equal number of allegorical statues representing, respectively, War, History, Peace, and Plenty.

War is personified by a statue of the American soldier, who, resting from the conflict, relates to History the story of the battle which this monument is intended to commemorate.

History, in listening attitude, records with stylus and tablet the achievements of the field and the names of the honored dead.

Peace is symbolized by a statue of the American mechanic, characterized by appropriate accessories.

Plenty is represented by a female figure, with a sheaf of wheat and fruits of the earth, typifying peace and abundance as the soldier's crowning triumph.

The main die of the pedestal is octagonal in form, panelled upon each face. The cornice and plinth above are also octagonal, and are heavily moulded. Upon this plinth rests an octagonal moulded base bearing upon the face, in high relief, the national arms. The upper die and cap are circular in form, the die being encircled by stars equal in number with the States whose sons contributed their lives as the price of the victory won at Gettysburg.

STATE APPROPRIATIONS.

The States made the following appropriations for the enclosing, laying out, ornamenting, and maintenance of the cemetery, between 1864 and 1872 :

Maine		$4,300.00
New Hampshire		2,255.34
Vermont		2,600.00
Massachusetts		9,471.83
Connecticut		3,000.00
Rhode Island		1,600.00
New York		26,072.86
New Jersey		4,205.30
Pennsylvania: For the purchase of lands	$2,324.27	
Treatment and care of the dead	835.40	
Proportionate share for enclosing, ornamenting, maintenance, etc.	20,000.00	
Removal of Confederate dead to Washington Cemetery, Maryland	3,000.00	
		26,159.67
Michigan		6,000.00
Maryland		4,205.30
Illinois		11,961.00
Wisconsin		2,526.36
Minnesota		1,686.50

In 1872 the cemetery was transferred to the care of the National Government, since which time it has not only been kept in the manner originally designed, but improvements have been made from time to time, and to-day, with its high and prominent location, its beautiful and artistically arranged trees and shrubbery, its well-kept lawns, it is one of the most attractive cemeteries of the land. In one end of the cemetery is a unique rostrum constructed of stone pillars, covered with creeping and blooming vines, which is used for the services of Memorial Day and similar occasions.

The following persons have delivered the Memorial Day orations in the cemetery:

Year	Speaker	Location
1868.	Rev. J. A. Brown, D.D.	Gettysburg.
1869.	Professor H. Louis Baugher	Gettysburg.
1870.	Rev. C. A. Hay, D.D.	Gettysburg.
1871.	Rev. J. B. Young	Gettysburg.
1872.	Rev. J. A. Brown, D.D.	Gettysburg.
1873.	Rev. S. S. Palmer	Gettysburg.
1874.	Rev. M. L. Gunoe	Gettysburg.
1875.	Fred. Staley, Esq.	Gettysburg.
1876.	Fred. Staley, Esq.	Gettysburg.
1877.	J. M. Vanderslice, Esq.	Philadelphia.
1878.	General Benj. F. Butler	Boston, Mass.
1879.	General Wm. McCandless	Philadelphia.
1880.	Hon. C. G. Williams	Wisconsin.
1881.	Hon. Julius Burrows	Michigan.
1882.	General Joseph Hawley	Connecticut.
1883.	Edward Gearhardt, Esq.	Danville, Pa.
1884.	Major Martin Maginnes	Montana.
1885.	Hon. S. Mc. Swope	Gettysburg.

1886. Major Wm. H. Lambert . . . Philadelphia.
1887. Colonel A. Wilson Norris . . . Philadelphia.
1888. Hon. T. E. Tarsney . . . . . Missouri.
1889. Hon. S. L. Woodford . . . . New York.
1890. Hon. Rufus Ingalls . . . . . Kansas.
1891. Rev. George Morrison . . . . Baltimore.
1892. General R. M. Henderson . . . Carlisle, Pa.
1893. George E. Reed, D.D., LL.D. . Carlisle, Pa.
1894. Hon. J. D. Dolliver . . . . . Iowa.
1895. Hon. Marriott Brosius . . . . Lancaster, Pa.
1896. Governor D. H. Hastings . . . Pennsylvania.

GETTYSBURG BATTLE-FIELD MEMORIAL ASSOCIATION.

The Legislature of Pennsylvania, on April 30, 1864, conferred upon the Memorial Association the rights of a corporation by the following Act of Assembly:

"AN ACT

"TO INCORPORATE THE GETTYSBURG BATTLE-FIELD MEMORIAL ASSOCIATION.

"SECTION 1. *Be it enacted*, etc., That Joseph R. Ingersoll, T. D. Carson, D. McConaughy, Wm. McSherry, A. D. Buehler, R. G. McCreary, J. B. Danner, George Arnold, J. L. Shick, James H. Marshall, Henry C. Carey, J. G. Fell, Alexander Henry, Edmund A. Souder, Theodore Cuyler, Wm. Strong, S. A. Mercer, H. C. Baird, Thomas M. Howe, N. B. Craig, John P. Penny, Wm. H. Robinson, Jr., James L. Graham, Harvey Childs, George G. Meade, Thomas J. Bingham, A. O. Heister, James Worrall, James L. Reynolds, S. W. Crawford, Winfield S. Hancock, John L. Atlee, William Kinsey, Samuel Small, F. M. Kimmell, P. Frazier Smith, J. McD. Sharp, H. C. Johnson, John Cessna, B. B. Vincent, John Scott, Wm. A. Wallace, George W. Householder, John S. McCalmont, Daniel Agnew, Wm. Hopkins, John P. Crozier, Wm. H. Miller, A. K. McClure, John D. Cochran, J. N. McAlister, C. L. Pershing, R. A. McMurtrie, their associates, who have subscribed and all others who shall hereafter subscribe to the fund devoted to the preservation of the battle-field of Gettysburg, and their successors, be and they are hereby made a body politic and corporate, by the name, style, and title of the Gettysburg Battle-field Memorial Association, and by that name shall be able and capable, in law, to have, and use, a common seal, to sue and be sued, plead, and be impleaded, and to do all such other things as are incident to a corporation.

"SECTION 2. That the object of said Association shall be, to hold and preserve, the battle-grounds of Gettysburg, on which were fought the actions of the first, second, and third days of July, Anno Domini one thousand eight hundred and sixty-three, with the natural and artificial defences, as they were at the time of said battle, and by such perpetuation, and such memorial structures as a generous and patriotic people may aid to erect, to commemorate the heroic deeds, the struggles, and the triumphs of their brave defenders.

"SECTION 3. That for its said purpose, the said Association shall have power to take, and to hold, by gift, grant, devise, purchase, or lease, such personal property and effects, and all such portions of said battle-grounds as may be necessary, or convenient, to promote and accomplish the object of its incorporation, to enclose, and perpetuate, said grounds and defences, to keep them in repair and a state of preservation, to construct and maintain ways and roads, to improve and ornament the grounds and to erect and promote the erection by voluntary contributions of structures and works of art and taste thereon, adapted to designate the spots of special interest, to commemorate the great deeds of valor, endurance, and noble self-sacrifice, and to perpetuate the memory of the heroes, and the signal events, which render these battle-grounds illustrious; and, to these ends, to make such by-laws, rules, and regulations as may be necessary, and proper, for the government of the affairs and promotion of the purposes of said Association; the property of said Association shall not be subject to attachment, or execution, and the lands acquired for the purposes of said Association, with its personal property, and the improvements and appurtenances shall be forever exempt from taxation, and also from the payment of an enrolment tax.

"SECTION 4. That the property, and affairs, of said Association shall be managed by a president and a board of thirteen directors, with a secretary, treasurer, and other necessary officers, by them to be selected; to be chosen annually, from the subscribers, by a majority of the votes given, each subscriber to be entitled to a single vote; the said officers to serve one year, or until successors are elected; the election to be held annually, on the first Monday of June, at Gettysburg; public notice thereof to be given by publication, in one newspaper in Gettysburg, Philadelphia, Harrisburg, and Pittsburg, at least two weeks previous to such election.

"SECTION 5. That said Association shall have power to issue certificates of membership to all persons who shall subscribe one or more shares to the said Battle-field Memorial Fund; the amount of a single share to be fixed by the board of directors, and not to exceed ten dollars; and all subscribers, upon payment, and receipt of such certificates, shall be entitled to vote at all elections of said Association.

"SECTION 6. That the president, directors, and treasurer, shall make annual reports, on the day of the annual election, to be presented to the members, and read and published, which shall be duly certified, and shall exhibit fully and accurately the receipts, expenses, and expenditures of the said Association.

"*Approved* The thirtieth day of April, Anno Domini one thousand eight hundred and sixty-four.

"A. G. CURTIN,
"*Governor.*"

"A SUPPLEMENT

"To an act entitled 'An Act to incorporate the Gettysburg Battle field Memorial Association,' approved April 30, 1864.

"SECTION 1. *Be it enacted*, etc., That if any person shall wilfully destroy, mutilate, deface, injure, or remove any monument, column, statue, memorial structure or work of art that shall be erected or placed upon the battle-ground held, or which shall be held, by said Association, or shall wilfully destroy or remove any fence, railing, enclosure, or other work for the protection or ornament of said battle-ground, or any portion thereof that may be held by said Association, or shall wilfully destroy, cut, hack, bark, break down, or otherwise injure any tree, bush, or shrubbery that may be growing upon said battle-ground, or shall cut down, or fell, and remove any timber, tree, or trees, growing or being upon such battle-grounds, or shall wilfully remove or destroy any breastworks, earthworks, or other defences or shelter, on any part thereof, constructed by the armies or any portion of the forces engaged in the battle of Gettysburg; any person so offending, and found guilty thereof before any justice of the peace of the county of Adams, shall, for each and every such offence, forfeit and pay a fine, in the discretion of the justice, according to the aggravation of the offence, of not less than five nor more than fifty dollars, one-half to the use of said company, and the other half to the informer, to be enforced and recovered, before said justice, in like manner as debts of like are now recoverable, in any action of debt, brought in the name of the commonwealth, as well for the use of said company as of the person suing.

"SECTION 2. That in addition to the penalty provided in the first section of this act, for the offences therein prohibited, any person who shall be guilty of either of the offences therein named, shall be deemed guilty of a misdemeanor, and on conviction thereof, in the court of quarter sessions of the said county of Adams, shall be punished by fine, not exceeding one hundred dollars, or imprisonment for not more than thirty days, or both, in the discretion of the said court.

"SECTION 3. That the president and directors of the said Gettysburg Battle-field Memorial Association shall have power and authority, by themselves, committees, engineer, surveyor, superintendent, or agents, by them to be appointed, to survey, locate, and lay out roads and avenues from any public road or roads in the vicinity of Gettysburg, or of the said battle-grounds, to and upon, and also in and through, any portion or portions of said battle-grounds, not, however, passing through any dwelling-house, or any burying-ground, or any place of public worship, and to open and fence, or otherwise enclose, such roads and avenues, the latter of a width not exceeding three hundred feet; and the same may be laid out so as to embrace any breastworks, or lines of defences, or positions of the forces engaged in the battle of Gettysburg, and with power to plant rows or colonnades of trees upon said roads and avenues; *Provided*, That it shall be lawful for such Association to enter upon adjoining lands and take materials necessary for the construction and repair of such roads and avenues, in like manner, and with like power, as in the case of railroads, under the act regulating railroad companies, approved the nineteenth of February, Anno Domini one thousand eight hundred and forty-nine, and its supplements; *Provided further*, That before such Association shall enter upon and take possession of any such lands for roads, or avenues, or such materials, they shall make ample compensation to the owner or owners thereof, or tender adequate security therefor; *And provided further*, That when the said company cannot agree with the owner or owners of any such lands which said Association may enter upon, use, or take for any such roads or avenues, the like proceedings shall be had to ascertain, determine, and recover damages, on account of the taking and appropriating such lands for roads or avenues as are provided for ascertaining and recovering damages by landowners from railroad companies by the said act regulating railroad companies, and its supplements. *Approved* The twenty-fourth day of April, Anno Domini one thousand eight hundred and sixty-six.

"A. G. CURTIN,
"*Governor.*"

There is no record of any meeting for organization of the gentlemen named above as incorporators. This may be due to the fact that immediately afterwards the great campaign in Virginia was inaugurated, and the whole attention of the people was concentrated upon the prosecution of the war during the memorable "battle summer of 1864," and that their time and means were given to the care and alleviation of the wounded and suffering. Upon the termination of the war, in the year following, there was for a time a complete diversion of public attention from everything connected with or pertaining to war.

However, the Legislature of Pennsylvania, in 1867, appropriated the sum of three thousand dollars "to be applied to the purchase of portions of the battle-grounds, and the general purposes for which said Association was incorporated," and in 1868 a like sum for the same purpose, this being all that it was asked to appropriate.

This money was presumably used in the purchase of that portion of Culp's Hill upon which the breastworks were still standing, of East Cemetery Hill where Stewart's, Reynolds's, Ricketts's, and Weidrick's batteries were posted, and where the lunettes or redans still remain, and also a small piece of ground on the slope and summit of Little Round Top, as these grounds were purchased during that period.

The first meeting of the Association of which there is any record was held on June 10, 1872, when the following persons were elected as officers and directors: President, Governor John W. Geary; Vice-President, David McConaughy; Directors, Henry C. Carey, Edmund Souder, General J. Watts De Peyster, Wm. M. Hirsh, A. D. Heister, David McConaughy, Joel B. Danner, George Arnold, Alex. D. Buehler, Dr. Charles Horner, J. Lawrence Schick, and John M. Krauth. George Arnold was subsequently elected treasurer, and John M. Krauth secretary.

The Board met on June 11, 1872, in the office of Mr. McConaughy, the following being present: Governor John W. Geary, Hon. A. D.

Heister, H. M. McAlister, J. B. Danner, David McConaughy, George Arnold, A. D. Buehler, Dr. Charles Horner, J. L. Schick, and John M. Krauth. George Arnold had evidently been elected treasurer in some preceding year, as he at this meeting submitted his report, which was referred to a committee for audit.

By a resolution, Mr. David McConaughy was appointed counsel and actuary, with full power to use every honorable effort to procure from every State interested appropriations to defray the expenses of carrying out the views and plans of the Board, and his compensation was fixed at one thousand dollars per annum.

By a resolution, the commander-in-chief of the army, with his staff and the commanders of corps, divisions, and brigades, were elected honorary directors of the Association.

The officers of the Association were instructed to make application to the President and proper officers, and to the governors of the States, for condemned ordnance for the redans and other works upon the battle-field.

Reference is also made in the minutes to appropriations which had been made by the States of New York and Minnesota. That of New York, of $6000, appears never to have been paid, but that of Minnesota, of $1000, was paid the following year to Governor Hartranft, of Pennsylvania, and handed by him to the Association.

At a subsequent meeting, held May 20, 1873, at which were present Messrs. McConaughy, Arnold, Danner, Buehler, Horner, Schick, and Krauth, resident directors, a resolution was passed that Dr. J. Rutherford Wooster be for the present relieved of his duties as co-operating agent under the direction of Mr. McConaughy, the actuary, and the thanks of the Board were tendered Dr. Wooster for the energy and zeal which he had directed to the work of cooperation. At this meeting, General Charles K. Graham, of New York, was elected to fill the vacancy caused by the death of H. N. McAlister, Esq.

Resolutions were passed instructing the officers to continue their exertions in behalf of the memorial effort, and to procure the erection on the field of an historical structure, in high art, as a memorial tribute to the Army of the Potomac, to be surmounted with an equestrian statue of Major-General George Gordon Meade, the commander-in-chief.

On July 26, 1873, a meeting was held, which was attended by the resident members, at which it was resolved that the actuary be authorized to receive the co-operation of Dr. J. Rutherford Wooster, and to accept his overtures to visit the capitals and Legislatures of the States of Connecticut, New Hampshire, and Rhode Island, and press upon the Legislatures of those States the memorial efforts at an early period of their sessions, the terms to be the same as heretofore.

When Dr. Wooster was first appointed to this position, and what, if anything, he ever accomplished, are not shown by the record.

At the next annual meeting of the stockholders, held June 16, 1873, Governor J. F. Hartranft was elected president, *ex officio*, and the Board of Directors of the previous year was re-elected, except that General Alexander S. Webb, of New York, was elected instead of Mr. Hirsh. The resident members of the Board, subsequent to the election, met at the office of Mr. McConaughy, and George Arnold was re-elected treasurer, and John M. Krauth secretary. At this meeting a resolution was passed that the Board would not be justified in incurring expenditure exceeding $500 for the expenses of Dr. J. Rutherford Wooster in visiting State Legislatures.

On July 19, Dr. Wooster was paid an additional sum of $100, which is the last reference to him in connection with the Association.

At the annual meeting, on June 18, 1874, the same Board was re-elected, except that General

Horatio G. Sickel was elected instead of Mr. Souder.

On August 26, at a meeting of the resident members, Mr. McConaughy, in view of the financial condition of the Association, declined to receive any salary thereafter.

In June, 1875, the Board was re-elected, except that Hon. Edward McPherson was elected instead of Mr. Danner, as it was again in 1876, except that R. G. McCreary, Esq., was elected instead of Mr. McPherson. The same Board was re-elected in 1877, 1878, 1879, Governor Henry M. Hoyt being elected president, *ex officio*, in the latter year.

There is no record that any of the non-resident members attended any of the meetings of the Board; and there is no record of any meeting ot the Board whatever between August 26, 1874, and July 7, 1879, the work in the mean time being intrusted to Mr. McConaughy. At the meeting upon the latter date, on motion of Mr. McCreary, it was resolved that a committee be appointed to examine and report upon the amount, condition, and title of the lands held by the Association, and also to report its financial condition, as a basis of correspondence with the non-resident members of the Board of Directors, and to revive interest in the objects of the Association. Messrs. McCreary, Horner, and

Krauth were appointed as the committee, which reported at a meeting held July 19, 1879, and was authorized to prepare and have distributed an address embracing its recommendations. The report of the treasurer showed the Association to be in debt to the amount of $165.46.

In the mean time other influences for the advancement of the objects of the Memorial Association were being quietly exerted.

In the summer of 1878 the Grand Army of the Republic of Pennsylvania encamped for a week on East Cemetery Hill. J. M. Vanderslice, of Philadelphia, was the Assistant Adjutant-General of the department, and very active in the promotion of the Order at the time.

The scope and possibility of the Memorial Association attracted his attention, as did the apparent apathy or inactivity of those controlling it. After inquiring into the status of the Association and examining the act of incorporation, he determined upon having the Grand Army of the Republic assume control and direction of it. Circulars were issued to the Posts and letters were written to personal friends throughout the State.

At his suggestion, General Strong Vincent Post, No. 67, of Erie, Pennsylvania, had during the encampment erected upon Little Round Top a tablet to mark the spot where General

Vincent was killed, which was the *first* memorial of any kind erected upon the battle-field outside of the cemetery; and Colonel Fred. Taylor Post, No. 19, of Philadelphia, had placed a small tablet to mark the spot where Colonel Taylor fell while leading the Bucktail Rifle Regiment in front of Round Top.

During the summer of 1879 the 2d Massachusetts Infantry placed a bronze tablet upon a large rock on the edge of Spangler's meadow, with an inscription reciting the facts connected with the historic charge of that regiment across the meadow.

Before the annual election in 1880, about one hundred shares of stock had been purchased by Posts of the Grand Army and individuals in sympathy with it. Just prior to the election, proxies were procured from these stockholders, constituting as they did a majority, and sent to Major Robert Bell, of Gettysburg, with the suggestion to have a board of directors elected in which members of the Grand Army of the Republic should predominate.

At the meeting of the stockholders held June 21, 1880, the following Board was elected: President, *ex officio*, Governor Henry M. Hoyt; Vice-President, Robert G. McCreary; Directors, General W. S. Hancock, General S. W. Crawford, General Louis Wagner, John M. Vanderslice, Major Chill W. Hazzard, Captain John Taylor, Colonel C. H. Buehler, Major Robert Bell, N. G. Wilson, J. L. Schick, Dr. Charles Horner, and John M. Krauth.

The money realized from the sale of certificates of stock during the year had been sufficient to liquidate the debt and leave a balance of $515.97 in the treasury.

The Association now commenced its career of active and effective work. At the meeting held July 2, Sergeant N. G. Wilson, Superintendent of the National Cemetery, was appointed General Superintendent of the grounds of the Association, which at that time embraced only the pieces of ground upon Culp's Hill, East Cemetery Hill, and Little Round Top, before alluded to. Major Bell and Mr. Wilson were instructed to have the roads upon the ground put in good order and repair.

This summer, during the encampment of the Grand Army, General Zook Post, No. 11, of Norristown, Pennsylvania, erected a shaft to mark the spot where General Zook fell in the Wheat-Field, the marble being taken from the farm of the general's father, near Norristown. The 91st Pennsylvania Infantry also put up a monument on Little Round Top, being the *first regimental* monument erected after the tablet of the 2d Massachusetts.

The Grand Army of Pennsylvania encamped upon the field for a week each summer from 1880 to 1894, except in 1884 and 1891.

At a meeting held in the head-quarters tent in the camp of the Grand Army, upon East Cemetery Hill, July 23, Mr. Vanderslice, believing that Colonel John B. Bachelder, by reason of the many years he had given to the study of the field, would be an aid to the Association, tendered his resignation as a director and urged the election of Colonel Bachelder in his stead. The officers were instructed to issue a certificate of membership to Colonel Bachelder, and he was elected. The thanks of the Board were tendered Mr. Vanderslice for his services during the past year in promoting the objects of the Association. General Wagner and Major Hazzard were appointed a committee to secure appropriations from the several States for the purpose of purchasing additional territory, improving it, laying out the avenues, and making the battle-field more accessible, and, upon the request of the Board, Mr. Vanderslice consented to act with this committee and to aid the Association in every way possible. He communicated with the influential members of the Grand Army in those States which had troops at Gettysburg, and pressed upon them the objects and requirements of the Association. During the following winter he visited Harrisburg, and, with the aid of others, secured an appropriation of $10,000 by the State of Pennsylvania.

At the annual election, June 8, 1881, the same Board was re-elected, and at the meeting held July 28 a motion was passed requesting Mr. Vanderslice to meet regularly with the Board, which he did, without voting upon any question.

At this meeting it was determined to open an avenue along the line of battle from the Taneytown Road to Little Round Top, the avenue to be sixty feet wide, except where necessary to embrace important points, where the width was to be three hundred feet. It was also proposed that an avenue should be laid out in front of the cemetery wall from the Baltimore Pike to the Taneytown Road, but this was never carried into execution.

During the year, Posts and members of the Grand Army of the several States commenced to manifest an active interest and desire to aid the Association. Several regimental monuments were erected, notably those of the 14th Brooklyn, 124th New York, 17th Connecticut, 90th and 88th Pennsylvania Infantry. At the meeting held November 16, 1881, the terms of the property holders over whose land the proposed avenue passed were not accepted, and it was decided to commence condemnation proceedings in accordance with the Act of Assembly.

At a meeting held June 2, 1882, arrangements were made for the reception of a delegation of Confederate soldiers, who visited the field for the purpose of locating the position of several commands.

At the annual election, June 6, 1882, the Board of Directors of the previous year was elected, except that J. M. Vanderslice was elected instead of Colonel Bachelder. John M. Krauth and J. L. Schick were again respectively elected secretary and treasurer.

At the meeting held July 27, 1882, it was resolved to purchase the Wheat-Field ; also the balance of the ground on Little Round Top, and to construct an avenue from East Cemetery Hill, by way of Culp's Hill, to the extreme right of the position occupied by the Twelfth Corps.

It was also decided to have sign-boards painted to locate as nearly as possible the positions of the Pennsylvania and the 1st Minnesota regiments, and to also mark the prominent points on the battle-field.

The placing of these cheap boards had the desired effect. Visitors from other States, in passing over the field, would inquire with indignation whether there were no other troops than Pennsylvanians engaged in the battle, and, upon being informed that only the States of Pennsylvania and Minnesota had made appropriations, naturally became desirous of having their States properly represented. Public interest was thus gradually being awakened.

The Superintendent was instructed to have the works upon the field reconstructed wherever possible.

At the meeting held in June, 1883, it being believed that, as the Board of Directors was composed exclusively of Pennsylvanians, it might advance the interests of the Association to have residents of other States again upon the Board, General Hancock, Major Hazzard, Captain Taylor, and Mr. Vanderslice gave place to General Joshua L. Chamberlain, of Maine, General John C. Robinson, of New York, General George L. Stannard, of Vermont, and Colonel J. B. Bachelder, of Massachusetts, the balance of the old Board being re-elected. At this meeting Colonel Bachelder was elected Superintendent of Tablets and Legends.

At the meeting, August 28, 1883, it was resolved that the memorials to be erected upon the battle-field should be submitted to the Board of Directors for their approval of the historical accuracy of the inscription.

During this year an appropriation of $5000 was received from the State of Massachusetts.

The positions of all the Massachusetts commands were located, and it was decided to purchase the ground necessary for the erection of monuments, for each of which the State had made an appropriation of $500. This was the *first* State to appropriate money for the erection of monuments upon this field.

On January 4, 1884, a meeting was called to take action upon the death of R. G. McCreary, Esq., the vice-president, and appropriate resolutions were passed. Sergeant William Holtzworth, who had been for many years a guide upon the battle-field, was elected director to fill the vacancy caused by the death of Mr. McCreary, and David A. Buehler, Esq., was elected vice-president.

May 15, 1884, a communication having been received from the survivors of the 3d Pennsylvania Cavalry, informing the Association of their intention to erect a monumental shaft, with suitable inscriptions, upon the field on which Gregg's cavalry division fought, it was decided to purchase the necessary ground, with the right of access thereto.

A reward of $50 was offered for the detection of any one destroying, mutilating, or removing any property of the Memorial Association, and the Superintendent was directed to properly place notices of the reward.

At the annual meeting in June, 1884, as Generals Robinson, Chamberlain, and Stannard had not attended any of the meetings during the year, Messrs. Hazzard, Vanderslice, and David A. Buehler were elected in their stead, the balance of the Board being re-elected, as were the various officers.

At the meeting of the Board held October, 1884, General Wagner reported that he had corresponded with General S. W. Crawford as to the transfer to the Memorial Association of his land in front of Little Round Top, upon which the Pennsylvania Reserves had fought, but without success, as the general said that he had made other provision, and could not do it.

General Wagner and Mr. Vanderslice were appointed a committee to have maps of the battle-field printed, showing the land owned by the Association. On motion of Mr. Vanderslice, a committee of three, to be known as the Committee on Legislation, was appointed, its duty being to correspond with the officials and Legislatures of the several States, urging appropriations, and to adopt other measures to awaken more general interest, especially among soldiers, in the work of the Association. General Wagner, Colonel Bachelder, and Mr. Vanderslice were appointed as the committee.

At this meeting it was decided to open an

avenue from Oak Ridge, by way of Reynolds's Grove, to the extreme left of the First Corps line of battle.

On April 10, 1885, the following amendments to the charter were decreed by the court of Adams County:

"AMENDMENTS TO THE CHARTER.

"SECTION 1. The property and affairs of the Gettysburg Battle-field Memorial Association shall be managed by a President and a Board of Twenty-one Directors, to be chosen annually by the members of the Association by a majority of the votes given at the annual election, together with such *ex-officio* Directors as are hereinafter provided for; *Provided*, however, that the Association shall have power, by by-law or resolution, from time to time to enlarge or diminish the number of elective Directors, if deemed advisable.

"SECTION 2. The election for President and Directors shall be held annually on the first Monday of June, at Gettysburg; at which election each member of the Association shall be entitled to one vote in person or by proxy; and the Directors so elected shall serve for one year or until successors are elected. In case of failure, for any reason, to hold said election on the first Monday in June, an election may be held on such day thereafter as the officers or executive committee may designate. Public notice of said election shall be given by publication in one newspaper in Gettysburg, Philadelphia, Harrisburg, and Pittsburg, at least two weeks previous thereto.

"SECTION 3. The Governor of the Commonwealth of Pennsylvania shall be, *ex officio*, President of the Association; and the Governors of such States as shall, by legislative appropriation, contribute funds for the support of the Association, shall be, *ex officio*, members of the Board of Directors, with power (if unable to be present) to substitute, under the official seal of the State, some one of its citizens to represent the State in the meetings of the Board.

"SECTION 4. The Directors shall have power to choose from their number a Vice-President, Secretary, Treasurer, Executive Committee, and such other officers as may be deemed necessary, and to prescribe the respective duties and powers of said officers by resolution or by-law.

"SECTION 5. There shall be a meeting of the Board of Directors at least once in every year at Gettysburg, at such time as may be determined by resolution or by-law, of which meeting notice shall be given in writing, signed by the Secretary, and sent to each Director by mail or otherwise, at least two weeks before the time of such meeting. And if, at such meeting, eleven of the said Directors shall not be present, those of them who shall be present shall have power to adjourn to any other time as fully as if all the Directors were present; but if eleven or more of the said Directors shall meet at the appointed time, or at such adjourned meeting, such eleven or more Directors shall be a quorum of the Board, capable of transacting the business of the Association. Special meetings of the Board of Directors may be called, subject to like notice, on the request of the Executive Committee.

"SECTION 6. So much of the Act of Assembly of April 30, 1864, and the Supplement thereto, incorporating this Association, as may be inconsistent with these amendments, is hereby repealed."

At a meeting held May 5, Messrs. Wagner, Bachelder, and Vanderslice, the Committee on Legislation, reported that the State of Connecticut had appropriated the sum of $2500 to the Association; Rhode Island, $1000; Delaware, $500; besides making appropriations to the several regiments towards the erection of monuments; and that the State of Indiana had appropriated $3000 for the erection of monuments only.

The appropriations of the several States, and for what purpose, will be given hereafter in detail.

This committee also reported that the Legislature of New York, through the exertions of General Henry A. Barnum, had made an appropriation of $10,000, but that the bill had not been signed by Governor Hill because of some constitutional objection. Messrs. Wagner and Vanderslice were requested to visit Albany for the purpose of removing, if possible, the objections of the governor. General Wagner, in company with General Barnum, afterwards had an interview with Governor David B. Hill, and the governor signed the bill, and expressed a desire to aid the Association in every way in his power.

The Superintendent of Tablets and Legends was instructed to require each organization intending to erect a monument or tablet on the field to have a suitable inscription thereon, showing its historical relation to the battle as to time and service.

General Wagner was appointed a committee to obtain from the Secretary of War as many cannon as possible.

The Executive Committee was instructed to purchase all the lands necessary for all the proposed avenues, and also the two small fields south of East Cemetery Hill.

At the meeting in June, 1885, as the amendments to the charter provided for an increased number of directors, the following were elected: General S. W. Crawford, General Louis Wagner, Major Chill W. Hazzard, John M. Vanderslice, Captain John Taylor, Colonel Eli G. Sellers, Pennsylvania; Colonel W. W. Dudley, Indiana; Colonel John B. Bachelder, Massachusetts; General Henry A. Barnum, New York; Colonel Frank D. Sloat, Connecticut; Colonel Elisha H. Rhodes, Rhode Island; General Byron R. Pierce, Michigan; David A. Buehler, J. L. Schick, Colonel C. H. Buehler, N. G. Wilson, Chas. Horner, M.D.; Major Robert Bell, Wm. D. Holtzworth, Alex. D. Buehler, and John M. Krauth, Gettysburg, Pennsylvania. Captain John Taylor and Mr. Alexander D. Buehler afterwards resigned, and their places were filled by John C. Linehan, of New Hampshire, and Colonel Charles L. Young, of Ohio.

At a subsequent meeting of the Board, held June 16, 1885, David A. Buehler was elected vice-president, John M. Krauth secretary, J. L. Schick treasurer, J. B. Bachelder superintendent of tablets, and N. G. Wilson, superintendent of grounds. General Louis Wagner, John M. Vanderslice, General H. A. Barnum, and the resident members of the Board, were selected as an executive committee. N. G. Wilson, W. D. Holtzworth, and John M. Krauth were appointed a committee on location. The following by-laws were then adopted:

BY-LAWS—ADOPTED JUNE 16, 1885.

"1. At the first meeting of the Board of Directors held in each year after the annual election, there shall be chosen by ballot, unless otherwise directed, a vice-president, secretary, treasurer, superintendent of tablets, superintendent of grounds, and an executive committee of eleven directors, who shall continue in office until successors shall have been elected.

"2. The Vice-President, in the absence of the President, shall represent the Association in the execution of contracts, instruments of writing, etc., and in general discharge all official duties which would devolve on the President if personally present.

"3. The Secretary shall keep and record, in a book provided for that purpose, minutes of all proceedings of the Board of Directors and of the Executive Committee, conduct the correspondence of the Association, send written or printed notices to directors of their election and of all regular or special meetings of the Board, and attest all orders drawn on the Treasurer.

"4. The Treasurer shall have custody of the moneys of

the Association, and be authorized to receive and receipt for gifts of money, membership fees, and legislative appropriations, and shall pay out the same upon orders of the President or Vice-President, attested by the Secretary. He shall give bond in the sum of twenty-five hundred dollars, with sureties to be approved by the Executive Committee, for the faithful discharge of his duties, and shall make a detailed written report of all receipts and disbursements during the year, at the annual meeting of the Association.

"5. The duties of Superintendent of Tablets, and Superintendent of Grounds shall be such as may be prescribed by the Board of Directors or Executive Committee from time to time.

"6. The Executive Committee shall be charged with carrying out the action of the Board of Directors from time to time, and they shall have power (between the meetings of the Board) to transact all the business of the Association requiring immediate attention, subject, nevertheless, to and in accordance with the general rules, regulations, and policy of the Association which the Board from time to time may prescribe. Seven members of the Executive Committee shall be necessary to constitute a quorum for the transaction of business. They shall make report in writing at each meeting of the Board of Directors. The Vice-President of the Association shall be chairman of the Executive Committee, and the Secretary of the Association shall be secretary of the committee.

"7. No salaries shall be paid to the officers or directors, except the Secretary, who shall be paid annually the sum of $100; but they may be reimbursed for expenses incurred by them in attending to the business of the Association."

General Wagner reported that he and Mr. Vanderslice had visited Mr. Whitney and his attorney in fact, at Glassboro, New Jersey, with reference to the purchase of Reynolds's Grove and adjoining ground, and that they had received satisfactory assurances that the ground would be sold at an extremely reasonable price. Messrs. Wagner, Barnum, and Vanderslice were appointed a committee to devise the best mode of carrying into effect the requirements of the act of New York making an appropriation to the Association.

The secretary was directed to write to the Adjutant-General of Ohio, and request that action upon the expenditure of the appropriation by that State be deferred until a committee from the State visit the field and examine the ground.

Corporal Skelly, Post No. 9, of Gettysburg, was granted permission to erect a memorial shaft on the spot where General Reynolds fell, the State of Pennsylvania having appropriated $1000 to the post for that purpose.

Messrs. Wagner, Vanderslice, and Buehler were appointed a committee to confer with the Secretary of War as to the practicability of opening an avenue through the National Cemetery to the Taneytown Road. The committee failed at the time to accomplish the purpose, but the avenue was subsequently opened as desired.

Messrs. Barnum, Wagner, and Vanderslice

were appointed a committee to confer with the Comptroller of New York with regard to the proper disbursement of the $10,000 appropriated by that State, with full power to represent the Association.

Permission was granted the 2d Maryland Confederate Infantry to erect a monument to indicate its position on the field, subject to the rule of the Association in regard to historical accuracy and inscription.

On motion of Mr. Vanderslice, the following was adopted: That hereafter regiments that shall erect monuments on the battle-field shall be required at the time to mark the flanks of their position whenever practicable; that any regiment notifying the Association of its intention to erect a monument shall be informed by the secretary of the rule in reference to inscriptions, and, upon failure to comply with its requirements, the Association shall have the necessary inscription placed on said tablet or memorial.

On motion of General Wagner, it was resolved that a certificate of membership be issued to the governor, *ex officio*, of each State that had made an appropriation to the Gettysburg Battle-field Memorial Association. The appropriation of Connecticut of $2500 was received this year.

At the annual meeting held June 7, 1886, the Board of Directors of the previous year was re-elected, except that Colonel Silas Colgrove, of Indiana, was elected instead of Colonel W. W. Dudley. Colonel Eli G. Sellers, of Philadelphia, afterwards resigned to make place for General Lucius Fairchild, of Wisconsin.

At a subsequent meeting, held July 3, the officers were also re-elected, and the Executive Committee constituted as in the past year.

Messrs. Wagner, Bachelder, and Vanderslice were reappointed the Committee on Legislation.

After discussion as to the best means to procure an appropriation from Congress for marking the positions of the Regular commands, the matter was referred to the Executive Committee, with power to act.

The Secretary of War was requested not to permit the erection of any regimental monument or memorial in the Cemetery until the location and inscription had been approved by the Association.

Colonel Bachelder, Superintendent of Tablets and Legends, was requested to forward to the secretary of the Association, for proper record, all inscriptions approved by him.

At a meeting held September 22, 1886, on motion of General Wagner, it was decided to open an avenue along the Eleventh Corps line of battle.

During this year the appropriations of Rhode Island of $1000, New Hampshire of $1000, New Jersey of $3000, Delaware of $500, Ohio of $3000, New York of $10,000, were received, and the Association was in a condition to do considerable necessary and effective work in the acquiring of land and opening of avenues.

In the beginning of 1887 the Association met with a very severe loss in the death of its vice-president, David Buehler, Esq., of Gettysburg, who had manifested so much zeal and ability in the promotion of its work during the years that he was its vice-president.

At a meeting held January 2, 1887, Colonel C. H. Buehler was elected vice-president, to succeed his brother. Messrs. Vanderslice and Krauth were appointed a committee to draft a resolution upon the death of Mr. David Buehler.

The following was offered and unanimously adopted:

"*Resolved*, That the Gettysburg Battle field Memorial Association with profound sorrow expresses its regrets upon the death of David A. Buehler, Esq., who has been its Vice-President for the last three years, during which time his intelligent and energetic efforts, his wise and mature judgment, his courteous and considerate treatment of all interested in its purpose, have in a very great measure tended to the advancement of the Association and to the furtherance of the great work accomplished by it; that this Association has suffered an irreparable loss in the death of one whose patriotic and loyal devotion to the principles of his government makes his loss a public one, and whose integrity of character, sincerity of purpose, and kindly nature endeared him to all who knew him ; that we tender the widow and the family of the deceased in their deep bereavement our sincere sympathy; that a copy of this minute be sent to them and to the public press."

J. A. Kitzmiller, Esq., was elected a director, to fill the vacancy caused by the death of Mr. Buehler.

At the meeting on February 25, 1887, after hearing Mr. G. W. Conger, representing the Monumental Bronze Company of Bridgeport, Connecticut, who presented an application of that company to erect upon the battle-field monuments constructed of white bronze, the Board, after careful and mature consideration, took the following action :

"*Resolved*, That no monument or memorial constructed of other material than real bronze or granite shall be permitted on the grounds of the Association."

On motion of General Wagner, the Executive Committee was directed to inquire without delay as to the cost of opening an avenue, sixty feet wide, from the general line occupied by the

Confederate army on Seminary Ridge to the Emmittsburg Road, and, if the funds of the Association would permit, to purchase the land necessary for the opening of the avenue.

On motion of Mr. Vanderslice, Colonel Bachelder was requested to prepare and submit to the Association an appropriate design for a tablet descriptive of the engagement and movements of all the commands engaged in the assault of July 3, by Pickett's, Pettigrew's, and Trimble's Confederate commands, upon the line held by the Second Federal Corps.

The vice-president was authorized to have special officers appointed by the court.

The Superintendent of Tablets was instructed to require the list of casualties in monumental inscriptions to be in conformity with the official records of the battle, as they appear in the office of the Adjutant-General U.S.A.

The Secretary of War was respectfully requested to furnish the Association with an official statement of the number of troops, by separate commands, that were reported present for duty in the battle of Gettysburg, July 1, 2, and 3.

It being represented to the Association that the 4th Ohio Infantry had contracted for the erection of a white bronze monument before the action of the Board forbidding the use of that material, permission was granted to the regiment to erect the monument upon East Cemetery Hill.

At a meeting, March 25, 1887, a committee was appointed to secure an office for the exclusive use of the Association, where the survivors of regiments and others having business with the Association might meet the secretary or other officers.

A letter was received from the secretary of the Ohio Commission, appealing from the decision of the Superintendent of Tablets and Legends refusing permission to carve the Twentieth Corps badge upon the monuments to be erected by regiments of the Eleventh Corps. The request of the Ohio Commission was respectfully refused, and the secretary was directed to suggest that the allowance of its request would lead to confusion, as a large portion of the Eleventh Corps was afterwards assigned to other corps, and the Twentieth Corps did not participate in the battle of Gettysburg.

The vice-president was authorized to file a protest with the Secretary of War against the erection of the monument of the 74th Pennsylvania Infantry in the Cemetery, because the Association was opposed to any command erecting a monument in the Cemetery until it had erected one in the most important position occupied by it during the battle.

It was decided to open an avenue from between the two Round Tops to the extreme left of the line held by Russell's brigade of the Sixth Corps.

A letter was received from Mr. C. T. Cook, secretary of Pickett's Confederate Division Association, requesting permission to erect a monument on the ground of the Association; and the secretary was instructed to answer the communication and suggest that the Pickett Association should send a committee to meet with the members of the Memorial Association, to confer as to the location of the monument, and, further, that he should inform them of the precedent established in the case of the 2d Maryland Infantry.

At a meeting, May 5, 1887, it was resolved that hereafter regiments erecting monuments on the ground of the Association would be required to locate and place them in the position held by the regiment in the line of battle, but that they would not be prohibited from erecting such markers on the field, to indicate secondary or advanced positions, as the Association might determine.

At this meeting, Colonel R. C. Maury, Captain E. P. Reese, and Major Wm. I. Clopton appeared before the Board and requested permission to erect the monument of Pickett's division where General Armistead fell. It was suggested to this committee that, as the granting of their application would be in violation of the rule requiring all monuments to be on the line of battle, the proposed monument should be erected on the avenue to be opened along the Confederate line, and that a marker be placed to indicate the spot where General Armistead fell. The committee replied that they were not authorized to act, and would submit the proposition to their Association.

At the annual meeting, June 6, 1887, the Board of Directors of the previous year was re-elected, except that—to meet the requirements of the law of Pennsylvania prohibiting the directors of a corporation from receiving compensation—John M. Krauth, secretary, and N. G. Wilson, the superintendent, were not elected directors, but continued to serve in the capacities named. Captain William E. Miller was elected instead of Mr. Wilson, and Calvin Hamilton instead of Mr. Krauth. Major Robert Bell having removed from the town, his place was filled by Captain H. W. McKnight, D.D.

At a meeting, July 11, 1887, Generals Daniel E. Sickles, H. W. Slocum, Charles K. Graham, and Major C. A. Richardson, composing the

New York State Commission, appeared before the Board and submitted their proposed plan of work in the erection of the monuments that had been authorized by the Legislature of New York. The officers of the Association were instructed to afford them every facility possible, and to acquire any land that might be necessary. At this meeting all of the officers of the previous year were re-elected and committees reappointed.

At a meeting, July 12, 1887, the Committee on Purchase of Land was authorized to purchase the house used as head-quarters by Major-General George G. Meade, with the land connected therewith.

The Superintendents of Grounds and of Tablets and Legends were instructed to mark with suitable and durable tablets the flanks of each division.

The Committee on Location was authorized to mark with a suitable tablet the spot where General Armistead of the Confederate army fell mortally wounded while leading the assault of July 3, 1863.

This committee was also directed to remove monuments on the ground of the Association to their proper position in line, wherever said removal was practicable.

At a meeting on July 29, 1887, the Superintendent of Grounds was directed to open an avenue from the summit of Culp's Hill along the rear of the breastworks occupied by Greene's brigade of the Twelfth Corps.

On August 25, 1887, the officers were authorized to negotiate a temporary loan of $1000 to pay the indebtedness of the Association and to meet current expenses.

September 16, 1887, Colonel John B. Bachelder tendered his resignation as Superintendent of Tablets and Legends, and J. M. Vanderslice, Esq., of Philadelphia, was selected to fill the position.

At a meeting on November 4, 1887, the following names were selected for avenues: that on Culp's Hill to be called Slocum Avenue; from the Taneytown Road to Weikert's House, Hancock; from Weikert's House to the road north of Little Round Top, Sedgwick; from Round Top to Devil's Den, Sykes; from Devil's Den to the Wheat-Field, Sickles; from the Fairfield Road to the Mummasburg Pike, Reynolds; from the Mummasburg Pike to the Harrisburg Road, Howard; from the headquarters of General Meade to Hancock Avenue, Meade.

At a meeting on December 16, 1887, Mr. Vanderslice submitted the following, which was adopted: That the Committee on Location of

Monuments be enlarged to five, and such committee shall have charge hereafter of the approval of inscriptions in addition to their duties as a committee on location. The following were appointed: J. M. Vanderslice, Wm. D. Holtzworth, Calvin Hamilton, Superintendent Wilson, and Secretary Krauth.

Mr. Vanderslice submitted the following rules and regulations, which were adopted by the Executive Committee, and unanimously ratified at a subsequent meeting of the Board on July 3:

"The following rules regulating the erection of monuments and memorials must be strictly complied with:

"1. All persons are forbidden, under the penalty of the law, to place, change, or remove any stake or marker on the grounds under the control of the Memorial Association without the knowledge and consent of the Superintendent of Grounds.

"2. Any one who shall construct any foundation for, or erect any monument or memorial upon the grounds of the Association before the Superintendent of Grounds shall have designated the place and given a permit, will be regarded as a trespasser and be amenable to the severe penalties provided for in the charter of the Association.

"3. The Superintendent shall not permit the erection of any monument or memorial until its location and the inscription to be placed thereon shall have been approved by the proper committee of the Association.

"4. All monuments or memorials hereafter erected must be of granite or real bronze.

"5. On the front of each monument must be the number of the regiment or battery, State, brigade, division, and corps, in letters not less than four inches long, and, in addition thereto, the time the regiment held the position, and a brief statement of any important movement it made.

"If the regiment was actively engaged, its effective strength and casualties must be given, which must agree with the official records of the War Department. If it was in reserve it should be so stated.

"If the same position was held by other troops, or if the command occupied more than one important position, the inscription should explain it.

"All lettering must be deeply and distinctly cut.

"Any statue or figure of a soldier must be so placed as to face the enemy's line.

"6. The monument must be on the line of battle held by the brigade unless the regiment was detached, and, if possible, the right and left flanks of the regiment or battery must be marked with stones not less than two feet in height.

"If the same line was held by other troops, the monuments must be placed in the order in which the several commands occupied the grounds, the first being on the first line, the second at least twenty feet in the rear of it, and so on, the inscriptions explaining the movements.

"7. Where practicable, ground must be filled in to the top of the foundation and well and neatly sodded.

"8. Two copies of the inscription must be sent to the Secretary of the Association, one to be returned approved and the other to be placed on file with the Secretary, and they should be distinct from other written matter.

"RECOMMENDATIONS.

"As the memorials erected upon this field will not only mark the positions held by the several commands, but will also be regimental or battery monuments, and in most instances the only ones ever erected by them, the Memorial

Association strongly recommends that the inscription be not only historically accurate, but be sufficient in detail to give an idea of the services of the command. This may add slightly to the cost, but it will add much more to the completeness of the monument.

"In the years to come, when the identity of the regiment shall have been merged in the history of the battle, the visitor to this great battle-field will be interested to know just where the troops from his city or county fought, and to learn something of the services rendered by them.

"It is therefore recommended that upon one side of the monument should be stated the part of the State from which the regiment was recruited, dates of muster in and muster out, total strength and losses during its service, and the battles in which it participated.

"SUGGESTIONS.

"It is the desire and determination of the Gettysburg Battle-field Memorial Association to secure the greatest possible historical accuracy for the legends of the monuments erected on the field.

"It has been decided by the Board of Directors to adopt the official records of the battle, recently compiled at the Adjutant General's office, as to the strength and casualties of the several commands in the battle, believing that the historical data thus secured would generally be more accurate than that which individuals could furnish.

"The War Department record may not be absolutely correct,—men reported wounded afterwards died, others reported missing were afterwards found to be wounded or killed,—but it has been found necessary at the Adjutant-General's office to establish a limit, and that limit is the official return.

"There is nothing in this rule, however, to prevent monument committees from having the record of their commands revised at the War Department, and any changes furnished officially from the Adjutant-General's office will be cheerfully adopted by the Association. Or if it is known that a soldier reported wounded afterwards died of his wounds, or one who was reported "missing" is known to have been killed, a corresponding revision may be made in the inscription and the name added to a list designated "killed or mortally wounded." Or if wounded only, the name may be changed from the list of missing to the list of wounded, but the aggregate must remain unchanged and a report of the case must be submitted with the inscription.

"If monument committees add names of other battles, they must assume the responsibility of their accuracy, and the official name of the battle adopted at the War Department must be given. Such list it is desirable should be preceded by the date of the muster in and followed by the date of the muster out of the regiment.

"Deep and solid foundations are of the utmost importance. A strata of rock comes very near the surface on many parts of the field. Where it does not, a few dollars additional will secure a permanent and satisfactory foundation. A few dollars saved from the foundation may jeopardize the entire structure.

"The flank stones placed with the number of the regiment cut on the faces nearest the monument will readily determine the alignment.

"Permanence and durability in lettering should be the aim. Whether the letter is sunk or raised, it should be deep and sharp, that it may be easily read, and particularly that it may withstand the ravages of time.

"Each monument should stand high enough to secure ready drainage. No more proper setting or finish can be given it than a carpet of good sod, well enriched. The pleasing effect of a beautiful monument may be entirely neutralized by untidy surroundings, and if not put in order at first it will seldom be done afterwards.

"C. H. BUEHLER,
"*Vice-President.*
"Attest: JOHN M. KRAUTH, *Secretary.*"

The secretary was directed to have these rules and regulations printed in circular form, and to furnish a supply to all State commissions contemplating the erection of monuments upon the field, with the request to transmit copies to the several regimental organizations and to those applying for the same.

The superintendent was directed to open an avenue from a point on Hancock Avenue, near Weikert's Lane, by way of the line of Nevin's brigade of the Sixth Corps, and of McCandless's brigade of Pennsylvania Reserves.

The Committee on Purchase of Land was authorized to purchase the ground occupied by Neill's brigade of the Sixth Corps, on the extreme right of the line on Wolf's Hill, and the superintendent was instructed to open a driveway thereto.

The superintendent was also authorized, in addition to marking the flanks of the divisions, to place, at the intersection of all driveways and avenues, index boards stating the troops occupying the respective lines.

During this year the appropriation of the

State of Maine of $2500 was the only one received by the Association, and on March 23, 1888, the officers were authorized to borrow, temporarily, the sum of $5000, with which to carry on the work.

At a meeting, April 10, 1888, General John P. Taylor, General J. P. S. Gobin, Colonel John P. Nicholson, Colonel R. Bruce Ricketts, and Lieutenant Samuel Harper, composing the Pennsylvania State Commission, met with the Board for conference with reference to the erection of the monuments of the Pennsylvania commands for which the Legislature of the State had recently made a liberal appropriation. After consultation the Board and the Commissioners went over the field together, and it was decided to purchase the ground yet required for monuments of six infantry regiments, six cavalry regiments, and one battery.

At the annual meeting on June 4, 1888, the following Board was elected: General S. W. Crawford, General Louis Wagner, J. M. Vanderslice, Esq., Major Chill W. Hazzard, Captain Wm. E. Miller, of Pennsylvania; General Henry A. Barnum, New York; Colonel Frank D. Sloat, Connecticut; Colonel Charles L. Young, Ohio; John C. Linehan, New Hampshire; General Lucius Fairchild, Wisconsin; Major John P. Rea, Minnesota; Colonel

Wheelock G. Veazey, Vermont; Colonel George C. Briggs, Michigan; Colonel John B. Bachelder, Massachusetts; and Colonel C. H. Buehler, Sergeant W. D. Holtzworth, Sergeant J. A. Kitzmiller, Sergeant Calvin Hamilton, Captain H. W. McKnight, D.D., S. Mc. Swope, Esq., and J. L. Schick, Esq., of Gettysburg.

The Board as elected this year, with the exception of Major Rea and Captain Miller, continued to serve until 1895, unchanged, except by the deaths of Generals Crawford and Barnum, Colonel Bachelder, and Mr. Holtzworth.

At the meeting of July 3, 1888, the officers and committees of the previous year were re-elected.

The committee of the 9th New York Cavalry appeared before the Board and established, to the entire satisfaction of those present, that that regiment fired the first shot of July 1, 1863.

A committee of the survivors of the 72d Pennsylvania Infantry appeared and protested against having the regimental monument located in the second line of battle, on the crest of the ridge at the "copse of trees," and requested permission to place it in the front line. On motion of Colonel Bachelder, the Committee on Location was instructed to locate the principal monument of the 72d Pennsylvania Infantry on the line of battle occupied by it on the crest of the ridge, in compliance with the rules of this Association, and the regiment was authorized to place a marker at the advanced position obtained by it, with a proper inscription, subject to the approval of the committee on inscriptions.

It is to be regretted that, although the Association was able to satisfactorily remove any objections that were at any time raised by committees and others representing any of the other 309 Federal regiments and batteries, it was unfortunately unable to harmonize the difference between it and the committee representing the 72d Pennsylvania Infantry, which resulted in long and costly litigation instituted by the regiment. Eventually the Supreme Court, without going into the merits of the case, decided in favor of the regiment, upon a bare technicality, and it was able to place its monument at the stone wall at a point where a section of Cushing's battery had been posted, and where, after the disabling of the battery, General Armistead and some of his command crossed, and to which the regiment with others advanced in the final repulse of the assault. This was done notwithstanding that the same regiment, when represented by a committee on which was the adjutant-general of the brigade to which the regiment belonged, had previously, when there were no rules regulating the matter, placed a monument on the very line designated by the Association as the proper one, and where the regiment had so gallantly stood and had suffered so fearfully. This, however, as has been stated, was the only trouble or unpleasant difference that the Association had in its difficult and arduous work of properly marking the field, and it had the gratification of knowing that its action in this instance was approved by all the officers of the brigade, including General Webb, its commander, and of the division, and by all others correctly informed upon the subject.

At this meeting, upon motion of General Fairchild, it was resolved that corps, divisions, and other organizations which participated in the battle, should be requested to erect on the battle-field an appropriate memorial commemorative of the patriotic services of officers who distinguished themselves.

General James S. Robinson, of Ohio, appeared before the Board and protested against the Association naming the avenue along the Eleventh Corps line Howard Avenue, and requested that it be called the Eleventh Corps Avenue. A letter was read from Colonel A. D. Lee, secretary of the Ohio Commission, to the same effect. Upon motion of General

Fairchild, the naming of the avenues was postponed.

The rules adopted by the Executive Committee on December 16, 1887, were ratified, and, on motion of General Barnum, the Superintendent of Grounds was instructed to rigidly enforce the rules, unless authorized by the Executive Committee to modify them.

The Executive Committee was directed to take such action as might be necessary to acquire and vest in the United States good and sufficient title to the positions occupied by the several commands of the regular army.

The committee was also directed to open an avenue along the line occupied by Kilpatrick's cavalry division from Round Top to the Emmittsburg Road, and one along the line of the Confederate army from the Hagerstown to the Emmitsburg Road.

It was also ordered that all cannon that had been donated by the War Department, which was available, should be brought to the field at once.

On July 27, 1888, it was decided to plant 125 trees on the denuded portion of Zeigler's Grove, in order to restore it as nearly as possible to the condition in which it was during the battle.

During this year $8600 were received from New York, $2000 from Ohio, $1500 from Vermont, $2500 from Michigan, and $1500 from

Wisconsin; and on November 23 the officers were directed to borrow the sum of $4000 from the bank of Gettysburg.

At the annual meeting, June 3, 1889, the Board of Directors of the previous year was re-elected, except that General Slocum, of New York, was elected instead of Major Rea, of Minnesota, and Hon. Edward McPherson, of Gettysburg, instead of William Holtzworth, deceased.

At a subsequent meeting of the board, on September 10, 1889, the officers and committees were also re-elected.

Captains W. E. Miller and S. C. Wagner, of the 3d Pennsylvania Cavalry, were appointed a committee to locate and lay out the proposed avenues along the line of General Gregg's cavalry division.

The Superintendent of Grounds was instructed to have the monuments of the Massachusetts regiments, erected at the "copse of trees," removed to their proper positions, and also that of the 5th New York Cavalry to its position in support of Elder's United States battery.

After the transaction of other routine business, the Board, upon the invitation of Governor Beaver, adjourned to attend the exercises of the dedication of the Pennsylvania monuments.

At a meeting, September 11, Colonel Briggs, of Michigan, offered the following resolutions, which were unanimously adopted.

"That it is the sense of this Association that the Congress of the United States should authorize the purchase of such land as may be necessary to open avenues and driveways along the whole line of battle occupied by the Army of Northern Virginia during the battle of Gettysburg, and that the positions occupied by the several divisions, brigades, and regiments of such army should be marked with tablets.

"That a copy of this minute be communicated to each member of Congress."

The Superintendent of Grounds was authorized to open a drive-way from Reynolds Avenue, on the summit of Oak Ridge, past the monuments of the 104th New York and 13th Massachusetts Infantry, to the Mummasburg Road; also to open a road-way, sixty feet wide, to the Custer cavalry brigade monument. The secretary was directed to confer with the New York and Ohio Monument Commissions relative to the removal of the monuments of the 29th Ohio and 122d New York.

During this year the only appropriation received was one of $20,000 from Pennsylvania.

At a meeting, May 27, 1890, Calvin Hamilton, Superintendent of the National Cemetery, was elected secretary to fill the vacancy caused by the death of John M. Krauth, Esq. Messrs. Swope, Kitzmiller, and Hamilton were appointed a committee to draft suitable resolutions to be presented at the annual meeting of the Board.

Messrs. Corbin and Harrington, of the New Jersey Monument Committee, met with the Board, and asked the privilege of making certain improvements in the ground about the several New Jersey monuments, as well as in the structures themselves, which was granted.

The Committee on Purchase of Land was authorized to purchase that portion of the Peach Orchard required for the erection of the monuments of the several regiments engaged there.

At a full meeting of the Board, September 3, 1890, the officers and committees of the Board were re-elected. At this meeting, Hon. S. Mc. Swope read the following resolutions relative to the death of John M. Krauth, Esq., which were unanimously adopted.

"In June, 1872, John M. Krauth was elected a director of the Memorial Association, and from that time until his death, May 10, 1890, he was its able and efficient secretary. That since 1880 this Association has effected its great, its trying, and its commendable work, that of locating with historical accuracy and almost universal acceptance all the regimental and other memorials erected on

BATTLE-FIELD MEMORIAL ASSOCIATION. 249

this field; in the acceptance by the Association of all these memorials, in the purchase of grounds, in the care and attention given to visitors who came here for data and information, and in all the varied activities of our Association, we have been exceptionally helped by the unselfish, patriotic, and modest candor and the untiring correspondence and aid of Mr. Krauth.

"In our previous sessions he was always with us; his post was always filled. His genial presence was a comfort and pleasure, and his counsel and fund of useful information were always available. To-day we miss him, yet in the very face of this loss we feel like rejoicing that God did not call him hence until his great aid and assistance had helped us to happily consummate the above-mentioned and other very difficult tasks.

"That we testify to his modesty as a man, his unselfishness as a soldier, his fidelity as our secretary, and his worth as a companionable co-worker and friend.

"*Resolved*, That a copy of this minute be spread upon the records of the Association. That they also be published in the Gettysburg papers, and that a copy be sent to his bereaved family."

The Board adjourned to visit the field and harmonize the difference between the representatives of the 12th New Jersey and 111th New York Regiments, of Hays's division, Second Corps, relative to the location of the monument of the latter regiment.

After hearing the several participants on the ground, on which they had fought twenty-seven years before, it was decided that the 12th New Jersey was entitled to the line as indicated by its right and left flank markers, and that the 111th New York should be permitted to place its monument at the termination of the right flank of the 12th New Jersey, to enable it to take advantage of the large boulder for a foundation. This decision was accepted with great cheerfulness on the part of the representatives of both regiments.

On October 3, 1890, the officers were authorized to borrow the sum of $2000. During this year the only appropriation received was one of $1000 from Vermont.

At a meeting, May 10, 1891, Colonel Bachelder submitted the plan for the High-Water-Mark tablet, to be erected at the "copse of trees," which was approved.

At the annual meeting of the stockholders, June 2, 1891, the Directors were all re-elected.

At a meeting of the Board, on August 25, 1891, the officers and committees of the previous year were re-elected. At this meeting, General E. H. Rhodes, representing the governor of Rhode Island, General Stryker, the governor of New Jersey, and Colonel A. E. Lee, the governor of Ohio, were present.

General Barnum and Colonels Briggs and Young were appointed a committee to confer with the governor and legislative authorities of Indiana, with the view of getting an appropriation from that State, to compensate the Association for the purchase of ground on which the seven Indiana monuments stand, and to defray the expenses of maintenance, etc.

At this meeting, Colonel Buehler, the vice-president, submitted a very lengthy and satisfactory report, bearing upon the litigation of the 72d Pennsylvania Infantry with the Association.

W. C. Sheely, Esq., representing the Gettysburg Electric Railway, appeared before the Board and asked the right of way along the several avenues on the Association's ground. On motion of S. Mc. Swope, Esq., the request was not granted, and the secretary was directed to so notify the company.

On motion of Mr. McPherson, the following committee was appointed to devise a plan of raising means for the future maintenance of the field: Generals Sickles, Barnum, and Wagner, Colonels Veazey, Briggs, and Bachelder, and Mr. McPherson. Colonel Bachelder was requested to communicate with the quartermaster-general of the army, and urge the importance of opening an avenue through the National Cemetery from the Baltimore Pike to the Taneytown Road. The only appropriation of this year was one of Illinois of $600.

At a meeting held January 5, 1892, the Executive Committee passed a resolution of remonstrance to the court against the granting of a license for the sale of intoxicating liquors at Round Top Park, adjoining the grounds of the Association.

At the annual meeting of the stockholders, June 6, 1892, the Board of Directors was re-elected, except that General Joseph B. Carr was elected instead of General Henry A. Barnum, deceased, and that General Daniel E. Sickles was elected instead of Calvin A. Hamilton, who had resigned to accept the position of secretary, and Dr. C. E. Goldsborough was elected instead of Captain Miller.

At a subsequent meeting, on September 16, 1892, the officers and committees of the previous year were re-elected.

General J. B. Carr was placed on the committee on the future maintenance of the field in place of General Henry A. Barnum, deceased. Mr. Swope read the following resolutions on the death of General Barnum, which, after remarks on his life and character by General Carr and Mr. Vanderslice, were adopted by a rising vote.

"WHEREAS, Since the last annual meeting of our Association, death has removed from any further deliberations with us that brave and gallant soldier, that true and good citizen, and that courteous and chivalric gentleman, Major-General Henry A. Barnum; therefore, be it

"*Resolved*, That since his membership in this Association, General Barnum has always been one of our most willing, earnest workers.

"That, although at a sacrifice to himself, when others less interested than he would remain away, he was almost always present, and at our regular and special meetings his chair was rarely vacant. That his soldierly service, sacrifice, and suffering for his country, which never ended until his death, seemed to excite in him a special interest in the work of the Association, and we hereby most cheerfully acknowledge the great assistance and aid rendered by him in the work we have so nearly completed.

"That his military knowledge and marked sympathy for the purpose intended by the creation of our Association made him not only a useful and valued member, but that his pleasant, genial, and courteous manner made him a most companionable co-worker and an affectionate and loved friend.

"In appreciation of his work, and in testimony of our loss of so valued a member and friend, be it also

"*Resolved*, That a copy of these resolutions be spread upon the minutes of the Association, that they also be published in the Gettysburg and New York papers, and the *National Tribune*, and that a copy of the same be sent to his afflicted family."

At a meeting, June 31, 1893, General David McM. Gregg was elected to fill the vacancy caused by the death of General S. W. Crawford. Several communications were read from the War Department relative to procuring ground for the monuments of the United States Regulars, and the Board resolved to transfer land to the general government necessary for sites for monuments of the regular troops, with right of way thereto.

At a meeting, May 19, 1893, the officers were directed to petition the Legislature of Pennsylvania that in case it should pass the bill granting the right of eminent domain to electric railways, it should exempt the battle-field of Gettysburg from its operations.

The Board also placed upon record its protest against the construction of an electric railway over the field.

At the annual meeting of the stockholders, on June 5, the Board of Directors was re-elected, and at a subsequent meeting of the Board the officers were also re-elected.

At a meeting on July 4, 1893, General Wagner submitted the following :

"That the Gettysburg Battle-field Memorial Association does hereby condemn the land covered by avenues which have been projected but not opened by the Association, and that the officers of the Association are hereby authorized and directed to purchase the lands from the owners thereof, and if the purchase cannot be made, to file the necessary petitions for a jury to assess damages for the land so taken and to execute the required bond for the payment of such damages."

The secretary was directed to make a requisition on the Chief of Ordnance, United States army, for 880 shells for 12-pounder guns and 270 cylindrical shells for 3-inch rifles, under the Act of March 3, 1873, and request that they be turned over to the quartermaster-general of Washington, D. C., for use in marking the positions of the commands in the regular army.

At a meeting of the Executive Committee, December 18, 1893, Colonel Bachelder was authorized to receive all the cannon turned over to the Memorial Association by the Secretary of War, under the Act of Congress approved March 3, 1873, which was not actually in possession of the Association, and he was instructed to deliver them to the United States Battle-field Commission, for the purpose of marking the battle-field.

At the annual meeting on June, 4, 1894, the Board of Directors was re-elected, the officers and committees being subsequently also re-elected.

On August 21, 1894, Messrs. McPherson and Kitzmiller were appointed a committee to inquire into the feasibility of transferring the property belonging to the Association to the United States government, and to report at a meeting to be held October 3, 1894.

At a meeting of the full Board, on October 3, 1894, this committee reported in favor of transferring the 600 acres of land owned by the Association, with 17 miles of avenue constructed thereon, giving access to 320 monuments which had been erected by the various States and regimental associations, to the United States government, and the Executive Committee was authorized to communicate with the stockholders and secure their written consent to the transfer.

General Sickles called the attention of the Board to the death of Major-General H. W. Slocum, and suggested that a suitable minute of the same be made and recorded in the minutes of the Association and communicated to the widow of the deceased.

The president appointed General Sickles and Hon. Edward McPherson to prepare the said minute.

At a meeting held May 22, 1895,—at which the following were present: Vice-President Colonel C. H. Buehler, Generals Daniel E. Sickles and Alex S. Webb, of New York; D. McM. Gregg and Louis Wagner, of Pennsylvania; Colonel Frank D. Sloat, of Connecticut; Charles L. Young, of Ohio; George C. Briggs, of Michigan; W. G. Veazey, of Vermont; J. M. Vanderslice, Esq., Hon. Ed. McPherson, S. Mc. Swope, Esq., J. A. Kitzmiller, Esq., Dr. C. E. Goldsborough, J. L. Schick, Esq., Calvin Hamilton, Secretary; also Colonel John P. Nicholson,

Major W. M. Robins, and Major C. A. Richardson, constituting the United States Board of Battle-field Commissioners,—resolutions were passed instructing the officers to execute, under the corporate seal, good and sufficient deeds of conveyance to the United States government of all lands owned by the Association, and of rights of way and easements belonging to it or in any way connected with or pertaining to such lands. Colonel Nicholson and General George S. Greene, of New York, were elected directors to fill the vacancies caused by the deaths of Colonel John B. Bachelder and General Joseph B. Carr.

On motion of General Wagner, the Legislature of Pennsylvania, then in session, was respectfully requested to pass and the governor to approve the Act vesting in the United States government joint jurisdiction with the Commonwealth over such lands as may be necessary for a National Park at Gettysburg.

On motion of Mr. Vanderslice, it was

"*Resolved*, That the Board express its grateful appreciation of the generous support accorded the Association by the several States, by their appropriations to it, and by the erection of appropriate monuments to mark the positions upon the field of their several organizations."

Colonel Nicholson moved that a carefully prepared resolution of thanks be tendered

Colonel C. H. Buehler. Colonel Nicholson was instructed to prepare a resolution in accordance with his motion.

General Wagner moved that the thanks of the Association be extended to the secretary and treasurer of the Association for the services they had rendered.

On motion of Colonel Nicholson, the thanks of the Association were tendered J. M. Vanderslice, Esq., for the efficient service he had rendered during his many years of active work in the Association and as secretary of the Committee on Inscriptions.

General Sickles moved that a history of the Association be published, which motion was adopted.

There being no further business, the Board adjourned to partake of a banquet which had been prepared for this final meeting. This was the last meeting held by the Board of Directors.

Colonel C. H. Buehler, who had succeeded his brother, David A. Buehler, Esq., as vice-president, on January 29, 1887, and had served continuously and faithfully until the last meeting, died shortly thereafter, his loss being lamented by those who had served with him in the Association, as it was by the citizens of the town and by all who knew him and greatly appreciated his worth as a soldier and citizen.

DIRECTORS OF THE GETTYSBURG MEMORIAL BATTLE-FIELD ASSOCIATION, 1872–1880.

General John W. Geary, Governor of Pennsylvania, President, deceased	1872
David McConaughy, Gettysburg, Vice-President	1872–1879
Henry C. Carey, Esq., Philadelphia, deceased	1872–1879
General J. Watts De Peyster, New York	1872–1879
Wm. M. Hirsh, Gettysburg, deceased	1872–1879
Hon. A. D. Heister, Pennsylvania, deceased	1872–1874
Joel B. Danner, Gettysburg, deceased	1872–1874
George Arnold, Gettysburg, deceased	1872–1879
Alexander D. Buehler, Gettysburg	1872–1879
Charles Horner, M.D., Gettysburg, deceased	1872–1879
J. Lawrence Schick, Esq., Gettysburg	1872–1879
John M. Krauth, Esq., Gettysburg, deceased	1872–1879
Edward Souder, Gettysburg, deceased	1872–1873
H. N. McAllister, Esq., Gettysburg, deceased	1872
General Charles K. Graham, New York, deceased	1873–1879
General John F. Hartranft, Governor of Pennsylvania, President, deceased	1873–1878
General Alexander S. Webb, New York	1873–1879
General Horatio G. Sickel, Pennsylvania, deceased	1874–1879
Hon. Edward McPherson, Gettysburg, deceased	1875
R. G. McCreary, Esq., Gettysburg, deceased	1876–1879

There was no meeting of the Board from 1874 to 1879.

DIRECTORS FROM THE REORGANIZATION IN 1880.

General Henry M. Hoyt, Governor of Pennsylvania, President, deceased	1879–1882
R. G. McCreary, Esq., Gettysburg, Vice-President, deceased	1880–1883
John M. Krauth, Esq., Gettysburg, Secretary from 1872 to time of decease in 1890	1880–1887

GETTYSBURG.

General W. S. Hancock, Pennsylvania, deceased	1880–1884
General S. W. Crawford, Pennsylvania, deceased	1880–1892
General Louis Wagner, Philadelphia	1880–1896
John M. Vanderslice, Esq., Philadelphia	1880–1882, 1884–1896
Major Chill W. Hazzard, Pennsylvania	1880–1882, 1884–1896
Captain John Taylor, Philadelphia, deceased	1880–1884
Colonel Chas. H. Buehler, Gettysburg, Vice-President from 1887 to 1896, deceased	1880–1896
J. L. Schick, Treasurer from 1880 to 1896	1880–1896
Major Robert Bell, Gettysburg	1880–1886
Charles Horner, M.D., Gettysburg	1880–1887
N. G. Wilson, Gettysburg, Superintendent of Grounds, 1880 to 1894	1880–1886
John B. Bachelder, Massachusetts, deceased	1880–1881, 1883–1894
Robert E. Pattison, Governor of Pennsylvania, President 1883–1886,	1891–1894
General Joshua L. Chamberlain, Maine	1883
General John C. Robinson, New York, deceased	1883
General George Stannard, Vermont, deceased	1883
William S. Holtzworth, Gettysburg, deceased	1884–1888
D. A. Buehler, Gettysburg, Vice-President, deceased	1883–1887
Colonel Eli G. Sellers, Philadelphia	1885
Colonel W. W. Dudley, Indiana	1885
General Henry A. Barnum, New York, deceased	1885–1891
Colonel Frank D. Sloat, Connecticut	1885–1896
Colonel Elisha H. Rhodes, Rhode Island	1885–1887
General Byron R. Pierce, Michigan, deceased	1885–1887
John C. Linehan, New Hampshire	1885–1896
Colonel Charles L. Young, Ohio	1885–1896
Colonel Silas Colgrove, Indiana	1886–1887
General Lucius Fairchild, Wisconsin, deceased	1886–1896
General James A. Beaver, Governor of Pennsylvania, President	1887–1890
Captain Wm. E. Miller, Pennsylvania	1887–1892
Calvin Hamilton, Gettysburg, Secretary from 1890 to 1896	1887–1890
Captain H. W. McKnight, D.D., Gettysburg	1887–1896
Captain John P. Rea, Minnesota	1888
Colonel Wheelock G. Veazey, Vermont	1888–1896
Colonel George C. Briggs, Michigan	1888–1896
William A. Kitzmiller, Gettysburg	1888–1896

BATTLE-FIELD MEMORIAL ASSOCIATION. 261

Hon. S. Mc. Swope, Gettysburg 1888–1896
Hon. Edward McPherson, Gettysburg, deceased 1889–1896
General Henry W. Slocum, New York, deceased 1889–1894
General Daniel E. Sickles, New York 1892–1896
General Joseph B. Carr, New York, deceased 1892–1893
C. E. Goldsborough, M.D., Gettysburg 1892–1896
General David McM. Gregg, Pennsylvania 1893–1896
General Alexander S. Webb, New York 1893–1896
General Daniel S. Hastings, Governor of Pennsylvania,
President 1895–1896
Colonel John P. Nicholson, Philadelphia 1895–1896
General George S. Greene, New York 1895–1896

During the existence of the Association, from 1864 until 1895, it received,—

From the sale of certificates of stock . . .	$9,875.59
From various States by appropriation . . .	96,490.00
From the officers and men at Fort Snelling	125.00
From the survivors of Cushing's battery .	25.00
From the 2d Maryland Confederate Infantry	60.00
Making a total of	$106,575.59

All of this sum was expended in the purchase, restoration, improvement, and maintenance of the grounds. Less than $10,000 was spent in salaries and like expenses; the only salary being that of $1000 per annum for the last few years to the Superintendent, and the salary of $100 per annum to the secretary, except for three years when he received $400 per annum.

In addition to about 600 acres of land, embracing the most important parts of the battle-field, and the construction of 17 miles of avenues and drive-ways, the Association induced and supervised the erection of 320 monuments.

Every one of the 313 volunteer regiments and batteries of the Federal army, except the three of West Virginia, has its position upon the field marked by a monument or memorial, and several of the regiments have second positions also marked.

The visitor to the field is impressed by the originality, uniqueness, and suggestiveness of many of these memorials, nearly all of which are of granite and bronze, and, notwithstanding the large number of monuments, there are only four or five instances of duplication of style.

It should be borne in mind that, in addition to the aid received from the several States in appropriations for the erection of monuments, the Survivors' Associations of many of the regiments supplemented by liberal contributions the amount appropriated, and there are a large number of regimental monuments upon the field costing from three thousand to five thousand dollars each, and several costing much more.

HOW THE STATES WERE REPRESENTED UPON THE FIELD, AND WHAT THEY HAVE DONE TO MARK IT.

The manner in which each of the States was represented in the battle, as indicated by its regiments and batteries with their losses, and by the general officers from the State, is shown upon the following pages, as is also what each State has done, through appropriations to the Association, and for the erection of substantial monuments, permanently marking the positions of its regiments and batteries in the battle.

MAINE.

Regiment.	Brigade.	Division.	Corps.	Killed and wounded.	Missing.
1st Cav.	3d, Gregg.	2d, Gregg.	Cavalry.	5	..
3d Inf.	2d, Ward.	1st, Birney.	Third.	77	45
4th Inf.	2d, Ward.	1st, Birney.	Third.	70	74
5th Inf.[1]	2d, Bartlett.	3d, Wheaton.	Sixth.	..	..
6th Inf.[1]	3d, Russell.	1st, Wright.	Sixth.	..	..
7th Inf.[1]	3d, Neill.	2d, Howe.	Sixth.	..	..
10th Inf.[2]	......	......	......	..	..
16th Inf.	1st, Paul.	2d, Robinson.	First.	68	164
17th Inf.	3d, De Trobriand.	1st, Birney.	Third.	130	3
19th Inf.	1st, Harrow.	2d, Gibbon.	Second.	195	4
20th Inf.	3d, Vincent.	1st, Barnes.	Fifth.	120	5

[1] Not engaged.   [2] Three companies at Twelfth Corps head-quarters.

Batteries.

	Corps.	Killed and wounded.	Missing.
Hall's 2d Light	First.	18	..
Stevens's 5th Light	First.	16	7
Dow's 6th Light	Artillery Reserve.	15	..

General Officers.

General Oliver O. Howard, Commander of the Eleventh Corps.

General John C. Caldwell, Commander of the First Division, Second Corps. (Born in Vermont.)

General Albion P. Howe, Commander of the Second Division, Sixth Corps.

General Adelbert Ames, Commander of the First Division, Eleventh Corps (after wounding of General Barlow).

General Freeman McGilvery, Commander Reserve Artillery.

State Appropriations for Monuments.

1887.	Resolves making provisions for monuments, purchasing land and improving the same, on the battle-field of Gettysburg, including appropriation of $2500 to the Memorial Association	$15,000.00
1889.	Maine Gettysburg Commission	10,000.00
1891.	"High-Water-Mark Monument"	500.00
1891.	Change flanking-stone, 5th Maine Battery, Seminary Ridge	25.00
1891.	5th Maine Regiment. Change location, etc.	150.00
1891.	17th Maine Regiment, tablet	300.00
1891.	Expense of the Executive Committee	725.00
1891.	Printing, binding, etc., report of Commission	3,600.00
	Total	$30,300.00

The monuments of this State are all of a substantial character. That of the 17th Maine, in the Wheat-Field, is the costliest monument of the State, and is one of the most massive upon the field, being built of the finest granite. It represents a soldier kneeling in a wheat-field and firing over a stone wall.

That of the 19th Maine, on Cemetery Ridge, near the "copse of trees," while without any ornamentation, is also of an imposing character.

The monuments were dedicated on October 10, 1889.

NEW HAMPSPHIRE.

Regiment.	Brigade.	Division.	Corps.	Killed and wounded.	Missing.
2d.	3d, Burling.	2d, Humphreys.	Third.	157	36
5th.	1st, Cross.	1st, Caldwell.	Second.	80	..
12th.	1st, Carr.	2d, Humphreys.	Third.	81	11
Edgell's.	1st, Light Battery.		Artillery Reserve.	3	..

General Officer.

Colonel Edward E. Cross, Commander of the First Brigade, First Division, Second Corps (killed.)

State Appropriations for Monuments.

The State expended for monuments, etc., upon the battle-field of Gettysburg the following amounts:

1886.	Appropriation to the Gettysburg Memorial Association	$1000.00
1886.	For Monuments, 2d, 5th, and 12th Regiments	1500.00
1886.	Appropriation for Monument, New Hampshire Companies 1st and 2d United States Sharp-shooters	500.00
1886.	Appropriation for repairs to above monuments	1000.00
1886.	Appropriation for Monument at High-Water-Mark	500.00
	Total expenditure	$4500.00

The appropriations of this State only provided for an expenditure of $500 for each of its monuments, and were not supplemented by individual contributions, so the monuments are among the least costly upon the field.

That of the 5th regiment, erected upon the spot where its brigade commander and former colonel, General Cross, was killed, is in the edge of the woods near the Wheat-Field, and is of rather unique character, being a cairn.

VERMONT.

Regiment.	Brigade.	Division.	Corps.	Killed and wounded.	Missing.
1st Cav.	1st, Farnsworth.	3d, Kilpatrick.	Cavalry.	38	27
2d Inf.[1]	2d, Grant.	2d, Howe.	Sixth.	. .	. .
3d Inf.[1]	2d, Grant.	2d, Howe.	Sixth.	. .	. .
4th Inf.[1]	2d, Grant.	2d, Howe.	Sixth.	. .	. .
5th Inf.[1]	2d, Grant.	2d, Howe.	Sixth.	. .	. .
6th Inf.[1]	2d, Grant.	2d, Howe.	Sixth.	. .	. .
12th Inf.[1]	3d, Stannard.	3d, Doubleday.	First.	. .	. .
13th Inf.	3d, Stannard.	3d, Doubleday.	First.	113	10
14th Inf.	3d, Stannard.	3d, Doubleday.	First.	86	21
15th Inf.[1]	3d, Stannard.	3d, Doubleday.	First.	. .	. .
16th Inf.	3d, Stannard.	3d, Doubleday.	First.	118	1

[1] Not engaged.

General Officers.

General George J. Stannard, Commander of the Third Brigade, Third Division, First Corps.

Colonel Hannibal Day, Commander of the First Brigade, Second Division, Fifth Corps.

General L. A. Grant, Commander of the First Brigade, Second Division, Sixth Corps.

State Appropriations for Monuments.

1888.	Appropriation to the Gettysburg Battle-field Memorial Association	$1,500.00
1888.	Appropriation for State monument and statue . .	11,750.00
1888.	Appropriation towards the 1st Cavalry monument	1,000.00
1888.	Appropriation towards the 1st Brigade monument .	1,303.00
1888.	Appropriation towards Company F's, 1st United States Sharp-shooters, monument	1,200.00
1888.	Appropriation towards Companies E and H's, 2d United States Sharp-shooters, monument . . .	800.00
1888.	Appropriation for additional work on tablets . . .	400.00
	Total	$17,953.00

This State had the advantage of having its ten regiments of infantry in two Vermont brigades, as it was thus enabled to consolidate the appropriations in the erection of two monuments.

That of Stannard's brigade, of the First Corps, on Cemetery Ridge, is a pure classical, Corinthian column, surmounted by a bronze statue of General Stannard. Upon the face of the pedestal is the inscription referring to each of the regiments.

That of Grant's First Vermont Brigade, which was stationed in the rear of Big Round Top in expectation of an attack upon that flank, represents a lion looking towards the front, but aroused, as if listening to the battle raging along the line of the Second Corps.

The monuments were dedicated on October 9, 1889.

MASSACHUSETTS.

Regiment.	Brigade.	Division.	Corps.	Killed and wounded.	Missing.
1st Cav.[1]	1st, McIntosh.	2d, Gregg.	Cavalry.	. .	. .
1st Inf.	1st, Carr.	2d, Humphreys.	Third.	99	21
2d Inf.	3d, Colgrove.	1st, Ruger.	Twelfth.	132	4
7th Inf.[1]	2d, Eustis.	3d, Wheaton.	Sixth.	6	. .
9th Inf.[1]	2d, Sweitzer.	1st, Barnes.	Fifth.	. .	. .
10th Inf.[1]	2d, Eustis.	3d, Wheaton.	Sixth.	. .	. .
11th Inf.	1st, Carr.	2d, Humphreys.	Third.	119	10
12th Inf.	2d, Baxter.	2d, Robinson.	First.	57	62

[1] Not Engaged.

MASSACHUSETTS—*Continued.*

Regiment.	Brigade.	Division.	Corps.	Killed and wounded.	Missing.
13th Inf.	1st, Paul.	2d, Robinson.	First.	84	101
15th Inf.	1st, Harrow.	2d, Gibbon.	Second.	120	28
16th Inf.	1st, Carr.	2d, Humphreys.	Third.	68	13
18th Inf.	1st, Tilton.	1st, Barnes.	Fifth.	24	3
19th Inf.	3d, Hall.	2d, Gibbon.	Second.	70	7
20th Inf.	3d, Hall.	2d, Gibbon.	Second.	124	3
22d Inf.	1st, Tilton.	1st, Barnes.	Fifth.	30	1
28th Inf.	2d, Kelly.	1st, Caldwell.	Second.	65	35
32d Inf	2d, Sweitzer.	1st, Barnes.	Fifth.	75	5
33d Inf.	2d, Smith.	2d, Steinwehr.	Eleventh.	45	..
37th Inf.	2d, Eustis.	3d, Wheaton.	Sixth.	28	19

Batteries.

	Corps.	Killed and wounded.	Missing.
Walcott's 3d Light (C)	Fifth.	6	..
McCartney's 1st Light (A)[1].	Sixth.	..	..
Phillips's 5th Light (E)	Artillery Reserve.	21	..
Bigelow's 9th Light	Artillery Reserve.	26	2

[1] Not Engaged.

General Officers.

General James Barnes, Commander of the First Division, Fifth Corps.

Colonel William S. Tilton, Commander of the First Brigade, First Division, Fifth Corps.

Colonel Sidney Burbank, Commander of the Second Brigade, Second Division, Fifth Corps.

Colonel Henry L. Eustis, Commander of the Second Brigade, Third Division, Sixth Corps.

State Appropriations for Monuments.

Resolve 42, Acts of 1883, for the payment to the Gettysburg Memorial Association, for the purchase of additional ground of special interest on the battle-field of Gettysburg . . . $5,000

BATTLE-FIELD MEMORIAL ASSOCIATION.

Resolve, Chapter 24, Acts of 1884, for the payment of $500 each to the organizations of the State participating in the battle, for the purpose of erecting suitable monuments on the battle-field	22,000
Resolve, 1885, Chapter 39, for the expenditure to the Massachusetts Mozart Association of the 40th New York Regiment for the erection of a monument	500
Resolve, 1888, Chapter 58, for the purpose of procuring and erecting flank stones to mark the positions of the Massachusetts regiments	1,200
Resolve, 1891, Chapter 62, for the erection of a large tablet, etc., in commemoration of the services of certain Massachusetts regiments	400
Resolve 76, of the same year, for the erection of a bronze tablet	500
Resolve, 1892, Chapter 10, payment to the Gettysburg Battle-field Memorial Association for the purpose of completing and caring for the granite and bronze monument in the course of erection at a certain copse of trees on the crest of Cemetery Ridge, to be known as the "High-Water Monument"	400
Total	$30,000

The monument of the 1st Massachusetts, on the Emmittsburg Road, is one of the finest upon the field. It cost about $3000, and is a huge granite diamond, weighing 18 or 20 tons, and upon its face is a well-cut figure of a soldier upon the skirmish line, firing over a rail fence.

That of the 13th Regiment, upon the First Corps line on Oak Hill, is surmounted by a granite soldier, advancing with his flag unfurled, representing the youthful color-bearer of the regiment who was killed on the spot.

That of the 12th (Webster) Regiment, in the same locality, is a large granite Minié-ball partially wrapped in the flag. Upon its base is a medallion likeness of Daniel Webster.

Those of Eustis's brigade,—7th, 10th, and 37th Regiments,—on the avenue east of Round Top, are of beautiful design and finish.

The monuments of this State, being among the first erected upon the field, do not contain as full inscriptions as those that were erected subsequently.

The monument of the 20th Massachusetts, which lost so heavily near the "copse of trees" on the 3d, is a large "pudding-stone," brought from Roxbury, where the regiment was recruited, and which was a landmark on the playground of the town. It was taken to Gettysburg to mark the spot where the soldiers who had once played around it fought so gallantly, yet there is nothing in the inscription to convey the beautiful sentiment intended to be expressed by this simple memorial.

All of the Massachusetts monuments are of tasteful and appropriate design and well constructed. They were dedicated at different times.

RHODE ISLAND.

Regiment.	Brigade.	Division.	Corps.	Killed and wounded.	Missing.
2d Inf.	2d, Eustis.	3d, Wheaton.	Sixth.	6	1

Batteries.

	Corps.	Killed and wounded.	Missing.
Arnold's 1st Light (A)	Second.	31	1
Brown's 1st Light (B)	Second.	26	1
Randolph's, or Bucklyn's, 1st Light (E)	Third.	29	1
Waterman's[1] 1st Light (C)	Sixth.	..	..
Adams's[1] 1st Light (G)	Sixth.	..	..

[1] Not engaged.

General Officer.

General Frank Wheaton, Commander of the Third Division, Sixth Corps.

State Appropriations for Monuments.

April, 1885.	To the Gettysburg Battle-field Memorial Association, for purchase, care of grounds, etc.	$1000.00
April, 1885.	For monuments to 2d Regiment, and Batteries A, B, and E	2000.00
May, 1891.	State contribution to "High-Water-Mark Monument"	400.00
	Total	$3400.00

This State had but one regiment in the battle, and it was not actively engaged, but its three batteries—Arnold's, Brown's, and Randolph's—took a most prominent part in the battle. While the monuments cost but $500 each, they are all characteristic.

CONNECTICUT.

Regiment.	Brigade.	Division.	Corps.	Killed and wounded.	Missing.
5th Inf.	1st, McDougall.	1st, Ruger.	Twelfth.	2	5
14th Inf.	2d, Smyth.	2d, Hays.	Second.	62	4
17th Inf.	2d, Ames.	1st, Barlow.	Eleventh.	101	96
20th Inf.	1st, McDougall.	1st, Ruger.	Twelfth.	27	1
27th Inf.[1]	4th, Brooke.	1st, Caldwell.	Second.	33	4

[1] Four companies.

Batteries.

	Corps.	Killed and wounded.	Missing.
Sterling's 2d Light	Artillery Reserve.	3	2
Brooker's 1st Heavy B. S.[1]	Artillery Reserve.	..	..
Pratt's 1st Heavy M. E.[1]	Artillery Reserve.	..	..

[1] Not engaged.

General Officers.

General John Sedgwick, Commander of the Sixth Corps.
General Horatio G. Wright, Commander of the First Division, Sixth Corps.

State Appropriations for Monuments.

1885.	Gettysburg Memorial Association, for purchase of portion of the battle-ground at Gettysburg	$2500.00
1888.	5th Regiment Connecticut Volunteers, for monument	500.00
1889.	2d Light Battery Connecticut Volunteers, for monument	500.00
1890.	27th Regiment Connecticut Volunteers, for monument	1000.00
1890.	17th Regiment Connecticut Volunteers, for monument	1000.00
1894.	Gettysburg Battle-field Memorial Association tablet at Cemetery Ridge, "High-Water-Mark"	200.00
	Total	$5700.00

The monuments of this State, while substantial, are rather plain, except that of the 17th Regiment, on Barlow's knoll, upon the extreme right of the Eleventh Corps line. It was erected for the most part by private contributions, and upon it are cut the names of all those of the regiment who fell in the battle.

The monuments of this State were dedicated on October 22, 1889.

NEW YORK.

Regiment.	Brigade.	Division.	Corps.	Killed and wounded.	Missing.
2d Cav.[1]	2d, Huey.	2d, Gregg.	Cavalry.	. .	. .
4th Cav.[1]	2d, Huey.	2d, Gregg.	Cavalry.	. .	. .
5th Cav.	1st, Farnsworth.	3d, Kilpatrick.	Cavalry.	2	4
6th Cav.	2d, Devin.	1st, Buford.	Cavalry.	5	8
8th Cav.	1st, Gamble.	1st, Buford.	Cavalry.	24	16
9th Cav.	2d, Devin.	1st, Buford.	Cavalry.	4	7
10th Cav.	3d, Gregg.	2d, Gregg.	Cavalry.	6	3
10th Inf.[2]	2d, Smyth.	3d, Hays.	Second.	1	. .
14th Inf.[3]	2d, Cutler.	1st, Wadsworth.	First.	118	99
20th Inf.	1st, Biddle.	3d, Doubleday.	First.	146	24
33d Inf.[1]	3d, Neill.	2d, Howe.	Sixth.	. .	. .
39th Inf.	3d, Willard.	3d, Hays.	Second.	95	. .
40th Inf.[4]	3d, De Trobriand.	1st, Birney.	Third.	143	7
41st Inf.	1st, Von Gilsa.	1st, Barlow.	Eleventh.	73	2
42d Inf.	3d, Hall.	2d, Gibbon.	Second.	70	4
43d Inf.[1]	3d, Neill.	2d, Howe.	Sixth.	4	1
44th Inf.	3d, Vincent.	1st, Barnes.	Fifth.	108	3
45th Inf.	1st, Von Amsberg.	3d, Schurz.	Eleventh.	54	48
49th Inf.[1]	3d, Neill.	2d, Howe.	Sixth.	. .	. .
52d Inf.	3d, Zook.	1st, Caldwell.	Second.	28	10
54th Inf.	1st, Von Gilsa.	1st, Barlow.	Eleventh.	54	48
57th Inf.	3d, Zook.	1st, Caldwell.	Second.	32	2
58th Inf.	2d, Krzyzanowski.	3d, Schimmelfennig.	Eleventh.	17	3
59th Inf.[2]	3d, Hall.	2d, Gibbon.	Second.	34	. .
60th Inf.	3d, Greene.	2d, Geary.	Twelfth.	52	. .
61st Inf.	4th, Cross.	1st, Caldwell.	Second.	62	. .
62d Inf.	3d, Nevin.	3d, Wheaton.	Sixth.	12	. .
63d Inf.[5]	2d, Kelly.	1st, Caldwell.	Second.	15	8
64th Inf.	4th, Brooke.	1st, Caldwell.	Second.	79	19
65th Inf.	1st, Shaler.	3d, Wheaton.	Sixth.	9	. .
66th Inf.	3d, Zook.	1st, Caldwell.	Second.	34	10
67th Inf.	1st, Shaler.	3d, Wheaton.	Sixth.	. .	1
68th Inf.	1st, Von Gilsa.	1st, Barlow.	Eleventh.	71	67

---

[1] Not engaged.   [2] Four companies.   [3] Brooklyn Zouaves.
[4] Mozart Regiment, recruited in New York, Pennsylvania, and Massachusetts.
[5] Two companies.

NEW YORK—*Continued.*

Regiment.	Brigade.	Division.	Corps.	Killed and wounded.	Missing.
69th Inf.[1]	2d, Kelly.	1st, Caldwell.	Second.	19	6
70th Inf.[2]*	2d, Brewster.	2d, Humphreys.	Third.	113	4
71st Inf.[2]†	2d, Brewster.	2d, Humphreys.	Third.	178	13
72d Inf.[2]‡	2d, Brewster.	2d, Humphreys.	Third.	86	28
73d Inf.[2]‖	2d, Brewster.	2d, Humphreys.	Third.	154	8
74th Inf.[2]§	2d, Brewster.	2d, Humphreys.	. . . .	86	3
76th Inf.	2d, Cutler.	1st, Wadsworth.	First.	164	70
77th Inf.[3]	3d, Neill.	2d, Howe.	Sixth.	. .	. .
78th Inf.	3d, Greene.	2d, Geary.	Twelfth.	27	3
82d Inf.	1st, Harrow.	2d, Gibbon.	Second.	177	15
83d Inf.	2d, Baxter.	2d, Robinson.	First.	24	58
86th Inf.	2d, Ward.	1st, Birney.	Third.	62	4
88th Inf.[1]	2d, Kelly.	1st, Caldwell.	Second.	24	4
93d Inf.[4]	. . . .	. . . .	. . . .	. .	. .
94th Inf.	1st, Paul.	1st, Robinson.	First.	70	175
95th Inf.	2d, Cutler.	1st, Wadsworth.	First.	69	46
97th Inf.	2d, Baxter.	2d, Robinson.	First.	48	78
102d Inf.	2d, Greene.	2d, Geary.	Twelfth.	21	8
104th Inf.	1st, Paul.	2d, Robinson.	First.	102	92
107th Inf.	5d, Colgrove.	1st, Ruger.	Twelfth.	2	. .
108th Inf.	2d, Smyth.	3d, Hays.	Second.	102	. .
111th Inf.	3d, Willard.	3d, Hays.	Second.	235	14
119th Inf.	2d, Krzyzanowski.	3d, Schimmelfennig.	Eleventh.	81	59
120th Inf.	2d, Brewster.	2d, Humphreys.	Third.	184	19
121st Inf.[3]	3d, Bartlett.	3d, Wheaton.	Sixth.	2	. .
122d Inf.	1st, Shaler.	3d, Wheaton.	Sixth.	42	2
123d Inf.	1st, McDougall.	1st, Ruger.	Twelfth.	13	1
124th Inf.	2d, Ward.	1st, Birney.	Third.	85	5
125th Inf.	3d, Willard.	3d, Hays.	Second.	130	9
126th Inf.	3d, Willard.	3d, Hays.	Second.	221	10
134th Inf.	1st, Coster.	2d, Steinwehr.	Eleventh.	193	59
136th Inf.	2d, Smith.	2d, Steinwehr.	Eleventh.	106	3
137th Inf.	3d, Greene.	2d, Geary.	Twelfth.	127	10
140th Inf.	3d, Weed.	2d, Ayres.	Fifth.	115	18

[1] Two companies.
[2] * First, † Second, ‡ Third, ‖ Fourth, and § Fifth Excelsior.
[3] Not engaged.   [4] At head-quarters guarding trains.

NEW YORK—*Continued*.

Regiment.	Brigade.	Division.	Corps.	Killed and wounded.	Missing.
145th Inf.	1st, McDougall.	1st, Ruger.	Twelfth.	10	..
146th Inf.	3d, Weed.	2d, Ayres.	Fifth.	28	..
147th Inf.	2d, Cutler.	1st, Wadsworth.	First.	177	92
149th Inf.	3d, Greene.	1st, Ruger.	Twelfth.	52	3
150th Inf.	2d, Lockwood.	1st, Ruger.	Twelfth.	30	15
154th Inf.	1st, Coster.	2d, Steinwehr.	Eleventh.	22	178
157th Inf.	1st, Von Amsberg.	3d, Schurz.	Eleventh.	193	114

Batteries.

	Corps.	Killed and wounded.	Missing.
Reynolds's 1st Light	First.	16	1
Rorty's 1st Light (B)	Second.	26	..
Winslow's 1st Light (D)	Third.	10	8
Smith's 4th Light	Third.	12	1
Barnes's 1st Light (C)[1]	Fifth.	..	..
Cowan's 1st Light	Sixth.	12	..
Harn's 3d Light[1]	Sixth.	..	..
Weidrick's 1st Light (I)	Eleventh.	13	..
Wheeler's 13th Light	Eleventh.	8	3
Winegar's 1st Light (M)	Twelfth.	..	..
Martin's 6th	Horse Artillery, Cavalry.	1	..
Hart's 15th Light	Artillery Reserve.	16	..
Taft's 5th Light	Artillery Reserve.	3	..
Ames's 1st Light (G)	Artillery Reserve.	7	..
Fitzhugh's 1st Light (K)[2]	Artillery Reserve.	7	..

[1] Not engaged. [2] 11th New York Battery attached.

GENERAL OFFICERS.

Corps Commanders.

General Daniel E. Sickles, Commander of the Fifth Corps (wounded).

General Henry W. Slocum, Commander of the Twelfth Corps.

General Abner Doubleday, Commander of the First Corps (temporarily).

General Daniel Butterfield, Chief of Staff (wounded).

General Gouverneur K. Warren, Chief Engineer.

Division Commanders.

General James S. Wadsworth, Commander of the First Division, First Corps.

General John C. Robinson, Commander of the Second Division, First Corps.

General Romeyn B. Ayres, Commander of the Second Division, Fifth Corps.

General Francis C. Barlow, Commander of the First Division, Eleventh Corps (wounded).

General Adolph von Steinwehr, Commander of the Second Division, Eleventh Corps.

Brigade Commanders.

General Alexander S. Webb, Commander of the Second Brigade, Second Division, Second Corps (wounded).

Colonel Patrick Kelly, Commander of the Second Brigade, First Division, Second Corps.

General George S. Willard, Commander of the Third Brigade, Third Division, Second Corps (killed).

General Charles K. Graham, Commander of the First Brigade, First Division, Third Corps (wounded).

General Hobart Ward, Commander of the Second Brigade, First Division, Third Corps.

General P. R. de Trobriand, Commander of the Third Brigade, First Division, Third Corps. (Born in France.)

General Joseph B. Carr, Commander of the First Brigade, Second Division, Third Corps.

Colonel W. M. R. Brewster, Commander of the Second Brigade, Second Division, Third Corps.

General Stephen H. Weed, Commander of the Third Brigade, Second Division, Fifth Corps (killed).

General J. J. Bartlett, Commander of the Second Brigade, First Division, Sixth Corps.

General David A. Russell, Commander of the Third Brigade, First Division, Sixth Corps.

Colonel Leopold von Gilsa, Commander of the First Brigade, First Division, Eleventh Corps. (Born in Germany.)

Colonel Charles K. Coster, Commander of the First Brigade, Second Division, Eleventh Corps.

BATTLE-FIELD MEMORIAL ASSOCIATION.

Colonel W. Krzyzanowski, Commander of the Second Brigade, Third Division, Eleventh Corps. (Born in Poland.)

Colonel Archibald L. McDougall, Commander of the First Brigade, First Division, Twelfth Corps.

General George S. Greene, Commander of the Third Brigade, Second Division, Twelfth Corps. (Born in Rhode Island.)

Colonel Thomas C. Devin, Commander of the Second Brigade, Cavalry Corps.

State Appropriations for Monuments.

For the erection of New York State Monument in National Cemetery: Appropriation made by Chapter 420, Laws of New York, 1889	$50,000.00
Appropriation made by Chapter 302, Laws of New York, 1891	10,000.00
Total	$60,000.00

For Regimental and Battery Monuments.

For the erection of monuments to New York regiments and batteries: Appropriation made by Chapter 269, Laws of New York, 1887	$60,000.00
Appropriation made by Chapter 83, Laws of New York, 1888	67,500.00
Appropriation made by Chapter 420, Laws of New York, 1889	10,000.00
Total	$137,500.00

For the erection of tablets to Battery E, and 10th, 11th, and 14th Batteries: Appropriation made by Chapter 126, Laws of New York, 1889	$2,000.00

To the Memorial Association.

Appropriation made by Chapter 525, Laws of New York, 1885	$10,000.00
Appropriation made by Chapter 269, Laws of New York, 1887	10,000.00
Total	$20,000.00

For Marker Sites and Sodding.

Appropriation made by Section 1, Chapter 440, Laws of New York, 1889	$1,525.00
Appropriation for the erection of a memorial bronze tablet, under the supervision of the Gettysburg Battle-field Memorial Association, Chaper 302, Laws of 1891	2,400.00
Appropriation for completing above-described memorial bronze and granite monument, Chapter 365, Laws of 1892	1,000.00
Appropriation for New York's pro rata share, in conjunction with other States, of the cost of recasting the "High-Water Tablet" so as to add thereto the names of four companies of United States Sharp-shooters from the State of New York, Chapter 726, Laws of 1893	400.00
Total	$5,325.00
Total appropriation by the State, exclusive of those to the cemetery	$224,825.00

When this great State decided to erect monuments upon the field, there was a certainty that it would be done not only in a liberal, but in a most thorough manner.

A commission, consisting of Generals Sickles, Slocum, Graham, and Carr, and Major Richardson, was appointed to take charge of the matter. They not only gave great personal attention to it, but employed a civil engineer, Mr. A. J. Zabriskie, who remained at Gettysburg constantly during the erection of the monuments, carefully inspecting the foundations and rejecting any monument or stone which was not in exact accordance with the specifications. This careful supervision has made the New York monuments among the most costly and the best constructed upon the field. In addition to the appropriation of $1500 to each command, many regiments contributed largely towards the erection of their monuments.

Before the State made any appropriation the 14th Brooklyn and 124th Regiments had erected costly monuments. That of the former at the railroad cut, on the First Corps line, is a soldier in the zouave uniform of the regiment in the act of loading, while the latter, on the Third Corps line, on the knoll above the Devil's Den, is surmounted by a statue of its youthful commander, Colonel Ellis, standing in the position he was when killed on the 2d, as he stood with folded arms watching the approach of the Texas brigade, which was advancing over the rocks and through the bushes in the immediate front. The regiment, recruited in Orange County, was known as the "Orange Blossoms." The citizens of the county contributed liberally to the monument. Near it is the fine monument of the 86th Regiment.

The monument of the 44th Regiment and two companies of the 12th, upon the summit of Little Round Top, is probably the most expensive regimental monument on the field. It is a massive granite castle, in the lower chamber of which are bronze plates containing a complete muster-roll of each company. A winding stairway leads to the observatory on top. It was through the liberal contributions of General Butterfield, principally, that this splendid monument was erected.

Among other fine monuments of the State are the following: that of Sickles's old "Excelsior Brigade," near the Emmittsburg Road, in which is a column for each of the five regiments, with full and appropriate inscriptions; that of the "Irish Brigade," on the edge of the Wheat-Field, a large granite and bronze cross, with a bronze Irish wolf-dog lying at its foot; that of Smith's battery, on the knoll, near Devil's Den, a bronze cannoneer standing by his gun with rammer in hand; the tall and expensive shaft of the 83d, on the First Corps line, on Oak Ridge, and the costly monuments of the 6th and 9th Cavalry immediately in front of it, the former containing one of the largest bronze plates on the field, representing a cavalry charge, and the latter a similar plate with a figure of a cavalry vedette discovering the approach of the enemy.

Many other of the monuments on this line are also handsome and expensive.

On the Twelfth Corps line, on Culp's Hill, among the most characteristic are those of the 78th and 102d, constructed of granite, representing a soldier firing from behind a log breastwork; that of the 123d is a granite figure of History recording the events of the battle upon a large tablet.

On the Second Corps line is the large granite clover-leaf monument of the 108th and the bronze soldier of the 111th, and a short distance beyond is the costly monument of Cowan's battery, which was erected through the generosity of Colonel Cowan. It is a fine piece of bronze work, depicting a battery firing grape and canister into the ranks of the enemy at short range.

Near this is the monument of the 42d (Tammany) Regiment. It was erected by subscriptions of the Tammany Organization of New York, and is a large and finely finished piece of bronze work. The granite pedestal is surmounted by an immense bronze wigwam, an Indian warrior standing beside it. This monument is subject to criticism, as in the far future it may lead to misconception as to Indians participating in the battle.

In fact, there is hardly a New York regimental monument on the field that is not attractive.

In addition to these the State erected, at an expense of $60,000, a magnificent monument in the cemetery in honor of its dead. It is a splendid work of art, being a classic shaft, and upon the dies of the base are large bronze tablets representing the principal events of each day of the battle.

Upon the summit of Round Top is the bronze heroic statue of General Warren, then chief engineer of the army. It was erected through the efforts of the 5th New York (Duryee's Zouaves), his old regiment. It is of a very high order of art, well executed.

NEW JERSEY.

Regiment.	Brigade.	Division.	Corps.	Killed and wounded.	Missing.
1st Cav.	1st, McIntosh.	2d, Gregg.	Cavalry.	7	. .
1st Inf.[1]	1st, Torbert.	1st, Wright.	Sixth.	. .	. .
2d Inf.[1]	1st, Torbert.	1st, Wright.	Sixth.	6	. .
3d Inf.[1]	1st, Torbert.	1st, Wright.	Sixth.	2	. .
4th Inf.[2]	. . . . . .	. . . . . .	. . . .	. .	. .
5th Inf.	3d, Burling.	2d, Humphreys.	Third.	78	16
6th Inf.	3d, Burling.	2d, Humphreys.	Third.	33	8
7th Inf.	3d, Burling.	2d, Humphreys.	Third.	101	13
8th Inf.	3d, Burling.	2d, Humphreys.	Third.	21	3
11th Inf.	1st, Carr.	2d, Humphreys.	Third.	141	12
12th Inf.	2d, Smyth.	3d, Hays.	Second.	106	9
13th Inf.	3d, Colgrove.	1st, Ruger.	Twelfth.	21	. .
15th Inf.[1]	1st, Torbert.	1st, Wright.	Sixth.	3	. .

[1] Not engaged.   [2] Guarding reserve ammunition train.

Batteries.

	Corps.	Killed and wounded.	Missing.
Clark's 2d Light	Third.	17	3
Parson's 1st Light	Artillery Reserve.	9	. .

General Officers.

General Judson Kilpatrick, Commander of the Third Division, Cavalry Corps.

General George C. Burling, Commander of the Third Brigade, Second Division, Third Corps.

BATTLE-FIELD MEMORIAL ASSOCIATION. 283

State Appropriations for Monuments.

By the Acts of 1886 and 1887 the State appropriated to the Memorial Association	$3,000.00
For regimental monuments	15,450.00
To the latter appropriation there were added individual contributions amounting to	5,305.00
By the Act of 1890 there was an additional appropriation for the improvement of the monument of the 12th Regiment, of	1,000.00
For expenses of dedication of the monuments in 1888, including transportation and the subsistance of the surviving soldiers who had participated in the battle, the State appropriated the additional sum of	19,500.00
Total	$44,255.00

This State was fortunate in having as its most active commissioner the Hon. W. H. Corbin, who, though not a soldier, manifested the greatest interest, and most carefully supervised the erection of the monuments.

The appropriations for the five regiments of the 1st New Jersey Brigade of the Sixth Corps, which were in reserve in the rear of the left centre, were consolidated in the erection of an imposing brigade monument, a granite castle, which stands in a commanding position.

The monuments of the 11th, 12th, and 13th Regiments and of Clark's battery are very characteristic. That of the 11th, on the Third Corps line, on the Emmittsburg Road, is a heavy pedestal, upon which lies an open volume of history. That of the 12th, on the

Second Corps line, contains a bronze plate representing the regiment charging out to and burning the Bliss barn. That of the 13th is one of the most substantial monuments on the field. It is in the woods, on the extreme right of the Twelfth Corps line, at the edge of Rock Creek, and upon its face is well cut in relief the figure of a soldier firing from behind the trees.

PENNSYLVANIA.

Regiment.	Brigade.	Division.	Corps.	Killed and wounded.	Missing.
1st Cav.	1st, McIntosh.	2d, Gregg.	Head-q'rs.	. .	2
2d Cav.	. . . . .	. . . .	Head-q'rs.	. .	. .
3d Cav.	1st, McIntosh.	2d, Gregg.	Cavalry.	15	6
4th Cav.[1]	3d, Gregg.	2d, Gregg.	Cavalry.	. .	. .
6th Cav.	Merritt.	1st, Buford.	Cavalry.	10	6
8th Cav.[1]	2d, Huey.	2d, Gregg.	Cavalry.	. .	. .
16th Cav.	3d, Gregg.	2d, Gregg.	Cavalry.	6	. .
17th Cav.	2d, Devin.	1st, Buford.	Cavalry.	. .	4
18th Cav.	1st Farnsworth.	3d, Kilpatrick.	Cavalry.	6	8
11th Inf.	2d, Baxter.	2d, Robinson.	First.	70	62
23d Inf.[2]	1st, Shaler.	3d, Wheaton.	Sixth.	14	. .
26th Inf.	1st, Carr.	2d, Humphreys.	Third.	206	7
27th Inf.	1st, Coster.	2d, Steinwehr.	Eleventh.	34	77
28th Inf.	1st, Candy.	2d, Geary.	Twelfth.	24	3
29th Inf.	2d, Kane.	2d, Geary.	Twelfth.	58	
46th Inf.	1st, McDougall.	1st, Ruger.	Twelfth.	12	1
49th Inf.[1]	3d, Russell.	1st, Wright.	Sixth.	. .	. .
53d Inf.	4th, Brooke.	1st, Caldwell.	Second.	74	6
56th Inf.	2d, Cutler.	1st, Wadsworth.	First.	73	56
57th Inf.	1st, Graham.	1st, Birney.	Third.	57	58
61st Inf.[1]	3d, Neill.	2d, Howe.	Sixth.	1	1
62d Inf.	2d, Sweitzer.	1st, Barnes.	Fifth.	135	40
63d Inf.	1st, Graham.	1st, Birney.	Third.	30	4

[1] Not engaged.   [2] Birney's Zouaves.

BATTLE-FIELD MEMORIAL ASSOCIATION. 285

PENNSYLVANIA—*Continued.*

Regiment.	Brigade.	Division.	Corps.	Killed and wounded.	Missing.
68th Inf.	1st, Graham.	1st, Birney.	Third.	133	19
69th Inf.	2d, Webb.	2d, Gibbon.	Second.	120	8
71st Inf.	2d, Webb.	2d, Gibbon.	Second.	79	19
72d Inf.[1]	2d, Webb.	2d, Gibbon.	Second.	189	2
73d Inf.	1st, Coster.	2d, Steinwehr.	Eleventh.	34	..
74th Inf.	1st, Von Amsberg.	3d, Schimmelfennig.	Eleventh.	50	60
75th Inf.	2d, Krzyzanowski.	3d, Schimmelfennig.	Eleventh.	108	3
81st Inf.	1st, Cross.	1st, Caldwell.	Second.	54	8
82d Inf.	1st, Shaler.	2d, Wheaton.	Sixth.	6	..
83d Inf.	3d, Vincent.	1st, Barnes.	Fifth.	55	..
84th Inf.[2]	1st, Carr.	2d, Humphreys.	Third.	..	..
88th Inf.	2d, Baxter.	2d, Robinson.	First.	57	49
90th Inf.	2d, Baxter.	2d, Robinson.	First.	53	40
91st Inf.	3d, Weed.	2d, Ayres.	Fifth.	19	..
93d Inf.	3d, Nevin.	3d, Wheaton.	Sixth.	10	..
95th Inf.[3]	2d, Bartlett.	3d, Wheaton.	Sixth.	2	..
96th Inf.[3]	2d, Bartlett.	3d, Wheaton.	Sixth.	1	..
98th Inf.	3d, Nevin.	3d, Wheaton.	Sixth.	11	..
99th Inf.	2d, Ward.	1st, Birney.	Third.	99	11
102d Inf.[2]	3d, Nevin.	3d, Wheaton.	Sixth.	..	..
105th Inf.	1st, Graham.	1st, Birney.	Third.	123	9
106th Inf.	2d, Webb.	2d, Gibbon.	Second.	63	1
107th Inf.	1st, Paul.	2d, Robinson.	First.	67	98
109th Inf.	2d, Kane.	2d, Geary.	Twelfth.	9	1
110th Inf.	3d, De Trobriand.	1st, Birney.	Third.	53	..
111th Inf.	2d, Kane.	2d, Geary.	Twelfth.	22	..
114th Inf.[4]	1st, Graham.	1st, Birney.	Third.	94	60
115th Inf.	3d, Burling.	2d, Humphreys.	Third.	21	3
116th Inf.[5]	2d, Kelly.	1st, Caldwell.	Second.	13	9
118th Inf.	1st, Tilton.	1st, Barnes.	Fifth.	22	3
119th Inf.[2]	3d, Russell.	1st, Wright.	Sixth.	2	..
121st Inf.	1st, Biddle.	3d, Doubleday.	First.	118	61
139th Inf.	3d, Nevin.	2d, Wheaton.	Sixth.	30	..

[1] Baxter's Zouaves. [2] Not engaged. [3] Gosline's Zouaves, not engaged.
[4] Collis's Zouaves. [5] Four companies.

PENNSYLVANIA—*Continued.*

Regiment.	Brigade.	Division.	Corps.	Killed and wounded.	Missing.
140th Inf.	3d, Zook.	1st, Caldwell.	Second.	181	60
141st Inf.	1st, Graham.	1st, Birney.	Third.	128	21
142d Inf.	1st, Biddle.	3d, Doubleday.	First.	141	70
143d Inf.	2d, Stone.	3d, Doubleday.	First.	161	91
145th Inf.[1]	4th, Brooke.	1st, Caldwell.	Second.	76	8
147th Inf.	1st, Candy.	2d, Geary.	Twelfth.	20	..
148th Inf.	1st, Cross.	1st, Caldwell.	Second.	120	5
149th Inf.	2d, Stone.	3d, Doubleday.	First.	205	131
150th Inf.	2d, Stone.	3d, Doubleday.	First.	180	84
151st Inf.	1st, Biddle.	3d, Doubleday.	First.	233	102
153d Inf.	1st, Von Gilsa.	1st, Barlow.	Eleventh.	165	46
155th Inf.[2]	3d, Weed.	1st, Ayres.	Fifth.	19	..

[1] Seven companies.   [2] Pittsburg Zouaves.

Pennsylvania Reserves.

Regiment.	Brigade.	Division.	Corps.	Killed and wounded.	Missing.
1st Inf.	1st, McCandless.	3d, Crawford.	Fifth.	46	..
2d Inf.	1st, McCandless.	3d, Crawford.	Fifth.	36	1
5th Inf.[1]	3d, Fisher.	3d, Crawford.	Fifth.	2	..
6th Inf.	1st, McCandless.	3d, Crawford.	Fifth.	24	..
9th Inf.[1]	3d, Fisher.	3d, Crawford.	Fifth.	5	..
10th Inf.[1]	3d, Fisher.	3d, Crawford.	Fifth.	5	..
11th Inf.	3d, Fisher.	3d, Crawford.	Fifth.	41	..
12th Inf.[1]	3d, Fisher.	3d, Crawford.	Fifth.	2	..
1st Rifles.	1st, McCandless.	3d, Crawford.	Fifth.	46	2

[1] Not engaged.

Batteries.

	Corps.	Killed and wounded.	Missing.
Cooper's 1st Light (B)	First.	11	..
Knap's 6th Light (E)	Twelfth.	3	..
Thompson's Light Independent (C and F)	Artillery Reserve.	24	4
Ricketts's 1st Light (F and G)	Artillery Reserve.	20	3
Runk's 3d Light (H)	Unattached.		

GENERAL OFFICERS.

General George G. Meade, Commander of the Army.

Corps Commanders.

General John F. Reynolds, Commander of the First Corps (killed).

General Winfield S. Hancock, Commander of the Second Corps (wounded).

General David B. Birney, Commander of the Third Corps (after General Sickles was wounded).

Division Commanders.

General Thomas A. Rowley, Commander of the Third Division, First Corps.

General John Gibbon, Commander of the Second Division, Second Corps (wounded).

General Alexander Hays, Commander of the Third Division, Second Corps.

General Andrew A. Humphreys, Commander of the Second Division, Third Corps.

General S. W. Crawford, Commander of the Third Division, Fifth Corps.

General John W. Geary, Commander of the Second Division, Twelfth Corps.

General David McM. Gregg, Commander of the Second Division, Cavalry Corps.

Brigade Commanders.

Colonel Chapman Biddle, Commander of the First Brigade, Third Division, First Corps.

General Roy Stone, Commander of the Second Brigade, Third Division, First Corps (wounded).

General S. K. Zook, Commander of the Third Brigade, First Division, Second Corps (killed).

General John R. Brooke, Commander of the Fourth Brigade, First Division, Second Corps (wounded).

General J. B. Sweitzer, Commander of the Second Brigade, First Division, Fifth Corps.

General Strong Vincent, Commander of the Third Brigade, First Division, Fifth Corps (killed).

Colonel William McCandless, Commander of the First Brigade, Third Division, Fifth Corps.

Colonel J. W. Fisher, Commander of the Third Brigade, Third Division, Fifth Corps.

General Thomas H. Neill, Commander of the Third Brigade, Second Division, Sixth Corps.

General A. Schimmelfennig, Commander of the First Brigade, Third Division, Eleventh Corps.

General Thomas L. Kane, Commander of the Second Brigade, Second Division, Twelfth Corps.

General John B. McIntosh, Commander of the First Brigade, Second Division, Cavalry Corps.

Colonel Pennock Huey, Commander of the Second Brigade, Second Division, Cavalry Corps.

Colonel John Irwin Gregg, Commander of the Third Brigade, Second Division, Cavalry Corps.

State Appropriations for Monuments.

Act of April 11, 1866, "to provide for the painting of Rothermel's picture of the battle of Gettysburg"	$25,000.00
Act of April 11, 1867, "for the purchase of portions of the battle-grounds and the general purposes for which the Gettysburg Battle-field Memorial Association was organized"	3,000.00
Act of April 11, 1868, "for the purchase of portions of the battle-grounds and the general purposes for which the Gettysburg Battle-field Memorial Association was organized"	3,000.00
Act of April 11, 1877, "for the purchase of a collection of shot, shell, and bullets collected on the battle-field"	500.00
Act of June 29, 1881, "for the purchase of additional grounds of special interest upon said battle-field, and in acquiring rights of way, in constructing roads and avenues, for such purposes as are contemplated by the Act incorporating the Gettysburg Battle-field Memorial Association"	10,000.00
Act of June 15, 1887, "for the purpose of perpetuating the participation in, and marking by suitable memorial tablets, of bronze or granite, the position of each of the commands of Pennsylvania Volunteers engaged in the battle," being $1500 for each command	121,500.00

BATTLE-FIELD MEMORIAL ASSOCIATION.

Act of May 6, 1889, "for the purchase of land and maintaining and keeping in repair the battle-field"	20,000.00
Act of May 7, 1889, "for the erection, in connection with other States, of a memorial tablet to indicate the 'High-Water-Mark of the Rebellion'"	1,000.00
Act of May 7, 1889, "for the purpose of perpetuating the participation in, and marking by suitable memorial tablets, of bronze or granite, the position of, Pennsylvania commands in the battle"	4,500.00
Act of May 8, 1889, "to provide transportation to Gettysburg, at the time of the dedication of the monuments of the Pennsylvania organizations, for all surviving soldiers, residents in Pennsylvania, who participated in the battle, and expenses incident thereto"	50,000.00
Act of May 7, 1891, "cost of printing and binding 'Pennsylvania at Gettysburg,' books, engravings, 87 plates of monuments, printing and binding 38,000 copies"	43,877.22
Act of May 7, 1891, "for the publication of the report of the Gettysburg Battle-field Commission"	3,000.00
Act of May 20, 1891, "for the erection of a tablet to commemorate the services of the 21st Regiment of Pennsylvania Cavalry, six months' regiment"	1,500.00
Act of May 20, 1891, "for the erection of monuments to Major-General Meade, Major-General Reynolds, and Major-General Hancock"	100,000.00
Act of June 1, 1891, "for the erection of a memorial tablet or monument to mark the position of the 26th Pennsylvania Emergency Regiment"	1,500.00
Act of June 9, 1891, "for the payment of the expenses incurred by the Commission"	2,000.00
Act of June 20, 1893, "for the purpose of maintaining and keeping in repair the battle-field of Gettysburg"	5,000.00
Act of June 6, 1893, "for expenses of the Gettysburg Battle-field Monumental Commission under the Act of June 15, 1887"	2,000.00
Act of June 6, 1893, "for the purpose of keeping the Pennsylvania monuments in repair, guarding them from destruction, and preserving them in good order"	2,500.00
Total, exclusive of appropriations to cemetery	$399,877.22

The survivors of several regiments of this State had erected monuments upon the field before the State made an appropriation for that purpose.

The difficulty was not in having an act passed by the Legislature, but in repressing efforts to have such an act passed, especially after Massachusetts made an appropriation for such purpose.

Those in the State most actively interested well knew that there would be a just rivalry between the great States of New York and Pennsylvania, which together had more commands present at the battle than all the other States combined. They knew that when New York took action it would be upon a liberal basis, and that Pennsylvania would be certain to equal anything done by the Empire State. They were, therefore, desirous of deferring action until the latter State had made its appropriation, but it required considerable effort to accomplish it.

As soon as New York had made an appropriation of $1500 for each regimental monument, Mr. J. M. Vanderslice prepared a bill making a like appropriation by the State of Pennsylvania, and General Gobin introduced it in the State Senate, where it passed unanimously. Some enthusiastic friends had had a similar bill introduced in the House of Representatives, making, however, an appropriation of only $1000 for each regiment. This bill was passed by the House at first, but a committee of conference was appointed by the two Houses, which reported in favor of the passage of the Senate bill. The report of the committee was adopted, and the bill appropriating $121,500 passed, and was approved June 15, 1887. Under the provisions of this bill, General John P. Taylor, General J. P. S. Gobin, Colonel John P. Nicholson, Colonel R. Bruce Ricketts, and Lieutenant Samuel Harper, were appointed commissioners. This commission gave to its work not only untiring zeal, but most thorough supervision, and its work has been most creditably and satisfactorily done. The monuments are a credit to the State upon whose soil they stand.

Among the most attractive monuments are: that of the 56th infantry on the First Corps line, a bronze stack of muskets and equipments; the massive monument of the 151st, at the edge of Reynolds's Grove; the huge granite tree-trunk with bronze ivy twined around it, of the 90th, on Oak Ridge, near the Mummasburg Road; the granite cannon and other implements of war of the 88th, near it; the bronze soldier of the 11th, farther to the left, on the same line; that of the 17th Cavalry, of Devin's brigade, immediately in their front, a full-sized horse and rider upon an immense block of Westerly granite; that of the 74th, on the Eleventh Corps line, a granite figure of the color-bearer falling, but still holding his flag aloft; that of Ricketts's battery, on East Cemetery Hill, one of the largest and most expensive upon the field, cannon, gunner, etc., in granite, cut in full relief; that of the 73d, near it, a bronze plate representing the regiment charging from out the cemetery to the relief of the batteries; that of the 23d (Birney's Philadelphia Zouaves), on Culp's Hill, representing a soldier double-quicking towards the works at "trail arms;" those of the 28th, 29th, and 109th, near by; the large and substantial one of the 71st, near the "copse of trees" on the Second Corps line; the bronze zouave with clubbed musket of the 72d, near by; that of the 1st Pennsylvania Cavalry in front of Meade's head-quarters, a bronze dismounted trooper kneeling and firing; also the bronze dismounted cavalryman of heroic size in the act of loading his carbine, of the 2d Cavalry, at Meade's head-quarters; that of the 8th Cavalry, near Pleasonton's head-quarters, a granite horse and rider, of full size, cut out of one piece of granite, with bronze equipments; that of the 95th (Gosline's

Zouaves), to the right and front of Little Round Top; that of the 155th (Pittsburg Zouaves); the granite castle of the 91st, of the same brigade, and that of the 83d, on Little Round Top, the latter a bronze statue of General Vincent; that of the 9th Reserves, between the two Round Tops, a soldier standing by the grave of his comrade; that of the 10th Reserves, near by; those of the 5th, 8th, and 12th, on Big Round Top; the large granite keystone of the 99th, on the knoll above Devil's Den; that of the 18th Cavalry, on Kilpatrick's line; that of the 148th, in the Wheat-Field; those of the 53d and 145th, on the line of Brooke's brigade; that of the 116th, beyond the Wheat-Field, a soldier falling while crossing a wall; that of the 118th (Philadelphia Corn Exchange), near by; the fine bronze cannoneer of Thompson's battery, in the Peach Orchard; those of the 68th and 141st, near it; the bronze zouave of the 114th, in Sherfy's yard, on the Emmittsburg Road; and that of the 105th (the Wildcat Regiment), near it. There are many other monuments of this State, as of New York, which are very attractive and impressive.

In addition to the regimental monuments, the State, in 1891, appropriated $100,000 for equestrian statues of Generals Meade, Hancock, and Reynolds. The two former have been erected, and the latter is still in the hands of the artist, and will be erected in the summer of 1897.

That of General Meade stands near the centre of the line of battle, on the Second Corps line. It represents him uncovered, as he rides upon the field at the time of Longstreet's assault and repulse, receiving the wild greetings of his army.

That of General Hancock, on East Cemetery Hill, where he assumed command of the army on the evening of July 1, represents him pointing to positions and giving directions for the formation of a new line of battle.

These two statues are considered, by capable critics, as two of the finest works of art of the kind in America, and no doubt that of General Reynolds, which will stand upon the First Corps line, will be of equal merit.

The regimental monuments were dedicated September 11 and 12, 1889, in the presence of an immense number of citizens of the State. The State furnished transportation to all surviving soldiers of the State who had participated in the battle.

The statues of Generals Meade and Hancock were dedicated on June 5, 1896, the ceremonies being attended also by a large number of distinguished military officers and citizens of the country.

DELAWARE.

Regiment.	Brigade.	Division.	Corps.	Killed and wounded.	Missing.
1st Inf.	2d, Smyth.	3d, Hays.	Second.	64	13
2d Inf.	4th, Brooke.	1st, Caldwell.	Second.	72	12

A considerable portion of the two Delaware regiments was recruited in Philadelphia.

General Officers.

General A. T. A. Torbert, Commander of the First Brigade, First Division, Sixth Corps.

General Thomas A. Smyth, Commander of the Second Brigade, Third Division, Second Corps (wounded).

State Appropriations for Monuments.

In 1885 the Legislature appropriated $2000 for the purpose of erecting monuments on the battle-field of Gettysburg. The amount was expended as follows:

For monuments, 1st and 2d Regiments	$850.00
To the Gettysburg Battle-field Association, for purchase of sites for monuments and fee for Delaware membership in said Association	500.00
Expenses of Joint Committee of the General Assembly, Military Committee, Governor, and State officers in visiting Gettysburg, to select sites for the monuments and attending the ceremonies of dedication	650.00
In 1891, for "High-Water-Mark Monument"	200.00
Total	$2200.00

Unfortunately, the two monuments of Delaware are duplicates, being small dark granite shafts.

MARYLAND.

Regiment.	Brigade.	Division.	Corps.	Killed and wounded.	Missing.
1st Cav.	3d, Gregg.	2d, Gregg.	Cavalry.	2	1
1st Inf.[1]	2d, Lockwood.	1st, Ruger.	Twelfth.	103	1
1st E. S.[2]	2d, Lockwood.	1st, Ruger.	Twelfth.	23	2
3d Inf.	1st, McDougall.	1st, Ruger.	Twelfth.	8	..

[1] Potomac Home Brigade.   [2] Eastern Shore.

Battery.

	Corps.
Rigby's Light (A)	Artillery Reserve.

General Officers.

General George Sykes, Commander of the Fifth Corps.

General H. H. Lockwood, Commander of the Second Brigade, First Division, Twelfth Corps.

State Appropriations for Monuments.

The General Assembly of 1888 appropriated for the erection of memorial tablets or monuments to suitably mark the positions occupied by the various Maryland military organizations serving with the Army of the Potomac at Gettysburg	$5000.00
To the Battle-field Memorial Association, for the purchase of land upon which to erect said monuments, laying out avenues leading thereto, and for taking care of said monuments after their erection	1000.00
Total	$6000.00

The monuments of this State are all of good character and substantially built. Those of the 1st Cavalry, of Gregg's division, on the right, and 1st Eastern Shore, on Culp's Hill, being particularly of excellent design and finish.

BATTLE-FIELD MEMORIAL ASSOCIATION. 297

WEST VIRGINIA.

Regiment.	Brigade.	Division.	Corps.	Killed and wounded.	Missing.
1st Cav.	1st, Farnsworth.	3d, Kilpatrick.	Cavalry.	8	4
3d Cav.[1]	2d, Devin.	1st, Buford.	Cavalry.	..	4
7th Inf.	1st, Carroll.	3d, Hays.	Second.	46	1

[1] Three companies.

Battery.

	Corps.	Killed and wounded.
Hall's Light (C)	Artillery Reserve.	4

State Appropriations for Monuments.

Appropriation $1000, expended as follows:

1892.	May 14, Colonel John B. Bachelder	$200.00
1893.	October 11, Thomas C. Miller, Secretary, etc	333.33
	Total	$533.33

No monuments have been erected up to this time.

OHIO.

Regiment.	Brigade.	Division.	Corps.	Killed and wounded.	Missing.
1st Cav.[1]	1st, Farnsworth.	3d, Kilpatrick.	Cavalry.	..	..
6th Cav.[2]	2d, Huey.	2d, Gregg.	Cavalry.	..	..
4th Inf.	1st, Carroll.	3d, Hays.	Second.	26	5
5th Inf.	1st, Candy.	2d, Geary.	Twelfth.	18	..
7th Inf.	1st, Candy.	2d, Geary.	Twelfth.	18	..
8th Inf.	1st, Carroll.	3d, Hays.	Second.	101	1
25th Inf.	2d, Ames.	1st, Barlow.	Eleventh.	112	72
29th Inf.	1st, Candy.	2d, Geary.	Twelfth.	38	..
55th Inf.	2d, Smith.	2d, Steinwehr.	Eleventh.	37	12
61st Inf.	1st, Von Amsberg.	3d, Schurz.	Eleventh.	42	12
66th Inf.	1st, Candy.	2d, Geary.	Twelfth.	17	..
73d Inf.	2d, Smith.	2d, Steinwehr.	Eleventh.	141	4
75th Inf.	2d, Ames.	1st, Barlow.	Eleventh.	94	92
82d Inf.	2d, Krzyzanowski.	3d, Schimmelfennig.	Eleventh.	102	79
107th Inf.	2d, Ames.	1st, Barlow.	Eleventh.	134	77

[1] Company F. Company A at Gregg's head-quarters.   [2] Not engaged.

Batteries.

	Corps.	Killed and wounded.	Missing.
Gibb's 1st Light (L)	Fifth.	6	..
Dilger's 1st Light (I)	Eleventh.	13	..
Heckman's 1st Light (K)	Eleventh.	13	2
Norton's 1st Light (H)	Artillery Reserve.	7	..

General Officers.

General Henry Hunt, Chief of Artillery. (Born in Michigan.)

General George A. Custer, Commander of the Second Brigade, Third Division, Cavalry Corps.

General Samuel S. Carroll, Commander of the First Brigade, Third Division, Second Corps. (Born in District of Columbia.)

General Orland Smith, Commander of the Second Brigade, Second Division, Eleventh Corps. (Born in Maine.)

General Charles Candy, Commander of the First Brigade, Second Division, Twelfth Corps.

State Appropriations for Monuments.

May 4, 1885.	"To purchase land upon which to erect a monument to the memory of the soldiers of Ohio who died upon the battle-field of Gettysburg"	$5,000.00
April 21, 1886.	Supplementary Act	35,000.00
	Total	$40,000.00

Of the above amount, $5000 was given to the Memorial Association and $35,000 was expended in the erection of monuments, expenses of commission, etc.

Although the appropriation to each command of this State was $2000, the monuments, with some exceptions, do not equal those of several of the other States in style and character. Among the finest are the combined monument of the 75th and 25th Regiments, on the Eleventh Corps line, and those of the 7th and 29th, on Culp's Hill. Probably the best piece of work is that of the 73d, near the cemetery wall, on the Taneytown Road,—a large pedestal, with the flag lying gracefully over it, cut from one piece of granite.

INDIANA.

Regiment.	Brigade.	Division.	Corps.	Killed and wounded.	Missing.
3d Cav.	1st, Gamble.	1st, Buford.	Cavalry.	27	5
7th Inf.[1]	2d, Cutler.	1st, Wadsworth.	First.	. .	. .
14th Inf.	1st, Carroll.	3d, Hays.	Second.	31	. .
19th Inf.	1st, Meredith.	1st, Wadsworth.	First.	160	50
20th Inf.	2d, Ward.	1st, Birney.	Third.	146	10
27th Inf.	3d, Colgrove.	1st, Ruger.	Twelfth.	109	1

[1] Not engaged.

General Officers.

General Solomon Meredith, Commander of the First Brigade, First Division, First Corps (wounded). (Born in North Carolina.)

General William Harrow, Commander of the First Brigade, Second Division, Second Corps. (Born in Kentucky.)

General Silas Colgrove, Commander of the Third Brigade, First Division, Twelfth Corps.

State Appropriations for Monuments.

The State appropriated $3000 on March 5, 1885, for the erection of monuments, but never contributed to the Association or paid anything towards the purchase of ground upon which the monuments are located.

The monuments of this State are plain, and

there seems to have been no effort towards originality or impressiveness.

ILLINOIS.

Regiment.	Brigade.	Division.	Corps.	Killed and wounded.	Missing.
8th Cav.	1st, Gamble.	1st, Buford.	Cavalry.	6	1
12th Cav.[1]	1st, Gamble.	1st, Buford.	Cavalry.	14	6
82d Inf.	1st, Von Amsberg.	3d, Schurz.	Eleventh.	23	89

[1] Four companies.

General Officers.

General John Buford, Commander of the First Division, Cavalry Corps. (Born in Kentucky.)

General Wesley Merritt, Commander of the Regular Brigade, First Division, Cavalry Corps. (Born in New York.)

General Elon J. Farnsworth, Commander of the First Brigade, Third Division, Cavalry Corps (killed).

General William Gamble, Commander of the First Brigade, First Division, Cavalry Corps.

State Appropriations for Monuments.

On May 29, 1889, the Legislature appropriated, to erect a suitable mark "upon the spot where the Illinois troops opened the battle of Gettysburg," the sum of $6000.

Of this amount, the sum of $600 was given to the Memorial Association, and the balance was expended on the three regimental monuments.

Though liberal appropriations were made for the three monuments, they are not of that character which was expected from this great State.

MICHIGAN.

Regiment.	Brigade.	Division.	Corps.	Killed and wounded.	Missing.
1st Cav.	2d, Custer.	3d, Kilpatrick.	Cavalry.	53	20
5th Cav.	2d, Custer.	3d, Kilpatrick.	Cavalry.	38	18
6th Cav.	2d, Custer.	3d, Kilpatrick.	Cavalry.	27	1
7th Cav.	2d, Custer.	3d, Kilpatrick.	Cavalry.	61	39
1st Inf.	1st, Tilton.	1st, Barnes.	Fifth.	38	4
3d Inf.	3d, De Trobriand.	1st, Birney.	Third.	38	7
4th Inf.	2d, Sweitzer.	1st, Barnes.	Fifth.	89	76
5th Inf.	3d, De Trobriand.	1st, Birney.	Third.	105	4
7th Inf.	3d, Hall.	2d, Gibbon.	Second.	65	..
16th Inf.	3d, Vincent.	1st, Barnes.	Fifth.	57	3
24th Inf.	1st, Meredith.	1st, Wadsworth.	First.	272	91

Battery.

	Corps.	Killed and wounded.
Daniel's 9th	Horse Artillery, Cavalry.	5

General Officers.

General Alpheus S. Williams, Commander of the First Division, Twelfth Corps. (Born in Connecticut.)

General Henry Baxter, Commander of the Second Brigade, Second Division, First Corps. (Born in New York.)

General Norman J. Hall, Commander of the Third Brigade, Second Division, Second Corps.

State Appropriations for Monuments.

The Legislature of 1887 appropriated the sum of $20,000 for marking by monuments the places occupied by Michigan troops at the battle of Gettysburg. This sum was subsequently used by the Commissioners from this State, as follows:

To the Memorial Association, for ground, etc.	$2,500.00
Michigan Cavalry Brigade (1st, 5th, 6th, 7th Michigan Cavalry) monument	5,400.00
To each of the seven regiments of infantry	1,350.00
Battery I, First Light Artillery	1,000.00
Total	$10,250.00

The balance of the appropriation was used in expenses of the commission.

The Legislature of 1889 appropriated the sum of $2000 for general expenses of dedication of the foregoing monuments, and $5000 to assist in paying the expenses of ex-soldiers attending such dedication.

Colonel George Briggs, of this State, a member of the Memorial Association, gave great personal attention and care to the designing and construction of the monuments, and they are among the best and most substantial upon the field. That of Custer's cavalry brigade,— 1st, 5th, 6th, and 7th Michigan,—on the line of Gregg's division, is one of the best-executed pieces of work on the field. It is particularly characteristic. That of the 24th, in Reynolds's Grove, is surmounted by a granite figure,—a soldier in action, wearing the army hat, the Iron Brigade and one or two other regiments being the only troops in the Army of the Potomac not wearing the fatigue cap. That of the 7th, near the "copse of trees," on the Second Corps line, that of the 16th, on Little Round Top, and that of the 4th, in the Wheat-Field, at the spot where its colonel, Jeffords, fell with a bayonet thrust through him, are well designed and constructed.

WISCONSIN.

Regiment.	Brigade.	Division.	Corps.	Killed and wounded.	Missing.
2d Inf.	1st, Meredith.	1st, Wadsworth.	First.	181	52
3d Inf.	3d, Colgrove.	1st, Ruger.	Twelfth.	10	..
5th Inf.[1]	3d, Russell.	1st, Wright.	Sixth.	..	..
6th Inf.	1st, Meredith.	1st, Wadsworth.	First.	146	22
7th Inf.	1st, Meredith.	1st, Wadsworth.	First.	126	52
26th Inf.	2d, Krzyzanowski.	3d, Schimmelfennig.	Eleventh.	155	62

[1] Not engaged.

General Officers.

General Carl Schurz, Commander of the Third Division, Eleventh Corps. (Born in Germany.)

General Thomas H. Ruger, Commander of the First Brigade, First Division, Twelfth Corps. (Born in New York.)

General Lysander Cutler, Commander of the Second Brigade, First Division, First Corps. (Born in Massachusetts.)

State Appropriations for Monuments.

1888.	To the Gettysburg Battle-field Association, for purchase of lands of especial interest on said battlefield	$1500.00
	For monument to each of the six regiments of infantry	1000.00
	Company G, Colonel Berdan's 1st United States Sharp-shooters	500.00
	Total	$3000.00

The six monuments of this State are among the best on the field. They are constructed in whole or in part of the red Montello (Wisconsin) granite.

Those of the 2d, 6th, and 7th, in Reynolds's Grove, that of the 5th, on the extreme left in rear of Round Top, that of the 3d, on Culp's Hill, and that of the 26th, on the Eleventh Corps line, while all of different style, are all equally fine.

MINNESOTA.

Regiment.	Brigade.	Division.	Corps.	Killed and wounded.	Missing.
1st Inf.	1st, Harrow.	2d, Gibbon.	Second.	223	1

State Appropriations for Monuments.

October 31,	1873.	To the Gettysburg Memorial Association	$1,000.00
May 3,	1893.	Paid for additional land	136.00
July and August,	1893.	Paid for large monument and bronze work, monument of 1st Regiment	16,384.00
		Paid for small monument and bronze work, monument of 1st Regiment	2,500.00
November 24,	1893.	Paid for grading and sodding grounds around monument . .	92.00
November 19,	1891.	Paid for bronze tablets, High-Water-Mark Monument . . .	200.00
		Total expenditures . . .	$20,312.00

While this State had but one regiment at Gettysburg, it was the first State, outside of Pennsylvania, to make an appropriation to the Memorial Association, and the State's liberality in expenditure for a monument for its regiment was unsurpassed.

The principal monument, which stands upon the Second Corps line, at the spot from which the regiment, by order of General Hancock, started upon its historic charge, cost over $16,000. It is a fine shaft surmounted by a bronze soldier double-quicking. It portrays great action, and is considered to be one of the best pieces of bronze work ever executed. The other monument is on the line where the regiment fought on the 3d. It cost $2500, and is of substantial character.

UNITED STATES REGULARS.

Regiment.	Brigade.	Division.	Corps.	Killed and wounded.	Missing.
1st Cav.	Merritt.	1st, Buford.	Cavalry.	10	5
2d Cav.	Merritt.	1st, Buford.	Cavalry.	10	7
5th Cav.	Merritt.	1st, Buford.	Cavalry.	4	1
6th Cav.	Merritt.	1st, Buford.	Cavalry.	34	208
2d Inf.[1]	2d, Burbank.	2d, Ayres.	Fifth.	61	6
3d Inf.[1]	1st, Day.	2d, Ayres.	Fifth.	72	1
4th Inf.[2]	1st, Day.	2d, Ayres.	Fifth.	40	..
6th Inf.[3]	1st, Day.	2d, Ayres.	Fifth.	44	..
7th Inf.[2]	2d, Burbank.	2d, Ayres.	Fifth.	57	2
8th Inf.[4]	.....	.....	.....	..	..
10th Inf.[5]	2d, Burbank.	2d, Ayres.	Fifth.	48	3
11th Inf.[1]	2d, Burbank.	2d, Ayres.	Fifth.	111	19
12th Inf.[6]	1st, Day.	2d, Ayres.	Fifth.	79	13
14th Inf.[6]	1st, Day.	2d, Ayres.	Fifth.	128	4
17th Inf.[7]	2d, Burbank.	2d, Ayres.	Fifth.	143	7
1st U. S.[8]	2d, Ward.	1st, Birney.	Third.	43	6
2d U. S.[8]	2d, Ward.	1st, Birney.	Third.	28	15

[1] Six companies. [2] Four companies. [3] Five companies.
[4] Head-quarters. [5] Three companies. [6] Eight companies.
[7] Nine companies. [8] Sharp-shooters.

The two regiments of sharp-shooters were composed of companies recruited in the several States, the majority of them being from Maine, Vermont, Michigan, and Wisconsin.

UNITED STATES BATTERIES.

	Corps.	Killed and wounded.	Missing.
Stewart's 4th (B)	First.	33	3
Woodruff's 1st (I)	Second.	25	..
Cushing's 4th (A)	Second.	38	..
Seeley's 4th (K)	Third.	21	4
Hazlett's 5th (D)	Fifth.	13	..
Watson's 5th (I)	Fifth.	20	2
Williston's 2d (D)[1]	Sixth.	..	..
Butler's 2d (G)[1]	Sixth.	..	..
Martin's 5th (F)[1]	Sixth.	..	..
Wilkeson's (Bancroft's) 4th (G)	Eleventh.	13	4
Rugg's 4th (F)	Twelfth.	1	..
Kinzie's 5th (K)	Twelfth.	5	..
Heaton's 2d (B & L)[1]	Horse Artillery, Cavalry.	..	..
Pennington's 2d (M)	Horse Artillery, Cavalry.	1	..
Elder's 4th (E)	Horse Artillery, Cavalry.	1	..
Randol's 1st (E & G)[1]	Horse Artillery, Cavalry.	..	..
Graham's 1st (K)	Horse Artillery, Cavalry.	3	..
Calef's 2d (A)	Horse Artillery, Cavalry.	12	..
Fuller's 3d (C)[1]	Horse Artillery, Cavalry.	..	..
Eakin's (Mason's) 1st (H)	Artillery Reserve.	9	1
Turnbull's 3d (F & K)	Artillery Reserve.	23	1
Thomas's 4th (C)	Artillery Reserve.	18	..
Weir's 5th (C)	Artillery Reserve.	16	..

[1] Not engaged.

No monuments or tablets have as yet been erected to mark the positions of the regiments and batteries of the Regular army.

LIST OF CONFEDERATE REGIMENTS AND BATTERIES ENGAGED IN THE BATTLE.

ALABAMA.

Regiment.	Brigade.	Division.	Corps.
3d Inf.	O'Neal.	Rodes.	Ewell.
4th Inf.	Law.	Hood.	Longstreet.
5th Bat.	Archer.	Heth.	Hill.
5th Inf.	O'Neal.	Rodes.	Ewell.
6th Inf.	O'Neal.	Rodes.	Ewell.
8th Inf.	Wilcox.	Anderson.	Hill.
9th Inf.	Wilcox.	Anderson.	Hill.
10th Inf.	Wilcox.	Anderson.	Hill.
11th Inf.	Wilcox.	Anderson.	Hill.
12th Inf.	O'Neal.	Rodes.	Ewell.
13th Inf.	Archer.	Heth.	Hill.
14th Inf.	Wilcox.	Anderson.	Hill.
15th Inf.	Law.	Hood.	Longstreet.
26th Inf.	O'Neal.	Rodes.	Hill.
44th Inf.	Law.	Hood.	Longstreet.
47th Inf.	Law.	Hood.	Longstreet.
48th Inf.	Law.	Hood.	Longstreet.

Batteries.

Reese's	Jeff Davis Artillery.
Hurt's	Hardaway Artillery.

ARKANSAS.

Regiment.	Brigade.	Division.	Corps.
3d Inf.	Robertson.	Hood.	Longstreet.

FLORIDA.

Regiment.	Brigade.	Division.	Corps.
2d Inf.	Perry.	Anderson.	Hill.
5th Inf.	Perry.	Anderson.	Hill.
8th Inf.	Perry.	Anderson.	Hill.

GEORGIA.

Regiment.	Brigade.	Division.	Corps.
Cobb's Legion.	Hampton.	Stuart's Cavalry.	. . . .
Phillips's Legion.	Hampton.	Stuart's Cavalry.	. . . .
2d Battalion, Inf.	Wright.	Anderson.	Hill.
2d Inf.	Benning.	Hood.	Longstreet.
3d Inf.	Wright.	Anderson.	Hill.
4th Inf.	Doles.	Rodes.	Ewell.
7th Inf.	Anderson.	Hood.	Longstreet.
8th Inf.	Anderson.	Hood.	Longstreet.
9th Inf.	Anderson.	Hood.	Longstreet.
10th Inf.	Semmes.	McLaws.	Longstreet.
11th Inf.	Anderson.	Hood.	Longstreet.
12th Inf.	Doles.	Rodes.	Ewell.
13th Inf.	Gordon.	Early.	Ewell.
14th Inf.	Thomas.	Pender.	Hill.
15th Inf.	Benning.	Hood.	Longstreet.
16th Inf.	Wofford.	McLaws.	Longstreet.
17th Inf.	Benning.	Hood.	Longstreet.
18th Inf.	Wofford.	McLaws.	Longstreet.
20th Inf.	Benning.	Hood.	Longstreet.
21st Inf.	Doles.	Rodes.	Ewell.
22d Inf.	Wright.	Anderson.	Hill.
24th Inf.	Wofford.	McLaws.	Longstreet.
26th Int.	Gordon.	Early.	Ewell.
31st Inf.	Gordon.	Early.	Ewell.
35th Inf.	Thomas.	Pender.	Hill.
38th Inf.	Gordon.	Early.	Ewell.
44th Inf.	Doles.	Rodes.	Ewell.
45th Inf.	Thomas.	Pender.	Hill.
48th Inf.	Wright.	Anderson.	Hill.
49th Inf.	Thomas.	Pender.	Hill.
50th Inf.	Semmes.	McLaws.	Longstreet.
51st Inf.	Semmes.	McLaws.	Longstreet.
53d Inf.	Semmes.	McLaws.	Longstreet.
59th Inf.	Anderson.	Hood.	Longstreet.
60th Inf.	Gordon.	Early.	Ewell.
61st Inf.	Gordon.	Early.	Ewell.
Cobb's Legion.	Wofford.	McLaws.	Longstreet.
Phillips's Legion.	Wofford.	McLaws.	Longstreet.

Batteries.

Carleton's . . . . Troup Artillery.
Frazier's . . . . Pulaski Artillery.
Milledge's.
Patterson's.
Ross's.
Wingfield's.

LOUISIANA.

Regiment	Brigade.	Division.	Corps.
1st Inf.	Williams.	Johnson.	Ewell.
2d Inf.	Williams.	Johnson.	Ewell.
5th Inf.	Hays.	Early.	Ewell.
6th Inf.	Hays.	Early.	Ewell.
7th Inf.	Hays.	Early.	Ewell.
8th Inf.	Hays.	Early.	Ewell.
9th Inf.	Hays.	Early.	Ewell.
10th Inf.	Williams.	Johnson.	Ewell.
14th Inf.	Williams.	Johnson.	Ewell.
15th Inf.	Williams.	Johnson.	Ewell.

Batteries.

Moody's . . . . Madison Light Artillery.
Green's . . . . Louisiana Guard Artillery.
Maurin's . . . . Donaldsonville Artillery.
Miller's . . . . Washington Artillery.
Norcom's . . . . Washington Artillery.
Richardson's . . . . Washington Artillery.
Squires's . . . . Washington Artillery.

MARYLAND.

Regiment.	Brigade.	Division.	Corps.
1st Battalion, Inf.	Steuart.	Johnson.	Ewell.

Batteries.

Brown's . . . . Chesapeake Artillery.
Dement's.
Breathed's.
Griffin's 2d.

MISSISSIPPI.

Regiment.	Brigade.	Division.	Corps.
2d Inf.	Davis.	Heth.	Hill.
11th Inf.	Davis.	Heth.	Hill.
12th Inf.	Posey.	Anderson.	Hill.
13th Inf.	Barksdale.	McLaws.	Longstreet.
16th Inf.	Posey.	Anderson.	Hill.
17th Inf.	Barksdale.	McLaws.	Longstreet.
18th Inf.	Barksdale.	McLaws.	Longstreet.
19th Inf.	Posey.	Anderson.	Hill.
21st Inf.	Barksdale.	McLaws.	Longstreet.
42d Inf.	Davis.	Heth.	Hill.
48th Inf.	Posey.	Anderson.	Hill.

Battery.

Ward's . . . . Madison Light Artillery.

NORTH CAROLINA.

Regiment.	Brigade.	Division.	Corps.
1st Cav.	Hampton.	Stuart.	. . . .
2d Cav.	W. H. F. Lee.	Stuart.	. . . .
1st Battalion, Inf.	Hoke.	Early.	Ewell.
1st Inf.	Steuart.	Johnson.	Ewell.
2d Inf.	Ramseur.	Rodes.	Ewell.
2d Battalion, Inf.	Daniels.	Rodes.	Ewell.
3d Inf.	Steuart.	Johnson.	Ewell.
4th Inf.	Ramseur.	Rodes.	Ewell.
5th Inf.	Iverson.	Rodes.	Ewell.
6th Inf.	Hoke.	Early.	Ewell.
7th Inf.	Lane.	Pender.	Hill.
11th Inf.	Pettigrew.	Heth.	Hill.
12th Inf.	Iverson.	Rodes.	Ewell.
13th Inf.	Scales.	Pender.	Hill.
14th Inf.	Ramseur.	Rodes.	Ewell.
16th Inf.	Scales.	Pender.	Hill.
18th Inf.	Lane.	Pender.	Hill.
21st Inf.	Iverson.	Rodes.	Ewell.
22d Inf.	Scales.	Pender.	Hill.
23d Inf.	Iverson.	Rodes.	Ewell.

NORTH CAROLINA—*Continued.*

Regiment.	Brigade.	Division.	Corps.
26th Inf.	Pettigrew.	Heth.	Hill.
28th Inf.	Lane.	Pender.	Hill.
30th Inf.	Ramseur.	Rodes.	Ewell.
32d Inf.	Daniels.	Rodes.	Ewell.
33d Inf.	Lane.	Pender.	Hill.
34th Inf.	Scales.	Pender.	Hill.
37th Inf.	Lane.	Pender.	Hill.
38th Inf.	Scales.	Pender.	Hill.
43d Inf.	Daniels.	Rodes.	Ewell.
45th Inf.	Daniels.	Rodes.	Ewell.
47th Inf.	Pettigrew.	Heth.	Hill.
52d Inf.	Pettigrew.	Heth.	Hill.
53d Inf.	Daniels.	Rodes.	Ewell.
54th Inf.	Iverson.	Rodes.	Ewell.
55th Inf.	Davis.	Heth.	Hill.
57th Inf.	Hoke.	Early.	Ewell.

Batteries.

Manly's . . . . North Carolina Artillery.
Latham's . . . . Branch Artillery.
Reilly's . . . . Rowan Artillery.
Graham's.

SOUTH CAROLINA.

Regiment.	Brigade.	Division.	Corps.
1st Cav.	Hampton.	Stuart.	. . . .
2d Cav.	Hampton.	Stuart.	. . . .
Jeff Davis Legion.	Hampton.	Stuart.	. . . .
1st Inf.	McGowan.	Pender.	Hill.
2d Inf.	Kershaw.	McLaws.	Longstreet.
3d Inf.	Kershaw.	McLaws.	Longstreet.
3d Battalion, Inf.	Kershaw.	McLaws.	Longstreet.
7th Inf.	Kershaw.	McLaws.	Longstreet.
8th Inf.	Kershaw.	McLaws.	Longstreet.
12th Inf.	McGowan.	Pender.	Hill.
13th Inf.	McGowan.	Pender.	Hill.
14th Inf.	McGowan.	Pender.	Hill.
15th Inf.	Kershaw.	McLaws.	Longstreet.
Orr's Rifles.	McGowan.	Pender.	Hill.

Batteries.

Bachman's	German Artillery.
Garden's	Palmetto Light Artillery.
Rhett's	Brooks Artillery.
Brunson's	Pee Dee Artillery.
Hart's	Washington Artillery.

TENNESSEE.

Regiment.	Brigade.	Division.	Corps.
1st Inf.	Archer.	Heth.	Hill.
7th Inf.	Archer.	Heth.	Hill.
14th Inf.	Archer.	Heth.	Hill.

TEXAS.

Regiment.	Brigade.	Division.	Corps.
1st Inf.	Robertson.	Hood.	Longstreet.
4th Inf.	Robertson.	Hood.	Longstreet.
5th Inf.	Robertson.	Hood.	Longstreet.

VIRGINIA.

Regiment	Brigade.	Division.	Corps.
1st Inf.	Kemper.	Pickett.	Longstreet.
2d Inf.	Walker.	Johnson.	Ewell.
3d Inf.	Kemper.	Pickett.	Longstreet.
4th Inf.	Walker.	Johnson.	Ewell.
5th Inf.	Walker.	Johnson.	Ewell.
6th Inf.	Mahone.	Anderson.	Hill.
7th Inf.	Kemper.	Pickett.	Longstreet.
8th Inf.	Garnett.	Pickett.	Longstreet.
9th Inf.	Armistead.	Pickett.	Longstreet.
10th Inf.	Steuart.	Johnson.	Ewell.
11th Inf.	Kemper.	Pickett.	Longstreet.
12th Inf.	Mahone.	Anderson.	Hill.
14th Inf.	Armistead.	Pickett.	Longstreet.
16th Inf.	Mahone.	Anderson.	Hill.
18th Inf.	Garnett.	Pickett.	Longstreet.
19th Inf.	Garnett.	Pickett.	Longstreet.

VIRGINIA— *Continued.*

Regiment.	Brigade.	Division.	Corps.
22d Battalion,Inf.	Brockenbrough.	Heth.	Hill.
21st Inf.	Jones.	Johnson.	Ewell.
23d Battalion,Inf.	Steuart.	Johnson.	Ewell.
24th Inf.	Kemper.	Pickett.	Longstreet.
25th Inf.	Jones.	Johnson.	Ewell.
27th Inf.	Walker.	Johnson.	Ewell.
28th Inf.	Garnett.	Pickett.	Longstreet.
31st Inf.	Smith.	Early.	Ewell.
33d Inf.	Walker.	Johnson.	Ewell.
37th Inf.	Steuart.	Johnson.	Ewell.
38th Inf.	Armistead.	Pickett.	Longstreet.
40th Inf.	Brockenbrough.	Heth.	Hill.
41st Inf.	Mahone.	Anderson.	Hill.
42d Inf.	Jones.	Johnson.	Ewell.
44th Inf.	Jones.	Johnson.	Ewell.
47th Inf.	Brockenbrough.	Heth.	Hill.
48th Inf.	Jones.	Johnson.	Ewell.
49th Inf.	Smith.	Early.	Ewell.
50th Inf.	Jones.	Johnson.	Ewell.
52d Inf.	Jones.	Johnson.	Ewell.
53d Inf.	Armistead.	Pickett.	Longstreet.
55th Inf.	Brockenbrough.	Heth.	Hill.
56th Inf.	Garnett.	Pickett.	Longstreet.
57th Inf.	Garnett.	Pickett.	Longstreet.
61st Inf.	Mahone.	Anderson.	Hill.

Cavalry.

Regiment.	Brigade.	Division.
1st Cav.	Fitzhugh Lee.	Stuart.
2d Cav.	Fitzhugh Lee.	Stuart.
3d Cav.	Fitzhugh Lee.	Stuart.
4th Cav.	Fitzhugh Lee.	Stuart.
5th Cav.	Fitzhugh Lee.	Stuart.
6th Cav.	Jones.	Stuart.
7th Cav.	Jones.	Stuart.
9th Cav.[1]	W. H. F. Lee.	Stuart.

---

[1] Commanded by Chambliss.

VIRGINIA—*Continued.*

Cavalry.

Regiment.	Brigade.	Division.
10th Cav.[1]	W. H. F. Lee.	Stuart.
11th Cav.	Jones.	Stuart.
12th Cav.	Jones.	Stuart.
13th Cav.[1]	W. H. F. Lee.	Stuart.
14th Cav.	Jenkins.	Stuart.
15th Cav.[1]	W. H. F. Lee.	Stuart.
16th Cav.	Jenkins.	Stuart.
17th Cav.	Jenkins.	Stuart.
34th Cav.	Jenkins.	Stuart.
35th Cav.	Jones.	Stuart.
36th Cav.	Jenkins.	Stuart.

[1] Commanded by Chambliss.

BATTERIES.

McCarthy's	1st Richmond Howitzers.
Blount's.	
Caskie's	Hampden Artillery.
Macon's	Richmond Fayette Artillery
Stribling's	Fauquier Artillery.
Jordan's	Bedford Artillery.
Parker's.	
Taylor's.	
Woolfolk's	Ashland Artillery.
Carrington's	Charlottesville Artillery.
Garber's	Staunton Artillery.
Tanner's	Courtney Artillery.
Carpenter's	Alleghany Artillery.
Raine's	Lee Battery.
Carter's	King William Artillery.
Fry's	Orange Artillery.
Page's	Morris Artillery.
Dance's	1st Virginia Artillery.
Cunningham's	Powhatan Artillery.
Griffin's	Salem Artillery.

VIRGINIA—*Continued.*

Graham's	Rockbridge Artillery.
Watson's	2d Richmond Howitzers.
Kirkpatrick's	Amherst Artillery.
Massie's	Fluvanna Artillery.
Grandy's	Norfolk Light Artillery Blues.
Lewis's.	
Moore's.	
Brooke's.	
Wyatt's	Albemarle Artillery.
Lusk's.	
Johnson's.	
Rice's	Danville Artillery.
Brander's	Letcher Artillery.
Crenshaw's.	
McGraw's	Purcell Artillery.
Marye's	Fredericksburg Artillery.
McGregor's.	
Chew's.	
Moorman's.	

"AN ACT

"TO ESTABLISH A NATIONAL MILITARY PARK AT GETTYSBURG, PENNSYLVANIA.

"*Be it enacted by the Senate and House of Representatives of the United States of America in Congress assembled,* That the Secretary of War is hereby authorized to receive from the Gettysburg Battle-field Memorial Association, a corporation chartered by the State of Pennsylvania, a deed of conveyance to the United States of all the lands belonging to said association, embracing about eight hundred acres, more or less, and being a considerable part of the battle-field of Gettysburg, together with all rights of way over avenues through said lands acquired by said association, and all improvements made by it in and upon the same. Upon the due execution and delivery to the Secretary of War of such deed of conveyance, the Secretary of War is authorized to pay to the said Battle-field Memorial Association the sum of two thousand dollars, or so much thereof as may be necessary to discharge the debts of said association, the amount of such debts to be verified by the officers thereof, and the sum of two thousand dollars is hereby appropriated out of any money in the Treasury not otherwise appropriated to meet and defray such charges.

"SEC. 2. That as soon as the lands aforesaid shall be conveyed to the United States the Secretary of War shall take possession of the same, and such other lands on the battle-field as the United States have acquired, or shall hereafter acquire, by purchase or condemnation proceedings; and the lands aforesaid shall be designated and known as the 'Gettysburg National Park.'

"SEC. 3. That the Gettysburg national park shall, subject to the supervision and direction of the Secretary of War, be in charge of the commissioners heretofore appointed by the Secretary of War for the location and acquisition of lands at Gettysburg, and their successors; the said commissioners shall have their office at Gettysburg, and while on duty shall be paid such compensation out of the appropriation provided in this Act as the Secretary of War shall deem reasonable and just. And it shall be the duty of the said commissioners, under the direction of the Secretary of War, to superintend the opening of such additional roads as may be necessary for the purposes of the park and for the improvement of the avenues heretofore laid out therein, and to properly mark the boundaries of the said park, and to ascertain and definitely mark the lines of battle of all troops engaged in the battle of Gettysburg, so far as the same shall fall within the limits of the park.

"SEC. 4. That the Secretary of War is hereby authorized and directed to acquire, at such times and in such manner as he may deem best calculated to serve the public interest, such lands in the vicinity of Gettysburg, Pennsylvania, not exceeding in area the parcels shown on the map prepared by Major-General Daniel E. Sickles, United States Army, and now on file in the office of the Secretary of War, which were occupied by the infantry, cavalry, and artillery on the first, second, and third days of July, eighteen hundred and sixty-three, and such other adjacent lands as he may deem necessary to preserve the important topographical features of the battle-field: *Provided*, That nothing contained in this Act shall be deemed and held to prejudice the rights acquired by any State or by any military organization to the ground on which its monuments or markers are placed, nor the right of way to the same.

"SEC. 5. That for the purpose of acquiring the lands designated and described in the foregoing section not already acquired and owned by the United States, and such other adjacent land as may be deemed necessary by the Secretary of War for the preservation and marking of the lines of battle of the Union and Confederate armies at Gettysburg, the Secretary of War is authorized to employ the services of the commissioners heretofore appointed by him for the location, who shall proceed, in conformity with his instructions and subject in all things to his approval, to acquire such lands by purchase, or by condemnation proceedings, to be taken by the Attorney-General in behalf of the United States, in any case in which it shall be ascertained that the same cannot be purchased at prices deemed reasonable and just by the said commissioners and approved by the Secretary of War. And such condemnation proceedings may be taken pursuant to the Act of Congress approved August first, eighteen hundred and eighty-eight, regulating the condemnation of land for public uses, or the Joint Resolution authorizing the purchase or condemnation of land in the vicinity of Gettysburg, Pennsylvania, approved June fifth, eighteen hundred and ninety-four.

"Sec. 6. That it shall be the duty of the Secretary of War to establish and enforce proper regulations for the custody, preservation, and care of the monuments now erected or which may be hereafter erected within the limits of the said national military park ; and such rules shall provide for convenient access by visitors to all such monuments within the park, and the ground included therein, on such days and within such hours as may be designated and authorized by the Secretary of War.

"Sec. 7. That if any person shall destroy, mutilate, deface, injure, or remove, except by permission of the Secretary of War, any column, statue, memorial structure, or work of art that shall be erected or placed upon the grounds of the park by lawful authority, or shall destroy or remove any fence, railing, inclosure, or other work for the protection or ornament of said park or any portion thereof, or shall destroy, cut, hack, bark, break down, or otherwise injure any tree, bush, or shrubbery that may be growing upon said park, or shall cut down or fell or remove any timber, battle relic, tree or trees, growing or being upon said park, or hunt within the limits of the park, or shall remove or destroy any breastworks, earthworks, walls, or other defences or shelter or any part thereof constructed by the armies formerly engaged in the battles on the land or approaches to the park, or shall violate any regulation made and published by the Secretary of War for the government of visitors within the limits of said park, any person so offending and found guilty thereof, before any justice of the peace of the county in which the offence may be committed, shall, for each and every such offence, forfeit and pay a fine, in the discretion of the justice, according to the aggravation of the offence, of not less than five nor more than five hundred dollars, one-half for the use of the park and the other half to the informer, to be enforced and recovered before such justice in like manner as debts of like nature are now by law recoverable in the county where the offence may be committed.

"SEC. 8. That the Secretary of War is hereby authorized and directed to cause to be made a suitable bronze tablet, containing on it the address delivered by Abraham Lincoln, President of the United States, at Gettysburg, on the nineteenth day of November, eighteen hundred and sixty-three, on the occasion of the dedication of the national cemetery at that place, and such tablet, having on it besides the address a medallion likeness of President Lincoln, shall be erected on the most suitable site within the limits of said park.

"And the sum of five thousand dollars, or so much thereof as may be necessary, is hereby appropriated out of any money in the Treasury not otherwise appropriated, to pay the cost of said tablet and medallion and pedestal.

"SEC. 9. That to enable the Secretary of War to carry out the purposes of this Act, including the purchase or condemnation of the land described in sections four and five of this Act, opening, improving, and repairing necessary roads and avenues, providing surveys and maps, suitably marking the boundaries of the park, and for the pay and expenses of the commissioners and their assistants, the sum of seventy-five thousand dollars, or so much thereof as may be necessary, is hereby appropriated out of any money in the Treasury not otherwise appropriated; and all disbursements made under this Act shall require the approval of the Secretary of War, who shall make annual report of the same to Congress.

Approved, February 11, 1895.

www.ingramcontent.com/pod-product-compliance
Lightning Source LLC
Chambersburg PA
CBHW031545300426
44111CB00006BA/176